SKI TRAILS IN THE CANADIAN ROCKIES

Gordon Rathbone on Lower Telemark Trail near Lake Louise. Photo Chic Scott

SKI TRAILS IN THE
CANADIAN
ROCKIES

CHIC SCOTT
& DARREN FARLEY

5th Edition

RMB

Trail to Skoki
by Ralphine Locke

By high mountain trails
Nestled in snowy hollows
White ptarmigan dream.

Skiers near Halfway Hut on the way to Skoki Lodge.
Photo WMCR Lloyd Harmon V108 1286

RMB | Rocky Mountain Books Ltd.
rmbooks.com
@rmbooks
facebook.com/rmbooks

Cataloguing data available from Library and Archives Canada
ISBN 978-1-77160-118-4 (pbk.)
ISBN 978-1-77160-119-1 (epub)

Front cover photo: Shawn McDonald and Dean Lister cross Amethyst Lake in the Tonquin Valley. Photo Chic Scott

Back cover photo: The warming hut located at the Golden golf course trailhead. Photo Darren Farley

Printed and bound in China

Distributed in Canada by Heritage Group Distribution and in the U.S. by Publishers Group West

For information on purchasing bulk quantities of this book, or to obtain media excerpts or invite the author to speak at an event, please visit rmbooks.com and select the "Contact Us" tab.

RMB | Rocky Mountain Books is dedicated to the environment and committed to reducing the destruction of old-growth forests. Our books are produced with respect for the future and consideration for the past.

We acknowledge the financial support of the Government of Canada through the Canada Book Fund and the Canada Council for the Arts, and of the province of British Columbia through the British Columbia Arts Council and the Book Publishing Tax Credit.

Nous reconnaissons l'aide financière du gouvernement du Canada par l'entremise du Fonds du livre du Canada et le Conseil des arts du Canada, et de la province de la Colombie-Britannique par le Conseil des arts de la Colombie-Britannique et le Crédit d'impôt pour l'édition de livres.

Disclaimer

The actions described in this book may be considered inherently dangerous activities. Individuals undertake these activities at their own risk. The information put forth in this guide has been collected from a variety of sources and is not guaranteed to be completely accurate or reliable. Many conditions and some information may change owing to weather and numerous other factors beyond the control of the authors and publishers. Individuals or groups must determine the risks, use their own judgment, and take full responsibility for their actions. Do not depend on any information found in this book for your own personal safety. Your safety depends on your own good judgment based on your skills, education, and experience.

It is up to the users of this guidebook to acquire the necessary skills for safe experiences and to exercise caution in potentially hazardous areas. The authors and publishers of this guide accept no responsibility for your actions or the results that occur from another's actions, choices, or judgments. If you have any doubt as to your safety or your ability to attempt anything described in this guidebook, do not attempt it.

CONTENTS

Preface   9

Acknowledgements   11

Introduction   12

   Snow Conditions   13

   Avalanches   13

   Weather   15

   Remoteness   15

   Environment   16

   Emergency Procedures   16

   Food, Gear and
      Other Supplies   16

   How to Use This Book   17

   Trip Planning   20

Waterton Lakes National Park   27

Fernie and the Crowsnest
   Pass   37

Calgary Nordic Trails   49

Mount Assiniboine
   Provincial Park   53

Kananaskis Country   80

Canmore to Banff   119

Banff to Castle Junction   142

Kootenay National Park   172

Columbia Valley   186

Lake Louise Area   200

Skoki   224

Yoho National Park   249

The Icefields Parkway   284

Jasper   311

Tonquin Valley   334

Mount Robson Provincial
   Park   348

Multi-Day
   Ski Adventures   352

Index   367

Calling For Assistance   370

Chic Scott   373

Darren Farley   375

Don Gardner and Joan Dunkley enjoy the sunshine in the Little Yoho Valley. Photo Chic Scott

PREFACE

By the time this edition of *Ski Trails in the Canadian Rockies* reaches the bookstores I will be 70 years of age and collecting my pension. Luckily I am still in good health and still out on the ski trails many days each winter. But it is time to begin to pass on the torch to a younger generation. Darren Farley, who is just 23 years old, is already very experienced and full of passion, and is responsible for much of the content of this book. It has been a real pleasure to work with Darren and he has brought a new perspective to this undertaking.

In this edition you will find a number of cross-country ski trail networks outside the national parks plus many new trails. In 2010, with three companions, I skied the Jasper to Banff traverse (as far as Lake Louise), so you will also find a greatly expanded guide to this historic traverse. Thanks to Rocky Mountain Books, this edition is printed in colour and contains excellent revised maps.

Since the publication of the first edition of *Ski Trails* back in 1977 there has been tremendous growth in the sport of cross-country skiing and now there are thousands of skiers on the trails each weekend. I hope all of you have a wonderful experience gliding across the snow and that you continue to enjoy winter in the Rocky Mountains for decades to come.

See you on the ski trail,
Chic Scott

Seana Strain, Karen Barkley, Heather Walter, Kathy Madill and Pat McCloskey ski along the Pipestone trails near Lake Louise. Photo Chic Scott

ACKNOWLEDGEMENTS

I would like to thank my best friend, Kathy Madill, for being such a pleasant ski companion and for sharing her excellent images with me. I would also like to thank the other photographers who have allowed me to use their images: Clive Cordery, Gill Daffern, Aileen Harmon, Sara Renner, Brad Kitching, Bow Valley Photography, Canmore Nordic Centre, Ken Chow, Alan Kane, Tomasz Gehrke, Gabriel Altebaeumer, Brad White, Orange Girl Photography, Jo Lunn, Tim Johnson, Josée LaRochelle and Matt Hadley. Once again I would like to thank the Whyte Museum of the Canadian Rockies and the Jasper/Yellowhead Museum & Archives for the use of several historic photos. Finally I would like to thank Don Gorman, Chyla Cardinal and Joe Wilderson at Rocky Mountain Books for all their hard work creating this volume.

"It is better to go skiing and think of God,
than go to church and think of sport."

— *Fridtjof Nansen*

INTRODUCTION

Skiing in the Canadian Rockies is a wonderful and varied experience. You can enjoy a safe and easy trackset trail or explore the high and wild backcountry. You can camp in the solitude of a remote valley or stay in the luxury and comfort of one of our historic lodges.

Skiing in these mountains offers you the opportunity to escape the noise and rush of our culture. In the winter you need venture only a few hundred metres from the road to enter a world of silence and beauty. In the winter all is clean, new and fresh. The purity of the snow formations, the wind and the clouds can put new life in your soul. The fresh air and hard exercise can put roses in your cheeks.

The Canadian Rockies have been home to ski adventure since the late 1920s. Long before the development of ski resorts and mechanical lifts, skiers from around the world journeyed to the Rockies to experience the winter wilderness. And much of that history is still around us. Thankfully most of the areas covered in this book are protected as national or provincial parks and little has changed over the years. You can still experience the same adventure and beauty that the pioneers enjoyed.

There are, however, serious hazards for ski tourers in the Canadian Rockies and you must be well prepared and use good judgment to venture safely into these mountains. The penalty for mistakes can be harsh indeed. Judgment comes with experience and it is advised that you begin slowly with modest trips, then gradually work your way into the more demanding ski tours.

The area covered by this book is very large and there are endless possibilities for ski adventure. We have collected only the most popular and obvious trails. You could spend a lifetime exploring the remote backcountry and you would rarely encounter a soul. Good ski touring skills and techniques are required for going far in these mountains. In addition, there are some distinctive characteristics of the Canadian Rockies that you should be familiar with.

SNOW CONDITIONS

The snow that falls in the Canadian Rockies is usually very dry, and during some years the snowfall can be minimal for long periods of time. The amount of snow can vary from place to place: along the Icefields Parkway, near Bow Summit, the snowpack can be several metres deep, while 150 km to the north, near Jasper, it can often be almost non-existent. Because temperatures are often low, the snow does not consolidate or settle fast. As a result of long periods of cold weather combined with a shallow snowpack, a loose and unstable type of snow, called depth hoar, often develops. Early season trail-breaking can be extremely frustrating and it is not uncommon to find yourself sinking into deep, unconsolidated snow. The best time to undertake longer ski tours is from mid-February on, when the snowpack is deeper and more settled. You should give serious consideration to the condition of the snowpack before you head out on a long-distance tour.

AVALANCHES

The snowpack in the Canadian Rockies is often unstable and unpredictable, and snow stability is difficult to evaluate, even for knowledgeable and experienced ski tourers. Avalanche accidents are a regular occurrence. You are advised to check Avalanche Canada's public forecast at www.avalanche.ca. You are also advised to take an avalanche awareness course, where you will learn to travel safely in avalanche terrain and to recognize signs of snow instability.

Ski tourers should all wear an avalanche beacon and carry a snow-shovel and probe when skiing in avalanche terrain. Your beacon should be switched on at the beginning of the tour and worn until you are safely back at your car. Batteries should be fresh and your group should do a beacon check at the beginning of each day. Everyone should know how to conduct a beacon search in the event of an avalanche incident. Avalanche beacons should not be an excuse to push the limits of safe judgment – remember that despite these electronic devices many avalanches still prove fatal.

You should ski with a high degree of awareness. Most of the tours in this book can be done without exposing yourself or your group to the possibility of being avalanched. If you find yourself anywhere that seems to be steep and dangerous, you are likely off route. If you are skiing terrain that makes you nervous, look for a more comfortable-feeling route. Keen observation, good route finding and caution are the keys to safe travel in these mountains.

PARKS CANADA'S AVALANCHE TERRAIN EXPOSURE SCALE

This exposure scale and the associated avalanche terrain ratings attempt to assess how serious the terrain is from the perspective of avalanche hazard. Used in conjunction with the daily avalanche forecasts it will enable you to evaluate the hazard and manage the risk when skiing the trails described in this book. For more information on the rating system, visit Parks Canada's Mountain Safety page at www.parkscanada.gc.ca/parksmountainsafety. The scale recognizes three levels of terrain:

Simple (class 1)

Exposure to low-angle or primarily forested terrain. Some forest openings may involve the runout zones of infrequent avalanches. Many options to reduce or eliminate exposure. No glacier travel.

Challenging (class 2)

Exposure to well-defined avalanche paths, starting zones or terrain traps; options exist to reduce or eliminate exposure with careful route finding. Glacier travel is straightforward but crevasse hazards may exist.

Complex (class 3)

Exposure to multiple, overlapping avalanche paths or large expanses of steep, open terrain; multiple avalanche starting zones and terrain traps below; minimal options to reduce exposure. Complicated glacier travel with extensive crevasse bands or icefalls.

In the trail names in this guidebook, the ATR (Avalanche Terrain

Rating) number 1, 2 or 3 following the type of skiing corresponds to the rating above.

To learn more about snow, avalanches and safe travel in avalanche country consult *Backcountry Avalanche Safety for Skiers, Climbers, Boarders and Snowshoers*, written by Tony Daffern and published by Rocky Mountain Books.

WEATHER

Weather in the Canadian Rockies can be extreme and there can be periods when the thermometer drops as low as –30°c. Chinook winds can change this in a matter of hours and raise the temperature above freezing. Carrying the proper protection against the wind and the cold is essential, and if your tour takes you above treeline you should be particularly well prepared. A night out in the Rockies is a serious matter, so carry survival equipment on all tours.

The average winter temperature in the Rockies is reasonable, however, and the area receives a large amount of sunshine. A typical Rockies day is perhaps –10°c and sunny. Springtime ski touring can be a real treat – often a sweater or windbreaker is all that is needed. An effective sun cream and quality sunglasses are required, particularly later in the season when the sun climbs higher in the sky.

Weather reports can be obtained in Banff by phoning 403-762-2088 and in Jasper at 780-852-3185. For online weather reports go to www.weather.gc.ca.

REMOTENESS

Many of the tours in this book take you through wilderness areas. There are no man-made facilities on most of these trails and often there will be no other skiers in the area. You will be on your own and you must deal with any eventuality with your own resources. This remoteness is indeed one of the great attractions of these mountains. For added security you may consider carrying a personal locator beacon. There is no cellphone reception in most of the areas included in this book.

ENVIRONMENT

Most of these trails are in national or provincial parks, where the environment is protected. Cutting of trees and branches is prohibited. All garbage must be packed out. Please practise "leave no trace" principles. Visit www.leavenotrace.ca for further information.

EMERGENCY PROCEDURES

Before venturing far into the backcountry you should obtain the knowledge and skills necessary to carry out a few emergency procedures. You should know how to build an emergency shelter, how to start a fire and how to stay warm and dry. You should also be familiar with avalanche rescue procedures, because it is unlikely that outside help will be able to do more than recover bodies.

Always let someone know where you are going and when you will return. In an emergency you can raise the alarm by phoning the appropriate number listed on page 370. Throughout most of Alberta the number to call in the event of an emergency is 911.

FOOD, GEAR AND OTHER SUPPLIES

The mountain communities of Banff, Canmore, Lake Louise, Jasper Golden, Invermere and Fernie have a wide variety of stores and shops to serve you. Ski equipment and backcountry gear can be purchased or rented at:

Monod Sports (Banff) 403-762-4571, 1.866.956.6663, www.monodsports.com

Patagonia (Banff) 403-985-5588, 1-855-541-4709,
www.patagoniaelements.ca/store/content/8/Banff

Gear Up Sports (Canmore) 403-678-1636, www.gearupsport.com

Trail Sports (Canmore Nordic Centre) 403-678-6764, www.trailsports.ab.ca

Valhalla Pure Outfitters (Canmore) 403-678-5610,
vpo.ca/t-VPO.StoreLocator.Canmore.aspx

Vertical Addiction (Canmore) 403-609-8226, vertical-addiction.com

Wilson Mountain Sports (Lake Louise) 403-522-3636, 1-866-929-3636, www.wmsll.com

Totem Ski Shop (Jasper) 780-852-3078, 1-800-363-3078, totemskishop.com

Gravity Gear (Jasper) 780-852-3155, 1-888-852-3155, www.gravitygearjasper.com

Dark Side Snow Skate Life (Golden) 250-344-4546

Summit Cycle (Golden) 250-344-6600

Selkirk Source for Sports (Golden) 250-344-2966

180 Mountain Sports (Golden) 250-344-4699

Inside Edge Boutique and Sports (Invermere) 250-342-0402, insideedgeboutiqueandsports.com

Columbia Cycle and Ski (Invermere) 250-342-6164

The Quest Outdoor Sports Rentals (Fernie) 250-423-9252

GearHub Sports (Fernie) 250-423-5555, gearhub.ca

The Guides Hut (Fernie) 250-423-3650, 1-888-843-4885, www.theguideshut.ca

If necessary you can drive to Calgary to get what you need from

Mountain Equipment Co-op, 403-269-2420, www.mec.ca

HOW TO USE THIS BOOK

TYPE OF SKIING

All trails have been designated as either Nordic skiing or ski touring. The following definitions apply..

Nordic skiing takes place on well-maintained trails that are usually packed and often trackset. The trails are normally near to a town or road and you will likely encounter other skiers along the way.

Ski touring takes you into the backcountry, usually below treeline but sometimes up into the subalpine. Trail-breaking is often required and you may go long distances without encountering any man-made facilities or other skiers. Route finding and wilderness survival skills are essential, as is proper equipment.

AVALANCHE RATING

Each trail has been given an avalanche terrain rating, or ATR. For more information on this scale, please refer to the explanation on page 14.

DIFFICULTY RATING

We have used a simple grading system of Easy, Intermediate and Advanced. But because it is not possible to globally apply such a system to 150 trails where conditions on the ground are constantly changing, there will be times when you must use your own discretion. The grading system also takes into account that Nordic skiing requires less knowledge and experience than ski touring. Consequently an easy ski along a trackset trail would be less challenging than an easy ski tour. The three difficulty grades should be interpreted as follows:

Easy trails are normally suitable for novice or inexperienced skiers (within the parameters of the above trail designations). Route finding is not difficult and there are few hills. The length of the trip should always be taken into consideration for beginner skiers.

Intermediate trails are more challenging and will often have steep hills which require more advanced skiing ability. For ski tours a more advanced level of route finding skills will be required.

Advanced trails may have extensive sections requiring advanced skiing skills and may also present serious route finding challenges. Often these tours will be in isolated and remote areas and you must rely solely on your own resources and abilities.

NAVIGATION

Directions are almost always given in the direction of travel (e.g., "ski along the right bank of the creek; turn left at the trail junction"). Sometimes a compass direction will be given in brackets (south) to add clarity. In a few instances the true left or right bank of a stream is referred to. In these cases the direction is derived from the direction of flow of the stream and may be different from the direction of travel of the skier. For example, if you are skiing upstream along what from your point of view is the right bank of a stream, you are actually skiing on the true left bank.

Times are given for an average party under average conditions. Times can vary greatly depending on the strength and ability of the party, the weight of their packs and the depth of the trail-breaking. What might take several days under one set of circumstances could be skied in a few hours on another day. You must integrate all the factors and arrive at your own estimate of the time your trip will require. The times given in this guidebook are only guidelines.

Distances are given in kilometres and are noted as being one-way, return or loop. All distances are approximate – we did not ski these trails with a tape measure. But they are accurate enough that with a little judgment you should be able to make correct decisions.

Elevations are given in metres and were determined from the contour lines on the map. They are intended to give you an idea of how much climbing will be required on a given trail and what the maximum elevation will be. Elevation gains given in the text are referred to as vertical metres to differentiate them from horizontal distances. These elevation gains are approximate and one should use discretion in interpreting them.

Grid References

Many specific objects such as huts are given a grid reference to help you accurately locate the object (e.g., Shangri La Cabin **447**800 E **5845**000 N). On the right-hand border of each map you will find instructions on how to use the Universal Transverse Mercator (UTM) grid system to locate the object on the map. In this book all grid references are derived from the newer NAD 83 (North American Datum 1983). If you have a map derived from NAD 27 (North American Datum 1927), a slight adjustment will be necessary.

Maps

Map references given are all for the 1:50,000 National Topographic Series. These can be obtained in hard copy form from Mountain Equipment Co-op (403-269-2420) or Map Town (403-266-2241) in Calgary or at the Alpine Club of Canada in Canmore (403-678-3200).

Many of the sports shops listed beginning on page 16 will also carry select maps.

Gem Trek maps are available for the Banff, Lake Louise, Jasper, Columbia Icefield, Yoho, Kootenay, Waterton Lakes and Kananaskis regions. These excellent maps are more accurate than the NTS series. These maps will also be available at sports shops and books stores in the region.

National Geographic produces excellent 1:100,000 scale maps to Jasper and Banff National Parks that can be purchased online at www.nationalgeographic.com.

GeoBC Maps are probably the most detailed maps commercially available, but also more expensive. They are based on the Terrain Resource Information Management (TRIM) data provided by the BC government. Unfortunately they only cover areas in British Columbia and cross the boundary into Alberta only for a few kilometres. These maps are available only online at www.geobc.gov.bc.ca.

The newly produced Summits and Icefields Map, created by Mark Klassen, T.J. Neault and Chic Scott, is mainly designed for high alpine ski tours on or near the Wapta Icefields. It could be used for a number of tours in this book as well. The scale is 1:50,000 and the contour interval is 20 m. This map is available at MEC, the ACC and other book and sports shops.

Maps can be acquired online from:

www.maptown.com

www.geobc.gov.bc.ca

www.gemtrek.com

www.nrcan.gc.ca/earth-sciences/products-services/mapping-product/11616

TRIP PLANNING

You should always have at least an informal plan in the back of your mind, even for the most casual day of skiing. The more serious the trip, the better planned it should be. If you do one of the multi-day ski tours, virtually nothing should be left to chance. The following are some of the items you should consider when planning your tour:

Register out Let someone know where you are going and when you will be back.

Route Study the map and any other information so as to be completely familiar with the route. Be aware of options and alternatives along the way.

Team Know the people you are skiing with and their skill and experience level. Don't get them in over their heads or allow them to get you in over yours.

Times Establish a start time and a finish time. Leave plenty of room in your schedule to deal with the unforeseen. Check your time along the way to gauge your progress. You should decide on a turn-back time and stick to it.

Equipment Run through an equipment check before departing. Check the rest of the group for proper skis, boots and clothing. Always do a beacon check before heading out.

Weather Obtain the latest weather forecast before starting out.

Snow stability Check the avalanche hazard and snow stability forecast before making a final decision on your route.

SKI TRAILS INFORMATION

For information on the state of ski trails try the following websites:

www.skierbob.ca

www.parkscanada.gc.ca

www.acmg.ca/mcr (Association of Canadian Mountain Guides mountain conditions report)

REGULATIONS

Most of the ski tours in this book are in areas where backcountry use is controlled to some degree. The majority of the tours lie within the boundaries of five national parks: Waterton, Banff, Yoho, Kootenay and Jasper, or are located in Mount Assiniboine or Mount Robson provincial parks (in British Columbia) or Kananaskis Country (in Alberta).

National Park entrance fees

Anyone stopping in a national park must pay an entry fee. Day passes for the parks cost a maximum of $9.80 for one adult or $19.60 for up to seven people arriving in the same vehicle. A one-year pass that is good for all the national parks in this book costs $67.70 for one person or $136.40 for up to seven people. (For Waterton only, adult admission is $7.80, with adult and group annual passes at $39.20 and $98.10 respectively.) Passes are available at park entrances or at park information centres.

National Park Wilderness Pass

In the national parks it is necessary to get a Wilderness Pass if you stay overnight in the backcountry. The cost is $9.80 per night or $68.70 for an annual pass that is good for one year from date of issue. These passes can be obtained at park information centres or, if you are staying at an ACC hut, from the Alpine Club of Canada. If you are just going skiing for a day trip, a Wilderness Pass is not required.

TRAVEL INFORMATION

Reaching the Canadian Rockies

There are international airports at both Edmonton and Calgary. It is possible to fly to these cities from nearly anywhere in the world. The areas described in this book are only a few hours drive from these airports, along excellent highways. In other words, it is possible to fly from Europe and be skiing in the Canadian wilderness the following day.

Once you are here

Public transportation in the Canadian Rocky Mountains is poor, particularly in winter. It is almost imperative that you have a vehicle if you want to reach most of the trailheads.

Cars can be rented from the major international chains (Hertz, Avis, Budget) in Calgary, Edmonton, Jasper and Banff. The highways in the Rockies are all well maintained in winter and driving is normally a reasonable proposition, but the cold can make extreme demands on both car and driver. Be sure your car has antifreeze adequate for –40°c and that it is equipped with snow tires (look for the snowflake symbol), a block heater and a strong battery. Snow tires are mandatory on the Icefields Parkway between November 1 and April 1. You should carry jumper cables in your trunk in the event of a dead battery. If the thermometer plunges it is advisable to plug your car in if possible. Propane and diesel powered vehicles can be hard to start on cold winter mornings. It is best not to park along the roadside, as high-speed snowplows regularly pass by.

There are regularly scheduled Greyhound buses along the Trans-Canada Highway (Highway 1). These buses stop at all the major centres between Calgary and Vancouver such as Canmore, Banff, Lake Louise and Golden. There are also regularly scheduled Greyhound buses that travel Highway 16 between Edmonton and Jasper. Check 1-800-661-TRIP (8747) or www.greyhound.ca for further information. Brewster Transportation (403-762-6700, 1-866-606-6700, www.brewster.ca) and Sundog Transportation & Tours (403-762-4343 in Banff, 780-852-4056 in Jasper or 1-888-786-3641, www.sundogtours.com) run scheduled buses along the Icefields Parkway between Banff and Jasper.

There is regularly scheduled train service from Toronto to Vancouver via Jasper. This is an excellent way to travel if you have the time. Contact VIA Rail at 1-888-VIA-RAIL (1-888-842-7245, www.viarail.ca).

Telephone numbers

The area code for southern Alberta is 403 and for northern Alberta (including Red Deer) it is 780. The area code for British Columbia is 250 except in the lower mainland, near Vancouver, where it is 604.

Where to stay

When you get off the plane in Calgary or Edmonton you are in a major city with a population over one million. There is an endless variety of accommodation, from five-star hotels to hostels. The five major mountain towns of Canmore, Banff, Lake Louise, Golden and Jasper all have a variety of hotels, bed and breakfast establishments and hostels. More information can be obtained from:

> Banff Lake Louise Tourism Bureau
> 403-762-8421, www.banfflakelouise.com
>
> Travel Alberta
> 1-800-ALBERTA, www.travelalberta.com
>
> Tourism British Columbia
> 1-800-435-5622, www.hellobc.com

The Alpine Club of Canada

The Alpine Club of Canada operates a clubhouse and many backcountry huts throughout the Rockies. The clubhouse is located on the outskirts of Canmore and has beds for about 50. There is a fully equipped kitchen, a comfortable reading room and a sauna. The huts tend to be rustic and lean towards a philosophy of self-reliance. Some of them are secured with a combination lock. Making a booking is a simple matter of exchanging your Visa or Mastercard number for the combination lock number. Bookings can be made through the ACC office:

> The Alpine Club of Canada
> Box 8040, Canmore, AB TIW 2T8
> 403-678-3200
> info@alpineclubofcanada.ca
> www.alpineclubofcanada.ca

Hostels

Hostelling International operates a number of facilities in the Rocky Mountains. These can be booked online at www.hihostels.ca or by phone at 1-866-762-4122. The hostels in the area covered by this book are:

The Kananaskis Hostel Located near Kananaskis Village, this comfortable hostel has dormitory accommodation for 30 and five four-person private rooms. 403-591-7333.

The Banff Alpine Centre is a large, modern facility with beds for 250. There is a restaurant, lounge and self-serve kitchen. 403-762-4123.

The Lake Louise Alpine Centre is owned and operated by Hostelling International in conjunction with The Alpine Club of Canada. This fully modern facility offers 155 beds, restaurant, sauna, library, lounge and a self-serve kitchen. 403-522-2201.

Castle Mountain Hostel, located along the Bow Valley Parkway at Castle Junction, is very comfortable and has beds for 28.

The Icefields Parkway Hostels are more rustic and are almost like backcountry cabins. These are located at Mosquito Creek, Rampart Creek, Hilda Creek, Beauty Creek and Athabasca Falls along the Icefields Parkway.

Jasper Hostels There are three hostels in the Jasper area. These are:

Jasper Hostel, located 7 km from the town of Jasper.

Maligne Canyon Hostel, located 11 km from Jasper.

Edith Cavell Hostel, located southwest of Jasper, is accessible only on skis (13 km from the trailhead). Open from February 15.

Commercial Lodges

The Canadian Rockies are blessed with a rich ski history and some very beautiful backcountry lodges. These are described in the book, with full contact information. They can provide a truly memorable experience and are highly recommended.

Miscellaneous Huts

There are several other huts included: the Egypt Lake and Bryant Creek shelters, administered by Parks Canada, and Naiset Huts, which are operated by Mount Assiniboine Lodge on behalf of BC Parks. Reservations are required and can be made up to three months in advance by phoning 403-762-1556 (Egypt Lake and Bryant Creek shelters) or 403-678-2883 (Naiset Huts). The Shangri La Cabin can be booked online at www.malignelakeskiclub.ca.

Campgrounds

Parks Canada plows several campgrounds and keeps them open all winter for folks with recreational vehicles. These are Tunnel Mountain (near Banff), Lake Louise and Wapiti (near Jasper). Contact the park information service for more current information.

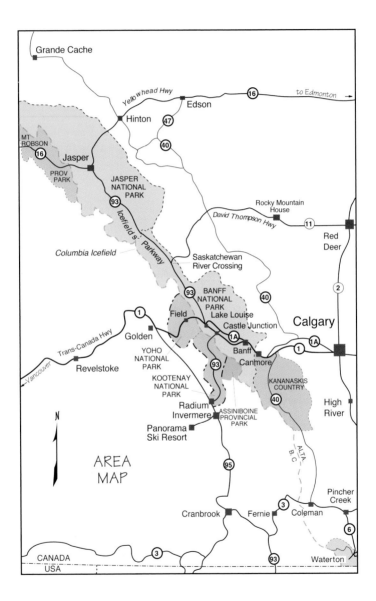

AREA MAP

WATERTON LAKES NATIONAL PARK

1. **Dipper** Intermediate, p. 28
2. **Cameron Lake** Easy, p. 29
3. **Summit Lake** Intermediate, p. 32
4. **Akamina Pass to Wall Lake and Form Lake**
   Easy/Intermediate, p. 33

Waterton Lakes National Park, the most southerly area covered in this book, is the Canadian section of the International Peace Park. Glacier National Park on the U.S. side of the border forms the southern portion. Situated in the extreme southwest corner of Alberta, this small park (505 square kilometres) is popular in summer for its backpacking and hiking trails but in winter it's very quiet and there are few amenities available.

In good snow years the skiing, especially in the Akamina Pass area, can be excellent. However, the area is affected by chinook winds, which, combined with less snowfall than in other mountain regions, may result in only marginal skiing.

Access: to Waterton Park is via Highway 6 from Pincher Creek, located 48 km north, or by Highway 5 connecting to Cardston, 45 km east. The Waterton townsite is located 8 km along a spur road off Highway 6. Chief Mountain Highway, which provides access from the United States, is closed in winter. Within the park, the Akamina Highway is the only road open, being plowed to a parking area 2.5 km short of Cameron Lake.

Facilities: There is little open in winter.

Accommodation: Crandell Mountain Lodge (www.crandellmountainlodge.com, 403-859-2288) and Waterton Lakes Resort (www.watertonlakeslodge.com, 402-859-2150) are both open in winter. Vimy's Lounge & Grill, located inside the Waterton Lakes Resort is also open in winter.

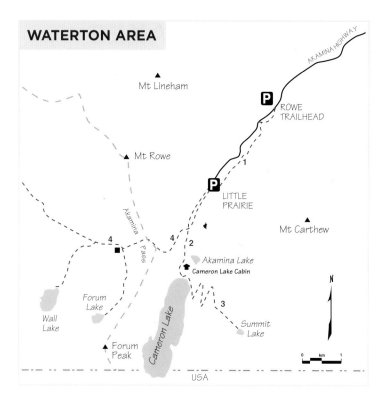

WATERTON AREA

Mt Lineham ▲

ROWE TRAILHEAD

AKAMINA HIGHWAY

Mt Rowe ▲

LITTLE PRAIRIE

Mt Carthew ▲

Akamina Pass

Akamina Lake
Cameron Lake Cabin

Forum Lake

Wall Lake

Cameron Lake

Summit Lake

Forum Peak ▲

N

0 km 1

USA

Information: Phone the visitor centre (403-859-5133) or visit www.pc.gc.ca/waterton. Phone or visit the parks office (403-859-5140), located on the right as you approach the townsite. In the event of emergency phone 403-762-4506 or 911.

1. DIPPER
Nordic Skiing, ATR 1

Grade Intermediate
Distance 6.5 km return
Time 2–3 hours

Elevation gain 50 m
Max elevation 1680 m
Map Sage Creek 82 G/1

This is a rolling and challenging trail that requires good snow conditions to be enjoyable. It is regularly trackset for classic skiing. The trail runs between the Little Prairie parking lot and the Rowe Creek trailhead and is downhill in that direction. You can use two cars and ski the trail one way if you choose. This trail is not recommended when snow conditions are icy or crusty.

Facilities: At the Little Prairie parking lot there are picnic tables, a camp shelter and toilets.

Access: Park at the Little Prairie parking lot, located at the end of the plowed section of the Akamina Highway, 13.5 km west of the town of Waterton.

From the picnic shelter, ski south for about 50 m (the opposite direction from what you would anticipate) to a large open meadow. Cross the meadow for about 100 m to find a bridge over Cameron Creek. Cross the bridge to the east side of the creek, then follow the trail north along the right bank. The trail rolls up and down little hills and is often narrow. If the snow is soft and powdery it can be a lot of fun, but if conditions are icy it can be very challenging. After about 3 km the trail crosses a bridge to the west side of the creek and ascends several hundred metres to the Rowe Creek trailhead.

2. CAMERON LAKE
Nordic Skiing, ATR 1

Grade Easy   **Elevation gain** Minimal
Distance 5 km return   **Max elevation** 1680 m
Time 1.5 hours   **Map** Sage Creek 82 G/1

This trail follows the unplowed section of the Akamina Highway from the Little Prairie parking lot to the north shore of Cameron Lake. It is a good trail for beginners and children and is regularly trackset for classic skiing.

Facilities: At the Little Prairie parking lot there are picnic tables, a camp shelter and toilets.

Kathy Madill at Cameron Lake. Photo Chic Scott

Options: On the return journey back to the Little Prairie parking lot you can follow an alternative trail that parallels the east side of the highway. This is an old road that gives you a nice downhill glide much of the way if skied south to north. It begins about halfway along the highway, opposite the Akamina Pass trailhead.

Access: Park at the Little Prairie parking lot, located at the end of the plowed section of the Akamina Highway, 13.5 km west of the town of Waterton.

Ski around the gate and continue along the unplowed section of Akamina Highway. The trail climbs very gently to begin with, then descends to the lake. Cameron Lake is a beautiful spot to eat your lunch and admire the scenery.

3. SUMMIT LAKE Ski Touring, ATR 2

Grade Intermediate
Distance 13 km return from Little Prairie
Time 6–8 hours return from Little Prairie
Elevation gain 310 m
Max elevation 1960 m
Map Sage Creek 82 G/1

This is a good trail for those who are looking for something a little more challenging. There is avalanche potential on this tour, so skiers should wear a beacon and be prepared to deal with the risks. This tour offers excellent terrain for making turns.

Access: Park at the Little Prairie parking lot, located at the end of the plowed section of the Akamina Highway, 13.5 km west of the town of Waterton.

Follow the Cameron Lake trail along the unplowed Akamina Highway to Cameron Lake. Continue along the trail around the northeast shore of the lake, crossing a bridge over Cameron Creek. Soon the trail begins to climb through the forest to the east and begins making long switchbacks. If it is a good snow year the trail will be difficult to follow. Work your way up the slope, following glades in the forest, for about 200 vertical metres. The angle of the slope is steep here and caution is advised. Eventually the angle begins to ease and the tour continues for about a kilometre in a southeast direction, crosses a low pass and then descends a short distance to Summit Lake. From here you have a good view across to the peaks in Glacier National Park. The descent back to Cameron Lake can provide excellent skiing and there are many options for descent routes.

4. AKAMINA PASS TO WALL LAKE AND FORUM LAKE
Ski Touring, ATR 1, 2

Grade Easy/intermediate

Distance 1.6 km from Akamina Highway to Akamina Pass; 4.7 km to Forum Lake; 5.6 km to Wall Lake one way

Time You can visit both lakes in a 5- to 6-hour day.

Elevation gain 220 m to Wall Lake; 360 m to Forum Lake

Max elevation 1800 m at Akamina Pass; 1780 m at Wall Lake; 2000 m at Forum Lake

Map Sage Creek 82 G/1

This trail has the best snow conditions in the area and is popular with

Kathy Madill on the trail to Akamina Pass. Photo Chic Scott

skiers who want something a little more challenging. When you cross Akamina Pass into British Columbia you are in Akamina–Kishinena Provincial Park. Snowmobiles are allowed here, so you may be sharing the trail with these machines. Forum Lake is perhaps a more exciting destination than Wall Lake, particularly if you are looking to make a few turns.

Facilities: At the Little Prairie parking lot there are picnic tables, a camp shelter and toilets.

Hazards: Snowmobiles.

Access: Park at the Little Prairie parking lot, located at the end of the plowed section of the Akamina Highway, 13.5 km west of the town of Waterton.

Follow the Cameron Lake trail along the unplowed Akamina Highway for about 1 km, then take the trail to the right toward Akamina Pass (trail sign). From here to the pass it is a moderate climb on a wide trail which runs through the trees with little in the way of views. At the pass, a cutline on the left marks the boundary of the park. The trail

Kathy Madill at Akamina Pass. Photo Chic Scott

now becomes Akamina Road, where there is a possibility of meeting snowmobiles.

To reach Forum Lake from Akamina Pass, descend gently down the BC side for about 1 km to where a trail branches off to the left. A trail sign at this point may be visible. Follow this trail for a short distance to reach a clearing where a ranger cabin is passed on the left. The trail now climbs for about 120 vertical metres where switchbacks through the trees will be hard to follow. When the angle begins to lay back, continue ahead, staying to the right to avoid a large, dangerous hillside on the left. The lake is tucked in an impressive cirque under Forum Peak.

To reach Wall Lake continue for several kilometres past the turn-off to Forum Lake, to the next trail branching to the left, which goes to Wall Lake (sign post). The route from here is obvious except at one point where a trail sign points up the ridge to Wall Lake. Do not take this cutoff but continue straight ahead along the obvious trail to the lake. The trail cuts the corner and climbs over the ridge, then runs along the creek to the lake. There is an impressive mountain wall behind the lake covered in frozen waterfalls.

"Why should we be in such desperate haste to succeed, and in such desperate enterprises? If a man does not keep pace with his companions, perhaps it is because he hears a different drummer. Let him step to the music which he hears, however measured and far away."

—*Henry David Thoreau,* Walden

FERNIE AND THE CROWSNEST PASS

5. **Fernie Alpine Resort** Easy/Intermediate, p. 39
6. **Fernie Golf Course** Easy, p. 41
7. **Island Lake** Easy/Intermediate, p. 42
8. **Boivin Creek** Easy, p. 43
9. **Allison Chinook** Easy/Intermediate, p. 45
10. **Syncline Cross Country Ski Area**
    Easy/Intermediate, p. 47

Fernie is located on the western side of the Canadian Rockies along Highway 3 (Crowsnest Highway). It is a town with about 5,000 residents and is best known for its downhill ski area, the Fernie Alpine Resort. Towering cedar forests and a humid climate give the Nordic trails a unique feel, unlike anywhere else in the Rockies.

The Municipality of Crowsnest Pass is the combination of five communities along Highway 3 which includes, from east to west, Bellevue, Hillcrest, Frank, Blairmore and Coleman. At one time the Crowsnest was one of Canada's premier coal mining regions. Today there are no working coal mines on the Alberta side of the Crowsnest Pass, but interest has once again begun to rise. The region is also known for its high winds that strip the land of its snow. Luckily most of the Nordic trails are sheltered in the trees and retain their snow even when the highway is bare.

Highway 3 runs east to west, passing through the Crowsnest Pass, Sparwood and Fernie. Elkford is located north of Sparwood on Highway 43 (Elk Valley Highway). The easiest access to the Crowsnest Pass is from Lethbridge, a 2-hour drive away on Highway 3. Calgary is a 3½-hour drive from the Crowsnest Pass following Highway 2 south from Calgary to Fort Macleod and then west on Highway 3.

Facilities: Fernie and the Crowsnest Pass have all the amenities

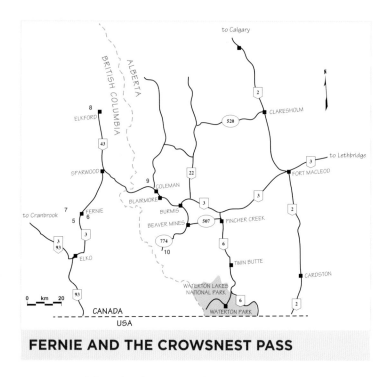

FERNIE AND THE CROWSNEST PASS

you may need for a ski adventure, with many gas stations, supermarkets and accommodations. The Crowsnest Pass does not have any stores selling or renting ski gear. Fernie, on the other hand, is well equipped with many locations where you can buy or rent ski equipment. Nordic rentals can be found beside the day lodge at Fernie Alpine Resort and at The Quest Outdoor Sports Rental (250-423-9252). A large selection of outdoor gear can be found at GearHub Sports (250-423-5555) and at The Guide's Hut (250-423-3650), both located in downtown Fernie.

Accommodation: Fernie and the Crowsnest Pass have many good places to stay, from quaint bed and breakfasts to large hotels. Budget accommodation can be found in Fernie at the Raging Elk Hostel (www.ragingelk.com, 250-423-6811).

A little history

On April 29, 1903, 90 million tons of rock came crashing down from Turtle Mountain, partially burying the town of Frank, Alberta. Seventy of Frank's 600 residents were killed, making this the deadliest landslide in Canadian history. Today the highway passes through the immense boulder field left by the calamity. The Frank was Canada's biggest landslide until the Hope Slide in BC in 1965.

Many of Canada's most tragic mining accidents occurred in the region's numerous coal mines. In 1914 an explosion killed 189 workers in the Hillcrest mine, claiming the title of Canada's worst mining accident. The Coal Creek Mine near Fernie also had its share of tragedy when, in 1902, 128 men were killed in an underground explosion.

5. FERNIE ALPINE RESORT NORDIC SKI TRAILS
Nordic Skiing, ATR 1

Grade Most routes are easy/intermediate.
Distance 10 km of trails
Max elevation 1100 m

Map Elko 82 G/6
Groomed for skate and classic skiing

This is a great trail system that feels as though it is a world away from the alpine resort it is situated beside. The trails wind through stunning cedar forests and are groomed frequently.

Facilities: There are toilets at the day lodge.

Note: Trail maps are located along the trail. You can also find maps and grooming reports at www.fernienordic.com.

Access: Drive down Highway 3 and turn at the well-signed Fernie Alpine Resort, a few kilometres south of Fernie. Continue left past the day lodge. The trailhead starts at parking lot number four.

TRAIL (SILK TRAIL)

1.5 km   Difficult

This trail links the parking lot with the Silk/Manchuria Loop. This is

Stephanie Vetsch skate skiing among the cedars at Fernie Alpine Resort. Photo Darren Farley

the steepest trail encountered, and can be daunting for beginners. The return to the trailhead can be challenging as well, especially when icy.

SILK/MANCHURIA LOOP

3.8 km   Easy

If skied counterclockwise, the Manchuria Trail starts with a steep but short uphill and then levels off. Pleasant skiing through cedar forest brings you to the connector trail offering a rather steep and exhilarating S bend turn before connecting with the Silk trail. Heading back on the Silk Trail offers a gradual uphill with a few steeper grades.

SCANDIA LOOP

4.5 km   Easy

In either direction, the Scandia Loop offers pleasant, rolling terrain. Near the farthest part of the loop, the cedars begin to dissipate, while birch and aspen trees become more prevalent. A wonderful view of Elk Valley emerges as the trees begin to thin, offering a nice reward.

6. FERNIE GOLF COURSE
Nordic Skiing, ATR 1

Grade Most trails are easy.   **Map** Fernie 82 G/11
Distance 12 km of trails   Groomed for classic skiing
Max elevation 1000 m

Fernie Golf Course is a great location for beginners or individuals wanting to get in a quick workout. The trails are all relatively flat but the open fairways allow for ample views of the surrounding valley.

Access: Coming from the east on Highway 3, turn left onto 6th Avenue shortly after crossing the Elk River. Continue onto Fairway Drive and follow it the end of the road, where you will find the clubhouse and parking area.

Note: The trails are groomed by the Fernie Nordic Society. There are trail maps on their website: www.fernienordic.com.

7. ISLAND LAKE
Nordic Skiing, ATR 1

Grade Easy/intermediate
Distance 16 km return
Time 2–4 hours
Height gain 300 m

Max elevation 1400 m
Maps Elko 82 G/6, Fernie 82 G/11
Groomed for skate and classic
skiing

This trail offers a pleasant ski into the heart of the Lizard Range. The upper section of the trail is blessed with many giant cedars, a rare sight in the Rockies.

Facilities: Island Lake Lodge offers lunch on Fridays and Saturdays. Reservations are required and are preferred 24 hours in advance: www.islandlakeresorts.com.

Hazards: Watch out for snowmobiles and snowcats frequenting the trail.

Access: Follow Highway 3 for a short distance west of Fernie, then turn right onto Cedar Valley Road. The road is well signed for both Island Lake Lodge and Mount Fernie Provincial Park. A parking lot is located a few kilometres along.

The trail begins at the left-hand side of the parking lot. Starting off relatively flat, the trail is good for beginners. It joins up and follows the cat track for a short distance before diving back into the forest. The trail swaps between the cat track and a designated Nordic trail for the rest of the way to the lodge. The final few kilometres to the lodge climb very steeply up switchbacks. Descending this section can be daunting in less than perfect snow conditions. Once you are at the lodge, there is a short loop that circumnavigates Island Lake. These trails are frequently groomed by the staff at Island Lake Lodge. If the Nordic trail is not groomed, the cat track is usually perfect for skate skiing, as it is driven daily bringing guests and employees to the lodge. The return to the parking lot from the lodge is very quick and, if conditions are good, can be done faster than guests taking a cat ride out from the lodge.

Stephanie Vetsch, Alberto Penate and Aaron Labovich start up the trail to Island Lake Lodge. Photo Darren Farley

8. BOIVIN CREEK
Nordic Skiing, ATR 1

Grade Easy
Distance 14 km return
Time 2–5 hours
Height gain 300 m

Max elevation 1645 m
Map Fording River 82 J/2
Groomed for classic skiing

This trail makes for a wonderful outing and is a great reason for visiting Elkford. Starting along a beautiful creek, the trail gradually climbs high into an alpine valley. Being near the Continental Divide, the trail gets snow early and keeps it late.

Facilities: There are two warming huts with outhouses. Boivin Hut is about 3 km up the trail, and Wildcat Hut is at 6.5 km. Overnighting in either hut is not allowed.

Boivin Hut. Photo Darren Farley

Skiing towards Wildcat Hut. Photo Darren Farley

Note: The trails are maintained and trackset by members of the Elkford Nordic Club. There is a donation box at the trailhead.

Access: Drive to Elkford along the Elk Valley Highway (Highway 43). After the highway crosses a bridge over Boivin Creek, take the first left onto Michel Road, then turn left onto Fording Drive, followed by a right turn onto Natal Road. Continue up Natal Road for 1.1 km. The trailhead is on the left-hand side of the road. Continuing along the road leads to the Wapiti Valley Ski Hill.

The trail begins by skirting along the banks of Boivin Creek. After a few hundred metres the track splits into two one-way trails that rejoin again soon after. After crossing a bridge over the creek, the trail begins to climb steadily, then becomes gentler as Boivin Hut is approached. The hut is approximately 3 km from the road and is just a short distance off the trail. Inside is a wood-burning stove and benches along the side walls. The hut makes a great destination for children or beginner skiers. After the hut, the trail climbs steadily, and as the elevation increases, the views improve. Several cutblocks are reached which provide good views of the magnificent surrounding peaks. The angle begins to ease as Wildcat Hut comes near. The trail splits into a one-way loop a few hundred metres before Wildcat Hut, located 6.5 km from the trailhead. The hut is almost identical to Boivin Hut, having a wood-burning stove in the middle and benches along the sides. The return journey down the creek is very quick.

9. ALLISON CHINOOK
Nordic Skiing, ATR 1

Grade Most routes are easy/intermediate.
Distance 30 km of trails
Max elevation 1400 m

Map Crowsnest 82 G/10
Groomed for classic and skate skiing

Allison Chinook is the Crowsnest Pass's premier Nordic trail system. The trails receive plenty of snow, which may be surprising, as the nearby town of Coleman rarely gets enough for a snowball fight. Aside from good snow, the vistas of the surrounding peaks are marvellous. Crowsnest Mountain looms overhead, adding a stunning backdrop to the forested trails.

Access: A few kilometres west of Coleman, turn right (north) off Highway 3 onto Allison Creek Road. The turnoff is signed "Chinook Lake Provincial Recreation Area 6 km." Follow the road for 2.6 km to reach a junction, then turn left (signed for ski trails) and continue along for 1 km. Parking is alongside the road, across from a fish hatchery.

Facilities: There are a couple of warming shelters and washrooms throughout the trail system.

Note: These trails were built and are maintained by the Crowsnest Pass Cross Country Ski Association and there is a $5 suggested donation for use by non-members. There is a sign-in station and donation box at the trailhead. The trails are groomed weekly from December 1 through March 31. Trail information and maps can be found at www.allisonwonderlands.ca.

Crowsnest Mountain looms over the trails at Allison Chinook. Photo Darren Farley

10. SYNCLINE XC SKI AREA
Nordic Skiing, ATR 1

Grade Most routes are easy/
   intermediate.
Distance 20 km of trails

Elevation 1300 m
Map Beaver Mines 82 G/8
Groomed for classic skiing

These are a collection of pleasant single-track trails a short distance from Castle Mountain Ski Resort. Snow quality can be variable and doesn't seem to last as long as a lot of other trail systems. It's a good idea to check the Syncline trail conditions blog or the Castle Mountain snow report before making the trip: synclinecastletrails.blogspot.ca; www.skicastle.ca.

Darren Farley skis along the West Castle River. Photo Darren Farley

Access: From Pincher Creek follow Highway 507 to Beaver Mines. Turn left at Beaver Mines onto Highway 774. Follow the road until it crosses the South Castle River (where the pavement ends). There are two parking areas. The first is on the left 700 m after the bridge. The main parking lot is also on the left, 1.7 km past the bridge.

Facilities: There are washrooms at the main parking lot.

Note: There is a kiosk at the main parking lot with trail maps and information. The trails are groomed and maintained by the Syncline Castle Trails Association. There is a donation box at the trailhead.

"On the other hand, there is a cleanness and virginity, an exquisite loneliness, about many of the Rocky Mountain peaks and valleys that has a peculiar charm. There is the feeling of having made a new discovery, of having caught Nature unawares at her work of creation, as one turns off from a scarcely-beaten route into one never trodden at all by the feet of white men; and this experience may be had in a thousand valleys among the Rockies."

—*A. P. Coleman,* The Canadian Rockies, New and Old Trails

CALGARY NORDIC TRAILS

11. **Canada Olympic Park** Advanced, p. 50
12. **Shaganappi Golf Course** Easy, p. 52
13. **Confederation Golf Course** Easy, p. 52
14. **Maple Ridge Golf Course** Easy, p. 52

Calgary is situated on the prairies about an hour's drive east of the Canadian Rockies. With over one million residents, the city houses a large portion of the recreationalists that use the mountain parks. Calgary also has an international airport, making it the gateway to the mountains for many visitors.

Even here in the land of suburbs and oil companies it is possible to get away and enjoy a few hours of Nordic skiing. Calgary has three golf courses that are regularly trackset by volunteers, and the trails at Canada Olympic Park are always in pristine condition. The frequent chinooks (warm westerly winds) that blow through town make snow conditions variable, so it is best to wait until after a snowfall to make use of the trail systems on the golf courses.

Highway 1 (Trans-Canada Highway) passes through Calgary and continues on to Canmore, Banff and Lake Louise. It is the quickest way to access the Rocky Mountains. Highway 1A (also known as Bow Valley Trail) begins at the northwest edge of Calgary and parallels Highway 1. The highway goes through the town of Cochrane and ends in the town of Canmore. It is a scenic option for those wanting a more relaxed journey to the mountains.

Facilities: Everything you need for a ski trip can be found in Calgary. Mountain Equipment Co-op is the go-to place for gear (www.mec.ca, 403-269-2420). Across from MEC is Atmosphere (www.atmosphere.ca, 403-264-2444). Spirit West has a selection of new gear as well as used outdoor equipment (www.outdoorspirit.ca, 403-263-1381). Equipment rentals can be found at both Mountain Equipment Co-op and the University of Calgary Outdoor Centre (www.calgaryoutdoorcentre.ca, 403-220-5038).

Accommodation: Calgary has accommodations for all budgets. Inexpensive options are listed at:

Hi Hostel Calgary (www.hihostels.ca/calgary, 778-328-2220, 1-866-762-4122)

Wicked Hostel (www.wickedhostel.com, 403-265-8777, 877-889-8777)

There are many companies offering shuttle service from the Calgary International Airport to Banff. Banff Airporter is a popular option (www.banffairporter.com, 1-888-449-2901).

11. CANADA OLYMPIC PARK
Nordic Skiing, ATR 1

Canada Olympic Park (COP) was built to host events for the 1988 Winter Olympics. But because the cross-country skiing and biathlon events were held at the Canmore Nordic Centre, no trail system suitable for races and long-distance skiing was ever created in Calgary. Today there is a small but strenuous loop for Nordic skiers located at the base of the ski jumps. The loop is approximately 2.5 km, trackset for both classic and skate skiing, and the grooming is impeccable. The trail is illuminated at night, but can be especially busy on weeknights, when Calgary's many ski clubs use the facilities for training and lessons. Because of their extensive use of snowmaking equipment, COP is the best option in the city for consistently good snow. More information can be found at www.winsport.ca.

Facilities: Toilets, food and water are available in the main day lodge. There is a small warming hut and gear rental hut at the beginning of the Nordic trails.

Hours of operation:

Weekdays 9 am – 9 pm

Weekends 9 am – 5 pm

Cost: $114.28 adult season pass, $25 day pass (subject to weekday/weekend variations)

Access: Canada Olympic Park is located at the western edge of the city, just off of Highway 1 (Trans-Canada Highway). To access the Nordic ski trails, park at the first pullout along Canada Olympic Drive. The Nordic trails begin on the south side of the road.

Canada Olympic Park (88 Canada Olympic Rd. sw, Calgary, AB T3B 5R5, 403-247-5452).

GOLF COURSES

Three of Calgary's golf courses are routinely trackset by volunteers from local ski clubs. There are no fees for skiing on any of the golf courses.

Darren Farley admires the skyline of Calgary from the Shaganappi golf course trails. Photo Darren Farley

12. SHAGANAPPI GOLF COURSE
Nordic Skiing, ATR 1

This is an 18-hole course that is groomed for classic and skate skiing when there is enough snow. The trails are situated in a lovely location overlooking the Bow River and downtown Calgary. There are maps along the trails. More information can be found at https://calgaryskiclub.org/useful-links.

Location: 1200 26 St. sw. It is possible to use the clubhouse parking lot. There are no facilities open in winter.

13. CONFEDERATION GOLF COURSE
Nordic Skiing, ATR 1

This is a nine-hole course that is groomed for classic skiing. Confederation also hosts the Lions Festival of Lights, which takes place on the fairway along 14th Street from November 29 through January 8. You can ski along the light displays, which are turned on nightly from 7 pm to midnight.

Location: 3204 Collingwood Dr. nw. Parking is along the road, as the gate to the clubhouse parking area is usually closed. The gate is left open just wide enough for skiers to squeeze through.

14. MAPLE RIDGE GOLF COURSE
Nordic Skiing, ATR 1

This is an 18-hole course located at the corner of Deerfoot Trail and Anderson Road. The course is only trackset for classic skiing.

Location: 1240 Mapleglade Dr. se. The clubhouse parking lot is closed in the winter. It is possible to park along the road at the end of Mapleglade Drive. The gate is left open wide enough for skiers to squeeze through.

MOUNT ASSINIBOINE PROVINCIAL PARK

15. **Shark to Assiniboine via Bryant Creek**
    Intermediate/Advanced, p. 63

16. **Sunshine to Assiniboine via Citadel Pass**
    Advanced, p. 67

17. **Banff to Assiniboine via Allenby Pass**
    Advanced, p. 69

18. **Assiniboine to Banff via Spray River**
    Intermediate, p. 71

19. **Og Pass** Easy/Intermediate, p. 72

20. **Dead Horse Canyon** Easy/Intermediate, p. 73

21. **Moose Bath** Easy/Intermediate, p. 74

22. **Jones Bench** Easy/Intermediate, p. 75

23. **Wonder Pass** Easy, p. 76

24. **Ely's Dome** Advanced, p. 77

Getting some turns at Assiniboine, p. 79

Mount Assiniboine Provincial Park offers some of the finest ski touring in the Rockies. There is always plenty of snow, the terrain is rolling and open and the scenery is outstanding.

For information about Mount Assiniboine Provincial Park, navigate from the BC Parks main webpage, www.bcparks.ca.

Access: The park cannot be accessed by motor vehicle. The usual methods of approach are either by helicopter or on skis. The helicopter is quick and comfortable but costly. As a compromise many parties fly in but ski out. For helicopter information or reservations, contact Mount Assiniboine Lodge (403-678-2883).

There are three ski access routes described in this guidebook. The route from Shark Mountain is the shortest and most popular. The route

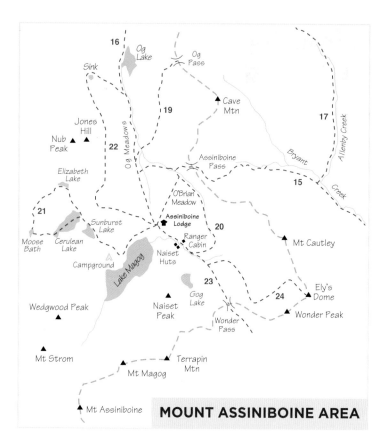

MOUNT ASSINIBOINE AREA

from Sunshine Village Ski Resort is longer and more difficult but still sees some traffic. The route from Banff over Allenby Pass, although the historic way to Mount Assiniboine, is now rarely used.

Facilities: There are several overnight possibilities offering varying degrees of comfort and cost: Mount Assiniboine Lodge, the Naiset Huts or camping. The lodge is historic and very comfortable; the Naiset Huts are rustic but much more affordable; and there is also a designated camping area on the meadows. All of these are administered by Mount Assiniboine Lodge.

Mount Assiniboine towers above a cabin at Mount Assiniboine Lodge. Photo Chic Scott

Regulations: Helicopter access to the park is restricted to landings at Mount Assiniboine Lodge or the Naiset Huts three days of the week only: Wednesdays, Fridays and Sundays. On long weekends flights are allowed on Mondays instead of Sundays. If you are skiing to Mount Assiniboine Park and are planning on spending a night at the Bryant Creek shelter, you will need a reservation from Banff National Park.

A little history

The meadows below Mount Assiniboine and the mountain itself have been a destination for adventure seekers for over 100 years. Mount Assiniboine was first climbed in 1901 by British clergyman James Outram, led by his Swiss guides Christian Bohren and Christian Hasler Sr. Their ascent was a remarkable tour de force – in only five days they travelled from Banff via Sunshine Meadows, traversed the mountain (up the southwest face and down the north ridge), then returned to Banff.

In 1922 the BC government created Mount Assiniboine Provincial Park, and in 1925 A.O. Wheeler (founder of The Alpine Club of

Canada) built several cabins (now called the Naiset Huts) which he used for his guided walking tours. Eventually these cabins were sold to The Alpine Club of Canada for a minimal amount.

In March of 1928 a young ski adventurer, Erling Strom, and his aristocratic partner, the Marquis d'Albizzi, led four clients to Mount Assiniboine over Allenby Pass. After spending several weeks skiing in the meadows below the striking tower of Mount Assiniboine, Strom was hooked. He returned that summer and, in partnership with the Canadian Pacific Railway, built Mount Assiniboine Lodge, which opened for business the following spring. If you visit the lodge today you can see the names of the early guests carved into the logs high over the main entrance to the dining room.

The 1930s was a growth decade for skiing in the Canadian Rockies and folks came from all over North America to experience the beauty and grandeur of the area. In those days guests and their guides would ski 60 km from Banff, over Allenby Pass, staying at two smaller cabins along the way (Ten Mile and Halfway). Fresh supplies were packed in the same way (on men's backs!) but staples were brought in on horseback the previous autumn and stored in the root cellar. During this era, if you came to Assiniboine, you were there for two, three or even four weeks. You could relax and adjust to a wilderness pace of life.

Strom operated the lodge for about 50 years, but the winter trade never became a large part of the operation, likely because the travel distance from Banff or Sunshine village was so far. Eventually Strom sold the lodge to the province of British Columbia, which then leased it out to commercial operators. For almost 30 years, beginning in 1983, Swiss-born mountain guide Sepp Renner and his wife Barb operated the lodge. Today their son André and his partner Claude Duchesne and wife Annick operate Mount Assiniboine Lodge. In 2010 and 2011 BC Parks undertook a major restoration project, putting a proper cement foundation underneath the lodge. With the advent of helicopter access, ski traffic has picked up and now forms a large portion of the yearly business.

Meanwhile the ACC cabins, which came to be known as the Naiset Huts, fell into disrepair over the years. In 1971 they were sold to the

A reunion of old-timers at Mount Assiniboine Lodge (left to right) Catharine Whyte, Lizzie Rummel, Aileen Harmon, Ken Jones, Sam Evans and Ray Bagley. Photo Aileen Harmon Collection

BC government, which completely refurbished them. In recent years a communal cook shelter has been built in the centre of the group of cabins. Today the Naiset Huts are operated by Mount Assiniboine Lodge, which charges a modest overnight fee.

A little more history

Erling Strom was born in 1897 in Norway and emigrated to the United States in 1919. For years he was a ski instructor at Lake Placid and ran a lodge at Stowe, Vermont. He is noted for making the second ascent of Denali (Mount McKinley, North America's highest peak) in 1932 using skis high on the mountain. Strom, however, will always be associated with Mount Assiniboine and his beautiful lodge in the meadows below the peak.

And again

Sepp Renner, a mountain guide originally from Andermatt, Switzerland, and Barb MacGougan of Calgary met in 1972 at Stanley Mitchell Hut in the Little Yoho Valley and were married two years later. Three children

MOUNT ASSINIBOINE LODGE

Mount Assiniboine Lodge is what one imagines the postcard picture of a Canadian Rockies ski lodge should look like. This historic log building sits in the meadows beneath the impressive tower of Mount Assiniboine, one of the most spectacular peaks in the world. The accommodation is very comfortable, with gourmet meals and guiding service.

Location In the meadow along the NE shore of Lake Magog (597100 E 5640500 N)

Map Mount Assiniboine 82 J/13

Facilities A central lodge surrounded by seven guest cabins. There is a separate washroom building that is propane heated, with showers and a large sauna. The lodge is equipped with a telephone.

Capacity about 30

Hosts André Renner, Claude Duchesne and his wife Annick

Season February to the beginning of April

Cost About $230/person/night, which includes guiding and all meals; minimum two-night stay; beer and wine available for purchase; helicopter flight is about $150 each way

Reservations Mount Assiniboine Lodge,
Box 8128, Canmore, AB T1W 2T8
403-678-2883, fax 403-678-4877
info@assiniboinelodge.com
www.assiniboinelodge.com

The owners and operators of Mount Assiniboine Lodge: (l to r) André Renner, Annick Duchesne and Claude Duchesne. Photo Chic Scott.

Mount Assiniboine Lodge. Photo Chic Scott

Erling Strom. WMCR NA66-1366

soon followed: André (1974), Sara (1976) and Natalie (1978). Sepp worked many years for Canadian Mountain Holidays as a heli-ski guide, but in the autumn of 1983 he and Barb took over management of Mount Assiniboine Lodge. For 30 years the couple made the lodge their home and livelihood, giving guests a magical experience in this mountain paradise. Summer and winter, through flower-filled meadows and across snowy peaks, Sepp and Barb safely guided their guests, then brought

NAISET HUTS

A large, modern cook shelter surrounded by five small, rustic cabins.

Location In the trees above the east end of Lake Magog (597200 E 5640400 N)

Map Mount Assiniboine 82 J/13

Facilities The cook shelter is heated and has two large tables. Two small stovetops are available, as well as pots and utensils. The five sleeping cabins are small and simple, with wooden bunks and foam pads. There are small heating stoves in the sleeping cabins. "Fire logs" to use in the cabins can be purchased at Assiniboine Lodge.

Capacity There is one cabin for 5 people, plus two cabins for 6 and two for 8, for a total capacity of 33.

Cost $25/person/night

Water From a hole in the ice in Magog Creek about 100 m from the cook shelter

Reservations Mount Assiniboine Lodge, 403-678-2883

Jonesy, one of the Naiset Huts, is an inexpensive place to stay. Photo Chic Scott

Sepp and Barb Renner ran Mount Assiniboine
Lodge for 30 years. Photo Sara Renner

Lizzie Rummel. WMCR NA66-2248

them home to gourmet meals in the historic lodge. Their children grew up here beneath the spectacular peak of Mount Assiniboine. In 2010 Sepp and Barb retired and their son André and guide Claude Duchesne and his wife Annick won the contract to manage Mount Assiniboine Lodge. Under Sepp and Barb's guidance the lodge has earned a world-wide reputation for excellence in mountain hospitality.

A little history

Sunburst Lake Camp was owned operated by Lizzie Rummel for 20 years, from 1951 to 1970. As well as the cabin there were several tent cabins and her famous tipi. Lizzie became a legend in the Canadian

Rockies and eventually had a school, two lakes and a street in Canmore named after her. People would journey from around the world to spend time with her on the shores of Sunburst Lake. She could always remind us of what was really important and beautiful in life.

> At Sunburst Lake Lizzie was completely at home. She was one with the trees, the flowers and the deer that would visit her place. In the winter she loved the snow that almost covered her cabin, and she enjoyed to glide on skis through the larches and over the hills around her. I think there has seldom been a situation where a person was so much a part of a place. In a way she was like Mount Assiniboine itself. She stood out above all around her – not domineering but like a beautiful spirit.

> —Hans Gmoser

15. SHARK TO ASSINIBOINE VIA BRYANT CREEK
Ski Touring, ATR 1

Grade Intermediate/advanced

Distance 27 km one way

Time It is a very full day to ski to Mount Assiniboine, and many parties take two days. Most parties can ski back out to the Shark Mountain parking lot in one day if they get an early start.

Elevation gain 440 m

Max elevation 2180 m

Maps Mount Assiniboine 82 J/13, Spray Lakes Reservoir 82 J/14

Facilities: There are toilets at the Shark Mountain trailhead. The Bryant Creek Shelter is located about halfway along this tour. The Naiset Huts and Mount Assiniboine Lodge are located near Lake Magog.

Hazards: The slopes above the trail below Assiniboine Pass present some avalanche hazard.

Access: The trail to Mount Assiniboine starts from a large parking lot at the Shark Mountain cross-country ski trails. To reach this lot, drive through the town of Canmore and follow the Smith-Dorrien/

Margaret Gmoser and Skip Pessl ski along the
Bryant Creek trail. Photo Chic Scott

Spray trail up the hillside and through the narrow pass. After 38 km turn right at the turnoff for Engadine Lodge. Drive past the entrance to the lodge and continue down the road for 5 km to the parking lot.

Most parties who ski to Mount Assiniboine use this route and it is usually well packed. Often skiers will fly to Assiniboine and ski back out to their cars via this trail. The only real difficulty is the descent from Assiniboine Pass, which is very steep. Often it is best to just remove your skis and walk down.

BRYANT CREEK SHELTER

This rustic cabin is often used as an overnight stop on the way to Mount Assiniboine.

Location At the far corner of a meadow, 600 m southwest of the warden cabin, on the west side of the trail along Bryant Creek (6**04**200 E 56**394**00 N)

Map Mount Assiniboine 82 J/13

Facilities Wood heating stove, axe and woodpile. There are no cooking stoves, pots or utensils. Bare wooden bunks with no foamies.

Capacity 18

Water Bryant Creek

Reservations Banff Visitor Centre, 403-762-1550

Bryant Creek Shelter. Photo Chic Scott

From the Shark Mountain parking lot follow the Watridge Lake trail (see page 114). It is a wide, trackset route with many signs marking the way. After about 3 km the trail climbs for a short distance and this is about as far as it will be trackset. The trail then descends steeply for about 100 vertical metres, crosses some flats and then crosses the Spray River on a bridge. From here the trail climbs briefly, then meanders through the forest for 500 m until it crosses Bryant Creek on another bridge.

From Bryant Creek, climb a short distance up the hillside, then turn left along the Bryant Creek trail. Soon there is another junction and here you stay right (the left fork goes down to a warden cabin). For the next 10 km the route stays on the right side of the valley and is easy to follow as it runs through the forest. After about 2 km the trail crosses a bridge over a creek, then continues for another 2 km and begins to climb. The grade is gentle at first but gradually the trail steepens. Just before reaching the Bryant Creek shelter the trail climbs a steep, open hillside and continues a short distance through forest before descending to a meadow. The Bryant Creek shelter is located about 600 m across the meadow to the left.

Cross the right flank of the meadow, enter the trees again and then ski past the Bryant Creek warden cabin. Follow the trail along the edge of the trees on the right side of the valley for about 3 km, then ski out left into the middle of the valley. Cross the meadows to the left-centre of the valley and continue for about 4 km to the hillside below the pass, sometimes following bits of trail through trees and sometimes open meadow.

The climb to Assiniboine Pass is steep and gains about 200 vertical metres. The trail follows the left side of the valley and eventually makes several switchbacks near the top. It works its way between two cliff bands, then traverses out to the right to the lowest point in the pass.

Ski through the pass and climb a small, steep hillside to a higher point. From here the trail descends a long slope out into O'Brien's Meadow. Cross the meadow and climb the hillside on the opposite side, then ski around a little pond before entering the trees. From here the trail heads south to the lodge, crossing meadows and traversing sections of forest. If it is early in the season and there has not been much traffic, this trail can be hard to follow.

Assiniboine Lodge is situated on a bench above Lake Magog. The Naiset Huts and the Ranger Cabin are about 300 m to the south of the lodge, along Magog Creek.

16. SUNSHINE TO ASSINIBOINE VIA CITADEL PASS
Ski Touring, ATR 3

Grade Advanced
Distance 30 km one way
Time Although this tour can be done in one long day, many parties will take two days.

Elevation gain 730 m
Elevation loss 760 m
Max elevation 2390 m
Maps Banff 82 O/4, Mount Assiniboine 82 J/13

The approach to Mount Assiniboine from Sunshine Village ski resort is not often used nowadays. It is hard for most of us to resist the appeal of the helicopter, and if we do, we usually opt for the shorter and easier route from Shark Mountain via Assiniboine Pass. However, if you are looking for some adventure and a long, hard tour, this trip might be for you.

Facilities: There are two cabins located at Police Meadow about halfway along this tour (590600 E 5648800 N). Note that these cabins are incorrectly marked on old topo maps. The structures were in good shape and the stove was in working order in the late 1990s but may have fallen into disrepair. These cabins are privately owned but are left open for use in emergency.

Hazards: There are a number of hazards on this tour. First of all you need good visibility to find your way across Sunshine Meadows to Citadel Pass. The descent from the pass to the Simpson River is subject to avalanche hazard, and good route finding skills are required. If you plan to stay at the Police Meadow cabins, you will find them tricky to locate, so leave yourself some daylight to get settled in. Finally, the route up Golden Valley and the Valley of the Rocks is famous for bottomless depth hoar and tricky route finding, so be prepared for hard trail-breaking. This tour will challenge most skiers.

Access: Begin at Sunshine Village and ski 10 km to Citadel Pass. (See the Citadel Pass tour beginning on page 148)

From Citadel Pass the route descends 600 m to the headwaters of the Simpson River. This descent is subject to avalanche threat from both sides, but the route itself is reasonably safe if you follow the best line. It is possible to stay on lower-angled or treed slopes almost all the way.

From the pass the route descends very gently for the first kilometre, past a lake, then climbs briefly to the brow of a steep hill. As you come down from Citadel Pass be sure to follow the drainage out to the left and not get drawn off to the right by an obvious line of meadows. Descend the steep hill using the safety of the trees wherever possible. There is some avalanche hazard at the top of the hill. From the bottom of this steep hill the remainder of the descent to the valley bottom stays in the centre of the drainage. However, there are serious avalanche paths on both sides, so exercise caution.

As you descend you can look directly south across the valley to a side valley where you will see a large meadow. This is Police Meadow, and if you look very closely you might be able to spot the cabin on the right flank of the meadow. If you intend to stay at the cabin, the best approach route in the winter is to follow the left bank of the creek downstream (serious bushwhacking) until it joins the Simpson River, then turn left and ski upstream along the river for about 1.5 km to reach the meadow.

The route up Golden Valley is a frustrating series of hills and sinks. There is no proper drainage to follow and you are continually climbing small hills only to descend again on the other side. It is recommended that you work your way along the left (northeast) side of the valley and attempt to ski near the edge of the trees if possible. Higher up in Valley of the Rocks the going gets easier: the trees spread out, the terrain is uniform and it is possible to make some headway.

About 1.5 km before Og Lake, the trail leaves the trees behind and from here to Lake Magog crosses open meadows. The route passes Og Lake and heads south through a narrow gap, then continues for about 3 km across flat, open meadows. The last kilometre ascends a draw (the entrance to the draw has cliffs on its west side) located at the south end of the meadow, which leads to Mount Assiniboine Lodge.

Margaret Gmoser and Barb Renner ski through Allenby Pass. Photo Chic Scott

17. BANFF TO ASSINIBOINE VIA ALLENBY PASS
Ski Touring, ATR 3

Grade Advanced
Distance About 50 km one way
Time Normally 2 days are required for this tour.
Elevation gain 1070 m over Allenby Pass; 260 m over Assiniboine Pass

Elevation loss 500 m from Allenby Pass to Bryant Creek
Max elevation 2440 m at Allenby Pass
Maps Banff 82 O/4, Mount Assiniboine 82 J/13

This is the original route to Mount Assiniboine that was followed by Erling Strom and his party in 1928. It was used for many years afterwards by guides and their guests, but today it is rarely travelled. It is a long way but if you have the time and energy and you like history it is recommended.

Facilities: Banff Sundance Lodge (403-762-4551) is located along Brewster Creek (593400 E 5661600 N) and is open in winter. Halfway Cabin is located along the creek in a high bowl 3 km north of Allenby Pass (599400 E 5649800 N) but is closed in the winter.

Access: Park your car 800 m along the Sunshine Village Ski Resort access road at the start of the trail along Old Healy Creek Road to Sundance Lodge (see page 134). (**Note:** The bridge over Healy Creek was washed out in the spring of 2013 but should have been rebuilt by the time this book reaches the stores in the winter of 2015.) Alternatively you can start from the Cave and Basin near Banff and follow the trail along Old Healy Creek Road to Sundance Lodge (see page 130).

Beyond Sundance Lodge the trail goes through the trees on the left bank of Brewster Creek for about 4 km, then crosses the creek on a bridge. From here the trail climbs steadily, staying on the west side of the valley above the creek. After about 6 km the trail (and the valley) curves around to the right and climbs up into a high bowl.

Here the route comes out into a big, open meadow. Halfway Cabin is located here on the west side of the creek just as you come out of the trees into the meadow. Note that the cabin is marked incorrectly on old topo maps. Halfway Cabin is closed in the winter but this is a good place to stop and camp.

From the cabin, ski down and across the creek. The climb to Allenby Pass is a steady grind for about 500 vertical metres. The trail gains elevation quickly and before long crosses two large avalanche slopes that are quite steep and could be very dangerous at the wrong time. The trail continues to climb steadily through the forest in long switchbacks, eventually reaching the edge of treeline, where it does a long traverse. Ascend through open trees in the centre of the valley, then angle left into a draw. Follow the draw to the pass.

On the far side of the pass, descend gentle slopes, staying generally to the right, then follow the creekbed for a long way. Travel is easy along here. At about 601600 E 5643900 N, as the creekbed narrows and turns into a canyon, climb up to the right and find the trail in the woods. The trail descends gently and steadily, curves to the right around a corner, then descends a south-facing slope in long switchbacks through open forest for about 150 vertical metres to the valley bottom. The way then continues gently downhill to the south to reach the Bryant Creek trail.

Follow the Bryant Creek trail over Assiniboine Pass to reach Mount Assiniboine Lodge (see page 58).

18. ASSINIBOINE TO BANFF VIA SPRAY RIVER
Ski Touring, ATR 2

Grade Intermediate
Distance 60 km one way
Time This tour can be done in one very long day but you have to move.
Elevation loss 810 m

Max elevation 2180 m at Assiniboine Pass
Maps Mount Assiniboine 82 J/13, Spray Lakes Reservoir 82 J/14, Canmore 82 O/3, Banff 82 O/4

This is an interesting way to ski right back to Banff. It is not done often and the Spray Valley is closed to skiers after April 15, as it is home to many carnivores. If you combine this tour with the Allenby Pass route to Assiniboine from the Cave and Basin, you can do a magnificent loop from Banff and never use your car. We did it in 2008 and found it to be an excellent four-day ski adventure.

Facilities: There is a derelict warden building called Fortune Cabin at about 612400 E 5641400 N and there is a functioning warden cabin (locked) at 606600 E 5650600 N about 23 km from Banff.

Follow the Bryant Creek trail in reverse from Mount Assiniboine toward Shark Mountain (route 15 on page 63).

At the point where the trail forks to the right and descends to cross Bryant Creek (609000 E 5635800 N), stay left. The trail descends toward Spray Lake and after about 1 km comes out in the open. Ski across marshy terrain with small trees. Likely the trail (road) is up on the left in the trees, but it is best to ski ENE across open terrain to reach the edge of Spray Lake. Continue easily along the lake, crossing a little bridge over the creek at 611200 E 5637600 N. Continue along the road, skirting around the edge of a rock bluff above the lake, then curve in a more northerly direction to the back end of a bay on the lake.

The road diverges here and starts to climb. We got lost at this point and wandered up the valley for a distance before we found the road again. Likely the Spray River road branches left (north) up the Spray Valley just after the junction where it starts to climb. Continue north following the old road. At about 612300 E 5641600 N the road comes down a hill, reaching an old derelict cabin (Fortune Cabin). The road turns back to the south for about 400 m, then curves left into Fortune Flats. In a short distance it crosses the Spray River on a bridge.

From here the road climbs gradually up the east side of the valley, occasionally crossing small creeks that no longer have bridges and can be tricky to negotiate. Eventually the road descends to the valley bottom, crosses some flats and then crosses the Spray River again on a bridge. Just after the bridge there is a warden cabin on the right. This section, from Spray Lake to the Spray warden cabin, is about 17 km and will likely be the crux of the tour – most likely the trail will not be broken and the going may be difficult. Luckily there is little deadfall across the road.

From the Spray warden cabin it is 23 km to Banff. It is just a matter of putting your head down, ignoring the pain and fatigue, and keeping going. The trail may be packed by snowmobile traffic to the warden cabin. About 10 km from Banff you reach the Goat Creek turnoff (see page 129) and from here the trail will be trackset. If you have the cash and the inclination, you can leave your skis at the door and have a drink in the lounge at the Banff Springs Hotel. You will certainly have earned it.

19. OG PASS
Ski Touring, ATR 1

Grade Easy/intermediate
Distance 10 km return
Time 4–5 hours return

Elevation gain 300 m
Max elevation 2300 m
Map Mount Assiniboine 82 J/13

This is a pleasant day trip through varied terrain. There are excellent views of Mount Assiniboine and a fun run down from the pass.

The trail starts just 100 m northwest of Mount Assiniboine Lodge. Descend the draw for about 500 m until the trail breaks out into Og Meadow. Ski across the meadow, heading north, for about 2 km. Then, just before the meadow narrows into a short "canyon," turn right. From here follow the drainage up to Og Pass.

On your return you can ski back down the creek from the pass, and then, for variation, just before reaching the meadow, turn south and follow another drainage to Assiniboine Pass. From Assiniboine Pass work your way back through meadows and forest to Mount Assiniboine Lodge (see 58).

20. DEAD HORSE CANYON
Ski Touring, ATR 2

Grade Easy/intermediate
Distance 5 km loop
Time 2-3 hours

Elevation gain 120 m
Max elevation 2290 m
Map Mount Assiniboine 82 J/13

This is a short and varied tour offering some climbing, a bit of a downhill run and some travel through forest

Hazards: The walls of the creekbed can be potentially dangerous during unstable snow conditions.

From Mount Assiniboine Lodge ski southeast past the cabins, cross the little creek, then ascend the hillside in front of the ranger cabin. Continue climbing up the open hillside and after about 500 m angle left through open trees to gain a bench at the edge of treeline. Ski across this bench for a short distance until you reach a prominent drainage that descends the hill to the north. The tour now follows the creekbed, losing about 120 m in elevation. It is a fun run but never too steep. Continue down the creekbed until you reach O'Brien's Meadow. Cross the meadow in a northwest direction, then follow the trail from Assiniboine Pass heading south to Mount Assiniboine Lodge (see 58).

21. MOOSE BATH
Ski Touring, ATR 2

Grade Easy/intermediate
Distance 8 km return
Time 4 hours return
Elevation gain The trail climbs 140 m as far as the pass above Elizabeth Lake, then descends 150 m to Moose Bath. It then climbs about 100 m to reach Cerulean Lake.
Max elevation 2290 m
Map Mount Assiniboine 82 J/13

Facilities: This tour passes by Sunburst Lake Cabin but the cabin will be locked. There is an outhouse there, though.

Hazards: The hillside descending to Elizabeth Lake has glades in the trees which could pose an avalanche threat in certain conditions. Straying too far to the right as you climb from Moose Bath up to Cerulean Lake would expose you to avalanches from the slopes of Sunburst Peak.

From Mount Assiniboine Lodge ski southwest along the rim of Lake Magog. After about 1 km (near the Lake Magog summer campground) work your way right, through some trees into a shallow drainage. Follow this drainage about 500 m until it pops over the crest of a hill to reach Sunburst Lake. About 100 m along the right shore of the lake you will find Sunburst Lake Cabin tucked in the trees. This is a pleasant spot for a break.

Continue northwest along the edge of the lake, then cross a short neck of land to Cerulean Lake. Traverse the east (right) edge of this lake for a short distance, then climb the hillside directly above its north corner. About 100 vertical metres of reasonably steep climbing through the trees brings you to a pass. Down the other side you will see Elizabeth Lake. Descend to the lake, taking a line a bit to the left. There is an opportunity for a few turns here, so have some fun.

Cross Elizabeth Lake and descend the creek that runs southwest. For most of the descent stay on the left bank of the creek, then work your way left (south) to a small pond shown on the map (Moose Bath!).

Cross the pond and work your way east through the trees, up the hillside above, to reach Cerulean Lake. Be careful not to get too close to the slopes of Sunburst Peak, as they pose an avalanche hazard. Cross the lake to rejoin your earlier tracks and follow them back to the lodge.

22. JONES BENCH
Ski Touring, ATR 2

Grade Easy/intermediate
Distance 13 km loop
Time 4–5 hours

Elevation gain 180 m
Max elevation 2350 m
Map Mount Assiniboine 82 J/13

This is a superb ski tour that ascends above timberline quickly and traverses high above the meadows for several kilometres. The views are excellent and there is opportunity to make a few turns along the way. Highly recommended.

From Mount Assiniboine Lodge, ski west across the meadows for about a kilometre until they begin to pinch out in the trees. Follow the drainage that curves up to the right toward a small peak called the Nublet (594900 E 5641900 N). Climb at a gradual angle up the creekbed, gaining about 120 vertical metres, until you reach treeline. From here work your way out right to a rounded shoulder. Above you now is the Nublet and the adventurous in your group can ski to its rounded and gentle summit. The leeward (southeast) side of this shoulder offers an excellent place to make a few turns.

Setting off from Mount Assiniboine Lodge. Photo Chic Scott

Carry on traversing the bench in a northerly direction for 3 km. After you pass beneath Jones Hill (on your left) you begin to descend gradually. To reach the valley bottom near Og Lake it is necessary to ski all the way to a sink that is marked on the map (595000 E 5644600 N) before descending to the right. Do not cut down into the valley before this point, as you will encounter very steep terrain. Just beyond the sink you can descend easily to the valley floor.

Return to the lodge across the meadows along the valley bottom. Just before reaching the lodge it is necessary to ascend a draw, ski though a section of trees and then pop through a little pass to the lodge.

A little history

Ken Jones was the first born-in-Canada Canadian to receive all the National Parks guide badges – for skiing, mountain climbing, river and bush craft and outfitting. For years he guided at Skoki and Mount Assiniboine lodges. He was also a log builder who worked on the expansion of Skoki Lodge in 1936 and the central building at Num-Ti-Jah Lodge at Bow Lake in 1948 and '49. From 1967 to 1974 he was the ranger at Mount Assiniboine Park. One of the Naiset Huts is in fact his old ranger cabin and is now called Jonesy's cabin. Jones Hill, Jones Bench (at Assiniboine) and Jones Pass (at Skoki) are all named for Ken. For the last two decades of his life he was often found at Mount Assiniboine Lodge chopping wood, shovelling snow and telling stories.

23. WONDER PASS
Ski Touring, ATR 1

Grade Easy
Distance 7 km return
Time 3 hours return

Elevation gain 210 m
Max elevation 2360 m
Map Mount Assiniboine 82 J/13

Wonder Pass is a short, very pleasant ski tour, perfect for a lazy day. The trail leads you high above the trees into beautiful alpine terrain where the views are excellent.

Facilities: The trail passes by the ranger cabin, and across the creek from here are the Naiset Huts.

From Mount Assiniboine Lodge, ski southeast past the cabins, then cross the creek and ascend the hill past the ranger cabin. Continue up the hillside above. The trail follows open terrain along the left bank of Magog Creek. After crossing the creek (where it turns east), the route stays high on the left for the last kilometre, then traverses into the pass.

On the return trip you can come back the same way or you can take a more direct line down the drainage below Wonder Pass. Both routes offer the opportunity to make a few turns.

24. ELY'S DOME
Ski Touring, ATR 3

Grade Advanced
Distance 8 km return
Time Full-day tour

Elevation gain 650 m
Max elevation 2830 m
Map Mount Assiniboine 82 J/13

This is a wonderful tour for a sunny spring day. It takes you to the top of the unnamed peak (601100 E 5639100 N) between Mount Cautley

Setting off for Ely's Dome. Photo Chic Scott

There are lots of places to get turns at Assiniboine. André
Renner shows his telemark style. Photo Chic Scott

and Wonder Peak, called Ely's Dome. The skiing can be excellent and there are marvellous views of Mount Assiniboine.

Hazards: There is avalanche potential on this tour, so use caution.

Ski up the hill past the ranger cabin as if going to Wonder Pass (see page 76), then work your way left across meadows towards the peak. The route up the peak ascends a ramp that traverses from right to left. If you chose a good line, the tour can be done in reasonable safety; however, there are steeper slopes nearby which can be dangerous in certain conditions. The descent offers excellent skiing.

A little history

Ely's Dome is named for the sister of Sam Evans, a packer and guide who worked at Skoki and Assiniboine in the 1930s and '40s. He came from Montana and was reputed to be enormously wealthy. Legend says he was an heir to the Dupont fortune, but he worked alongside the rest of the guides and never let on.

Getting some turns at Assiniboine
Ski touring, ATR 2

The Nublet

Excellent terrain for making turns can be found on the shoulder below the Nublet. These southeast-facing slopes are set at a reasonable angle, are protected from the wind and are in the sun all day. Highly recommended. See the Jones Bench tour page 75) for the approach.

The Cerulean Lake Hillside

The hillside above the north shore of Cerulean Lake offers some good terrain for turns. This is glade skiing (in the trees), so it is excellent for those cloudy and snowy days. See the Moose Bath tour, page 74) for the approach.

Mount Cautley

The west-facing slopes of Mount Cautley offer good terrain for making turns. You get lots of sun and the views of Mount Assiniboine are spectacular. See the Dead Horse Canyon tour, page 73) for the approach.

KANANASKIS COUNTRY

25. **West Bragg Creek Trails** Easy/Intermediate, p. 82
26. **Sandy McNabb Trails** Easy/Intermediate, p. 85
27. **Ribbon Creek Trails** Easy/Intermediate, p. 89
28. **Ribbon Creek to Skogan Pass** Intermediate, p. 92
29. **Peter Lougheed Provincial Park Trails**
    Easy/Intermediate, p. 95
30. **Elk Lakes Cabin Approach**
    Easy/Intermediate, p. 101
31. **Upper and Lower Elk Lakes** Easy, p. 103
32. **Gypsum Mine** Easy, p. 104
33. **Smith Dorrien (Sawmill) Trails**
    Intermediate/Advanced, p. 106
34. **Chester Lake** Intermediate/Advanced, p. 107
35. **Burstall Pass** Intermediate/Advanced, p. 108
36. **Commonwealth Creek** Intermediate, p. 109
37. **Commonwealth Lake** Easy, p. 111
38. **Rummel Lake** Intermediate, p. 111
39. **Mount Shark Trails** Easy/Intermediate, p. 113
40. **Watridge Lake** Easy, p. 114
41. **Marushka (Shark) Lake** Easy, p. 116

Kananaskis country encompasses 4000 square kilometres of superb mountain terrain directly west of Calgary in the front ranges of the Rocky Mountains. Peter Lougheed Provincial Park and Spray Valley Provincial Park are located in the heart of Kananaskis Country. This spectacular region has always been popular with Calgary hikers, climbers and skiers, and its recreational potential was vigorously developed

KANANASKIS COUNTRY

by the provincial government during the 1970s and '80s, most notably the wonderful network of ski trails at Kananaskis Lakes.

The area can be approached from Calgary via Highway 1 (Trans-Canada Highway) and Highway 40 (Kananaskis Trail) or from Canmore via Smith Dorrien/Spray Trail. Both of these secondary roads are maintained in good winter driving condition.

There is not a lot of commercial development in Kananaskis Country. There are two downhill ski resorts – Fortress Mountain (now closed) and Nakiska. Kananaskis Village has several hotels and restaurants, as well as a grocery store and sports shop. Gas and some groceries can be purchased at Fortress Junction, 42 km along Highway 40 from Highway 1. Engadine Lodge (mountengadine.com, 403-678-4080) along the Smith Dorrien/Spray Trail offers very pleasant accommodation. Ribbon Creek Hostel (www.hihostels.ca, 403-591-7333) is located near Kananaskis Village and offers excellent low-cost accommodation.

There is a Visitor Information Centre at Barrier Lake (403-673-3985) along Highway 40, which is open 9:00 am to 4:00 pm seven days a week in winter. There is another in Peter Lougheed Provincial Park (403-591-6322), open 9:30 to 4:30 seven days a week, and a third one at the Sandy McNabb trailhead, open 8:30 to 4:30 seven days a week (403-933-7172). Kananaskis also has a general information phone line at 403-678-0760.

There are six outstanding ski trail systems in Kananaskis Country: Ribbon Creek; Peter Lougheed Provincial Park; Mount Shark; Smith/Dorrien; West Bragg Creek; and Sandy McNabb. All of these offer excellent skiing for novice and expert alike and are very popular on weekends. You can ski here for a few hours or all day if you like. For more information, stop at the Visitor Information Centres at Barrier Lake, Peter Lougheed Provincial Park or Sandy McNabb, where you can also purchase excellent maps of these trail systems.

25. WEST BRAGG CREEK TRAILS
Nordic Skiing, ATR 1

Grade Most trails are easy/ intermediate
Distance 45 km of trails
Max elevation 1500 m
Groomed for classic and skate skiing

Maps Bragg Creek 82 J/15; Bragg Creek and Area Trails Map 2014; Gem Trek Bragg Creek and Sheep Valley

This is a beautiful and popular trail system that is regularly trackset. Snow quality can be variable, however, especially after chinooks (warm westerly winds). It is possible to be skiing through powder snow one weekend and be hitting rocks the next. Be sure to wait until after a good snowfall.

Access: 1. Main parking area. Drive west through the hamlet of Bragg Creek along Balsam Avenue. Turn left at a T-intersection after crossing the Elbow River. Continue straight along Township Road 232 for 9 km. The parking lot is at the end of the road.

2. Alternative trail access. Follow Elbow Falls Trail (Highway 66) for 15 km past Bragg Creek to Allen Bill Pond.

Facilities: There are toilets at both parking lots.

Note: These trails are groomed and maintained by the Greater Bragg Creek Trails Association, www.braggcreektrails.org.

MOOSE CONNECTOR

1.6 km   Difficult

In either direction, Moose Connector descends steep hills down to a bridge crossing over a creek. Be careful.

MOOSE LOOP

5.1 km   Intermediate

Moose Loop is one of Bragg Creek's finest trails. When you ski counterclockwise from the Moose Connector junction, the trail starts out skirting along the edge of some lovely meadows filled with willow bushes. Moose Mountain occupies the skyline to the west, making for a great backdrop. After a ways along the meadow, the trail climbs into the forest and connects with an old exploration road. The trail continues along the road until finally making a brisk descent to a creek crossing. The trail rises steeply after the creek, followed by a long, rolling descent. After the descent, the trail continues undulating through the forest until it makes a steep descent and a tight corner onto a bridge. The rest of the way to the starting junction is relatively flat.

CRYSTAL LINE

4.1 km   Easy, with one difficult section

This trail runs in a relatively straight line from west to east. The western portion is comprised of easy, rolling terrain, while the eastern part parallels the access road. At the farthest eastern section there is a very steep uphill which makes for a very exhilarating descent when skied in the opposite direction. From the top of this hill to the junction with the Sundog Loop is a gentle uphill.

SUNDOG LOOP

4.0 km   Intermediate

The west side of this trail rambles uphill when skied from north to south. Watch out for the ice flow at the bottom of the steep ravine. The eastern leg of the trail travels through pleasant meadows before a very steep downhill to Crystal Line.

ELBOW TRAIL

5.1 km   Intermediate

From the Sundog Loop, Elbow Trail runs beside a winding creek and pleasant meadows. The terrain is gentle. In the midsection of the trail is a short side trail which climbs up and then descends back to Elbow Trail, offering more of a challenge. From the southern junction with Iron Springs Trail, the route descends briskly. This section to Allen Bill Pond gets plenty of sunlight, making it one of the first trails to become unskiable in the spring. Soon a very steep hill with a steep corner in the middle is reached, which can be difficult to descend when it is icy. The rest of the way is flat, skirting along the bank of the Elbow River. The trail crosses under a bridge along Elbow Falls Trail (road), shortly before reaching the Allen Bill Pond parking area.

IRON SPRINGS TRAIL

5.8 km   Intermediate

From its southerly junction with Elbow Trail, Iron Springs Trail climbs steadily up a logged hillside. This section is often icy and can pose a challenge on the way down. The trail skirts along the perimeter of a large meadow to a bridge. Crossing the bridge leads to Elbow Trail along a small ungroomed but well marked trail through the forest. From the bridge the trail climbs steadily to the top of a hill, where there is a gate. The trail then descends down the other side through an old cutblock, presenting a long and enjoyable run.

TELEPHONE AND HOSTEL LOOP

Both trails are infrequently groomed, but are commonly skier-set.

Ian Kruger skiing along Moose Loop at West Bragg Creek. Photo Darren Farley

26. SANDY McNABB TRAILS
Nordic Skiing, ATR 1

Grade Most routes are easy/ intermediate

Distance More than 30 km of trails

Max elevation 1640 m

Map Mount Rae 82 J/10; Gem Trek Bragg Creek and Sheep Valley

Groomed for classic skiing

Nestled in the foothills of the Rockies, Sandy McNabb offers a unique skiing experience. Winding single-track trails meander through aspen-filled valleys and ascend to high ridgetops that offer stunning views of the mountains. These trails are much less popular than other trail systems, despite their close proximity to Calgary. Being in the foothills, the snow quality is often dictated by chinooks. Many of these routes have very thin snow cover throughout the year and may have rocky patches showing through. Wait until there is significant snow before going.

Facilities: There is an information centre at the parking lot. Public washrooms are outside.

Access: From the town of Turner Valley take Highway 546 west. After 18 km, turn right at the "Sheep River Park Headquarters" sign. Park at the information centre.

The Upper Trails

All of the trails north of the highway are single-lane tracks. Watch out for other skiers! The upper trails have more varied terrain than the lower ones, with skiing along scenic ridges and winding through pleasant ravines. Highly recommended.

ARCTIC HILL

1.2 km   Intermediate

From the information centre the trail ascends a hill through a beautiful aspen forest. This section can be tricky to descend when travelling in the opposite direction, because of the very narrow track. The trail gains and follows the crest of a ridge with some nice views of the Rockies. It then descends in a straight line to a hairpin turn (use caution). After the hairpin turn, the trail crosses a small ice flow, followed by some meadows.

MACABEE LOOP

4.1 km   Easy

This is an easy, gentle trail. It trends slightly downhill from north to south. Watch out for the ice flow near the Wolftree Link junction.

PINE RIDGE

2.5 km   Difficult

This trail follows a horseshoe ridge, climbing up one side and descending down the other. Both directions offer tricky downhills. At the top there is a picnic bench with a lovely view of the prairies stretched out below. The sprawling suburbs of Calgary can just be made out on the skyline. At 1640 m this is the highest point of the entire trail system.

BALSAM LINK

1.3 km   Intermediate

The descent from Pine Ridge Trail is steady and quick. Watch your speed! It makes for a long, gradual ascent in the other direction.

DEATH VALLEY LOOP

4.0 km   Difficult

Counterclockwise from Long Prairie Loop, this trail ascends to an embankment lined with aspen trees. Along the embankment are wonderful views of the Rockies poking out from behind the foliage. The trail then descends steeply. When conditions are not optimal, this descent can become very serious. Be careful. After the hill, the trail skirts along the bottom of a hillside. This is a beautiful place to be on a sunny day.

WOLFTREE LINK

800 m   Easy

This trail offers a gentle, meandering uphill when skied towards the north and a fun downhill run in the other direction.

LONG PRAIRIE LOOP

1.1 km   Easy

The northern section of this trail, running west to east, skirts above Long Prairie Creek, traversing open hillsides. The gentle downhill makes for pleasant skiing.

WHITETAIL

300 m   Intermediate

This trail offers a short and steep descent running from north to south through an open aspen forest. Be careful!

The Lower Trails

Most trails south of the highway are trackset with two lanes. The terrain here is much flatter than the trails above the highway, making it a good spot for beginners.

Overlooking the mountains of Sheep River
Provincial Park. Photo Darren Farley

Darren Farley skis through aspen forest at
Sandy McNabb. Photo Darren Farley

LOGGERS LOOP

5.3 km   Easy

This is a flat trail, good for beginners. The trail stays in the forest without much change in scenery and is double-tracked for two-way skier traffic.

MEADOW

1.4 km   Easy

This is a flat, double-tracked trail that parallels the main road.

SANDY MCNABB LOOP

6.2 km   Easy

This is a beautiful trail that skirts along an embankment overlooking the Sheep River. It is mostly flat, with easy skiing. There are beautiful vistas at the many viewpoints along the way. Unfortunately the trail is plagued with very thin snow cover, so watch out for rocks and branches. It's best to save this route for after a big snowfall.

27. RIBBON CREEK TRAILS
Nordic Skiing, ATR 1

Grade Most routes are easy/
    intermediate.
Distance 50 km of trails
Max elevation 2075 m

Map Spray Lakes Reservoir
    82 J/14
May be groomed for classic
    skiing

This was the first ski trail system developed in the Kananaskis Valley, created in 1972 by Don Gardner. When there is adequate snow it provides excellent cross-country skiing. Ranging across the lower slopes of mounts Collembola, Allan and Kidd there are plenty of viewpoints. Unfortunately, heavy snowshoe use has damaged the trails to the north in the vicinity of Troll Falls. The trails near Kananaskis Village can be excellent, however.

Facilities: There are plenty of amenities in the vicinity of the Ribbon

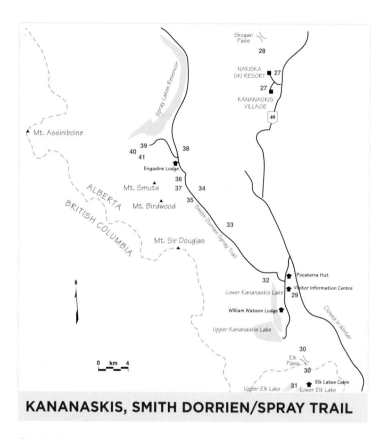

KANANASKIS, SMITH DORRIEN/SPRAY TRAIL

Creek ski trails at Kananaskis Village and at Nakiska Ski Resort. There are toilets at the Ribbon Creek trailhead.

Note: Trail maps are available at the Visitor Information Centres.

Access: Drive along Kananaskis Trail (Highway 40) for 23 km from the junction with the Trans-Canada Highway (Highway 1) and turn right for Kananaskis Village and Nakiska Ski Resort. You can park at four different lots to access these trails:

Keep right for Stoney parking.

Keep right for Nakiska Ski Resort.

Don Gardner, who designed the trails at Ribbon Creek and Kananaskis Lakes and played a big part in creating the Canmore Nordic Centre trails, is pictured at Ribbon Creek Hostel, where his old wooden skis from 1972 are mounted on the fireplace. Photo Kathy Madill

Don Gardner skis along the Ribbon Creek trails, which he designed in 1972. Photo Chic Scott

For Kananaskis Village, turn left, then cross the Ribbon Creek bridge.

For the Ribbon Creek parking lot, keep left initially, then turn right before you cross Ribbon Creek bridge.

Note: Many of the Ribbon Creek trails were damaged by the floods of 2013. At the time of publication some routes are still under reconstruction. Inquire at the Kananaskis Visitor Information Centre for current status.

28. RIBBON CREEK TO SKOGAN PASS
Ski Touring, ATR 1

Grade Intermediate
Distance 21 km to pass return
Time Full-day tour
Elevation gain 625 m

Max elevation 2075 m
Map Spray Lakes Reservoir
82 J/14

This is one of the classic tours in the Ribbon Creek area. It gets you up high and has great views. Unfortunately, the noise of the Nakiska resort and the jet airplanes overhead, on their way to Vancouver, detract from the experience.

Facilities: There are toilets and a camp shelter at the trailhead.

Options: It is possible to ski across the pass and descend the other side to Dead Man's Flats.

Access: Drive down Kananaskis Trail (Highway 40) for 23 km from the junction with the Trans-Canada Highway (Highway 1) and turn right to Kananaskis Village and Nakiska Ski Resort. Turn first left, then stay right before you cross the bridge to reach the Ribbon Creek parking lot.

There are actually two parking lots at Ribbon Creek, and the trail to Skogan Pass starts at the camp shelter between the two lots. Ascend a wide, gradual trail for about 500 m, then cross Nakiska Road. Descend a short distance to a junction and take the left-hand fork. The trail now goes along the brow of the hill for about 1 km, with great views out over the valley to the right, to a four-way trail junction. Carry on straight ahead and wind your way uphill for about 1 km to an intersection with a road (snowmobile traffic). Stay right for a short distance, then keep right again on a broad trail while the snowmobile road curves up to the left. There is a barrier across the trail here. Continue past the barrier for a short distance to another intersection. Take the right-hand fork and immediately cross a creek. The trail now starts to climb for more than a kilometre, eventually reaching a power line. Turn sharply left and climb steeply for a ways. The trail then levels off, crosses an open area, then curves right and climbs steeply to another intersection. Turn left and climb at a moderate angle. Ignore two roads that branch off to your right. After about 500 m the road comes out of the thick trees into an area of low trees and climbs straight up the hillside. The road then enters the forest again and in about 100 m comes to another trail junction. From here there are two choices:

1.   You can carry on straight ahead through the forest along a

Ian Daffern on the Skogan Pass trail. Photo Gill Daffern

level trail until it reaches the power line. Turn left up the power line and climb at a moderate grade for about 500 m until the road angles left into the woods. After about 300 m the road crosses the power line into the woods on the right. Continue along the road through the trees on the right of the power line for about 500 m until it comes out at the power line again. Continue up the power line for about 100 m to a trail intersection.

2. It is also possible to turn left and ski the 3.5 km Skogan Loop. This trail winds its leisurely way uphill through cutblocks and offers incredible panoramas. It eventually rejoins trail #1 at the power line. This is the end of the groomed trail.

To continue to the pass, ski at an angle into the trees on the left and carry on through the forest on a road that rolls up and down for about 1.5 km. Pass under the power line again and ascend moderately steeply through the trees for the last 500 m to the pass. If you are heading for Dead Man's Flats, continue straight ahead through the lowest point in the pass (see page 121). To get a great view, angle up and left, climbing steeply for about 100 m to the power line.

29. PETER LOUGHEED PROVINCIAL PARK TRAILS
Nordic Skiing, ATR 1

Grade Most routes are easy/intermediate.
Distance Nearly 80 km of trails

Max elevation 2125 m
Map Kananaskis Lakes 82 J/11
Groomed for classic skiing

This is a truly excellent system of Nordic ski trails, one of the best in North America. It was designed and built in the mid- to late seventies under the direction of Don Gardner. All of the trails, other than Fox Creek, Boulton Creek and Moraine, are 4 m wide with two classic tracks and a lane in the middle. The trails are well maintained and are groomed regularly. On a sunny weekend you will find hundreds of other skiers of all abilities enjoying themselves on these trails.

The Pocaterra warming hut. Photo Chic Scott

Note: Trail maps are available at the Visitor Information Centres.

Facilities: There are nine parking lots from which you can access these ski trails: Pocaterra, Visitor Information Centre, Elkwood, William Watson Lodge, Boulton Creek, Boulton Bridge, Lower Lake, Elk Pass and Upper Lake. Three parking lots have something to offer other than washrooms:

Pocaterra has a warming hut with a fireplace and benches.

The Visitor Information Centre has indoor washrooms, telephones, interpretive films, displays and a deluxe lounge with comfy chairs and couches and a fireplace. You can also get up-to-date reports on trail conditions and grooming here.

William Watson Lodge has low-cost accommodation for seniors and people with disabilities.

Access: Drive down Kananaskis Trail (Highway 40) for 50 km from the junction with the Trans-Canada Highway (Highway 1), then turn right onto Kananaskis Lakes Trail. The nine parking lots are scattered along each side of this road over the next 13 km: Pocaterra, Visitor Information Centre, Elkwood, Boulton Creek, Boulton Bridge, Elk Pass and Upper Lake are just off the road to the left, while William Watson Lodge and Lower Lake are a short distance off to the right.

Below is an overview of the main trails. Many of the smaller ones not included here are also worth skiing.

POCATERRA

10.5 seniors km   Easy/intermediate

Pocaterra is a long, popular trail starting at the Pocaterra parking lot and ending at Tyrwhitt. Along the way it connects with eight different trails. The first 3.6 km from the hut are popular with beginner skiers because of the gentle grade. After passing the turnoff for Lynx, the trail begins to climb steadily the rest of the way until Tyrwhitt.

PACKERS

3.1 km   Difficult

Packers trail connects Pocaterra with the junction for Whiskey Jack and Moraine. The trail descends from Pocaterra, with a few steep hills thrown in. There is an ice flow after one of the steep descents that can prove difficult to navigate, but it is usually well signed.

WHISKEY JACK

4.5 km   Difficult

Running east to west, Whiskey Jack connects Pocaterra and the Boulton Creek parking lot. The trail runs downhill from Pocaterra. The alternating gentle and steep hills make for a great downhill or a rather long uphill. In the middle of the trail there is a steep section with a notorious corner, the scene of many crashes. Don't be afraid to walk this section. There is a picnic bench at the Pocaterra/Whiskey Jack junction.

TYRWHITT

4.5 km   Intermediate

Tyrwhitt connects Elk Pass and Pocaterra. It is a lovely trail which gets snow early and holds it until late. From Pocaterra the trail climbs gently, passing through forests of (usually) snow-capped trees. The trail then begins to level off while passing through open meadows. This area boasts lovely views towards the often cloud-filled Elk River valley. The trail begins to steepen just before reaching Elk Pass.

LOOKOUT

5.2 km   Difficult

This trail has one of the best views you can get while track skiing. Lookout connects Tyrwhitt with Hydroline. From Tyrwhitt the trail climbs steadily, making for a very exhilarating downhill. At the top there is a fire lookout perched in a wonderful location giving a 360-degree view of the entire valley. This is an excellent place to eat lunch if the wind isn't too strong. Beside the trail at the top you will notice a mailbox. Inside is a guestbook for visitors. From the fire lookout down to the power line, the trail varies from steep to very steep. The author once broke a pair of skis here, so use caution.

Kathy Madill skis along trails in Peter Lougheed
Provincial Park. Photo Chic Scott

BLUEBERRY HILL

3.2 km   Difficult

This trail is another one of the gems found at Peter Lougheed. It is an out and back ski connecting to the Elk Pass trail. The trail gradually ascends, eventually leading to a viewpoint that overlooks Kananaskis Lakes. There is a picnic bench here. The descent back down is exhilarating.

HYDROLINE

3.9 km   Intermediate

Hydroline is a rather uninspiring trail connecting lower Elk Pass Trail, Lookout and Elk Pass itself. The trail follows a large string of power lines from which it has received its name.

ELK PASS

7.3 km   Intermediate

Elk Pass Trail connects Boulton Creek, Fox Creek, Hydroline and Blueberry Hill. Soon after leaving the parking lot and passing the Boulton Creek trailhead, the trail begins to steepen considerably. After cresting a hill, the track drops quickly and steeply down towards the Fox Creek trailhead. You can avoid this initial steep section by taking Boulton Creek and turning right onto Fox Creek Trail before connecting with Elk Pass Trail. From here the route gently meanders upwards through the bed of Fox Creek. A picnic bench awaits visitors at the Blueberry Hill turnoff. From this turnoff to the pass the trail begins to rise and parts of it get quite steep. At the pass you are rewarded with another picnic bench and satisfactory views. If you ski a few metres south of the pass, you will notice a sign marking the British Columbia/ Alberta boundary. You have reached the Great Divide, the hydrological apex of the Rockies. Snow on the Alberta side drains to Hudson's Bay, while snowmelt in BC flows to the Pacific Ocean.

FOX CREEK

1.6 km   Easy

Fox Creek is a wonderful single-track trail that ambles alongside its

A group of schoolkids set off on perfectly groomed Peter Lougheed Provincial Park ski trails. Photo Chic Scott

namesake stream, connecting Moraine and Elk Pass. The trail is tight, with lots of bumps and unexpected corners. This route makes you feel like you are in a true winter wonderland. A bench halfway along greets you just after you cross a small bridge over the creek. This is a great spot for tea. This trail does not seem to hold snow very well, so it is not always a good choice late in the season.

MORAINE

2.4 km   Easy

Moraine connects Fox Creek with the junction for Whiskey Jack and Packers. It is a lovely single-track lane that ambles through the forest. There are great views along part of it where the trail skirts along the top of a ridge that looks towards Upper Kananaskis Lake.

BOULTON CREEK

2.5 km   Easy/intermediate

Boulton Creek is a pleasant single-track trail connecting the Boulton parking area with Fox Creek. Boulton Creek was badly damaged in the floods of 2013. At the time of writing, the fate of the trail was still unknown. It is best to check with the information centre before skiing here.

Note: It is still possible to ski from Elk Pass Trail along Boulton and connect with Fox Creek.

30. ELK LAKES CABIN APPROACH
Ski Touring, Atr 1

Grade Easy/intermediate   **Height loss** 260 m
Distance 10 km one way   **Max elevation** 1900 m
Time 2–4 hours   **Map** Kananaskis Lakes 82 J/11
Height gain 200 m

The journey to the Elk Lakes Cabin is fairly straightforward and has little avalanche hazard, making it a popular trip for beginners. It is frequently done on cross-country skis, although metal edges are nice for

ELK LAKES CABIN

This is a pleasant log cabin a short distance from beautiful Elk Lakes.

Location Above a creek, 100 m west of the power line (636400 E 5601600 N)

Map Kananaskis Lakes 82 J/11

Facilities Fully equipped with foamies, cooking utensils, propane cookstoves and lanterns, and a wood stove for heat

Capacity 10 in winter

Water From the creek directly west of the hut (you must dig down in the snow)

Reservations The Alpine Club of Canada 403-678-3200

Note This hut is locked when no custodian is present; a combination number is required.

Elk Lakes Cabin. Photo Darren Farley

the descent along the power line. Although not popular with alpine ski tourers, the area does have the potential for turns. Directly east of the hut are a few cutblocks which offer good turns once there is enough snow to cover any stumps. The many drainages and bowls west of the hut also have the potential for good skiing.

Facilities: There are toilets at the parking lot. Elk Lakes Cabin is the destination of this trip.

Hazards: The final descent along the power line can be difficult when icy.

Access: Drive along Highway 40 (Kananaskis Trail) for 50 km from the junction with Highway 1 (Trans-Canada Highway), turn right onto Kananaskis Lakes Trail, then continue along the road and park in the Elk Pass lot.

Follow Elk Pass Trail 6 km to Elk Pass. The trail is trackset and is covered in the Peter Lougheed Provincial Park Trails section (see page 99). The initial kilometre of Elk Pass Trail ascends and descends a very steep hill, which can be tricky with a large pack on. You can bypass this section by going left onto Boulton Creek and then turning right onto Fox Creek. Fox Creek then joins up again with Elk Pass Trail. From Elk Pass ski directly south, following the power line. After about 3 km of gentle downhill, the trail begins to steepen and this section can be difficult when snow conditions are not the best. There is also a trail that traverses back and forth through the forest, crossing over the hydroline. The mellower grade of this trail is a good choice when snow conditions are less than ideal. Upon reaching the bottom, continue across a meadow following the hydroline until you reach a large sign and map. Turn right (west) here. The hut is a short distance away (636400 E 5601600 N).

31. UPPER AND LOWER ELK LAKES Ski Touring, ATR 1

Grade Easy
Distance 4 km return
Time 1–2 hours return

Height gain 20 m
Max elevation 1760 m
Map Kananaskis Lakes 82 J/11

This is a popular ski tour from the Elk Lakes Cabin. The views from both the upper and the lower lakes are spectacular.

Access: The trail begins at Elk Lakes Cabin.

From the cabin, ski down to the creek directly in front of the cabin door. There are two variations to get to the lower lake.

Option 1: Directly across from the cabin door, on the far side of the creek, is a trail that ascends steeply into the forest. The trail rolls through the forest for a ways before skirting alongside a meadow. The route then follows the right shoulder of a creek for the rest of the way to Lower Elk Lake.

Option 2: Ski north along the creek in front of the cabin. After about a hundred metres the trail cuts left (west) into the forest. The trail meanders westerly through the forest for about a kilometre before reaching Lower Elk Lake.

From Lower Elk Lake, ski along the right bank to the far end of the lake. Here the trail crosses a bridge over a creek. On the far side of the bridge is a sign and a junction. The left trail leads about 800 m to the top of a viewpoint (be careful on the descent!). The right trail continues through the forest, eventually traversing along the left side of a large creek that leads to Upper Elk Lake. The mountains around the lake are truly stunning.

32. GYPSUM MINE
Ski Touring, ATR 2

Grade Easy
Distance 15 km return
Time Full day

Height gain 470 m
Max elevation 2130 m
Map Kananaskis Lakes 82 J/11

This trip follows an old road leading to a long forgotten mining site. There are outstanding views along the entire length of the road, making for a very pleasant ski tour. The grade is gentle all the way to the top.

Hazards: The trail crosses several large avalanche paths while traversing along Gypsum Ridge. Don't linger. The final hundred metres to the actual mine site crosses large slide paths. It is best to avoid this section entirely.

Options: There are plenty of glades along the entire road that offer opportunities for turns. The slide paths and trees on Gypsum Ridge are a very popular deep-powder destination. Closer to the mine there are many mellow, gladed slopes good for beginners.

Access: Drive down Kananaskis Trail (Highway 40) for 50 km from the junction with the Trans-Canada Highway (Highway 1), then turn right onto Kananaskis Lakes Trail. At the bottom of the hill turn right onto Smith Dorrien/Spray Trail. Continue for 4 km and park on the south side of the highway where there is a small opening in the trees.

From the side of the road ski south across a meadow until you reach the mining road. Turn right (west) and ski along the road until you reach a creek. Ski south across the creek and ascend a short ways through the trees until regaining the road. There is often a trail that follows the creek westward before entering the forest. This trail is to be avoided, as it is used by skiers coming down from Gypsum Ridge and goes straight up a slide path. Follow the road as it gently ascends towards the south. The road makes a hairpin turn before contouring the hillside of Gypsum Ridge. Be careful here, as the road crosses some large slide paths. After traversing along Gypsum Ridge, the route makes a few switchbacks, levelling out for a bit, then switchbacking again. The road leads all the way to the mine site along the slopes of Mount Invincible. It is best to turn around at the highest point of the road, just before it leaves the trees and descends the short distance to the mine. This last section crosses some very large avalanche slopes and is not worth the risk. There isn't much to see at the mine site that can't be observed from the safe side of the slide paths.

A little history

In 1920 George Pocaterra, one of the first non-natives to venture into the wilds of Kananaskis, discovered the large gypsum deposit on the side of Mount Invincible. In 1966 Alberta Gypsum acquired a lease and subsequently built the road to the mining site. The company lost their lease in 1970, however, after failing to pay their land restoration deposit.

33. SMITH-DORRIEN (SAWMILL) TRAILS Nordic Skiing, ATR 1

Grade Intermediate/advanced
Distance 29 km of trails
Max elevation 2110 m

Maps Spray Lakes Reservoir
82 J/14, Kananaskis Lakes
82 J/11

This network of trails offers many hours of enjoyable skiing. The routes are all old logging roads and occasionally have long, leg-burning downhills. The tracks are not groomed anymore, so you may be breaking trail.

Facilities: There are toilets at the parking lots.

Note: Trail maps are available at the Visitor Information Centres.

Access: These trails can be accessed from two parking lots. At the south end the Sawmill parking lot is located on the east side of Smith-Dorrien/Spray Trail 14 km from the Kananaskis Lakes Trail junction or 47 km from Canmore.

At the north end the Chester Lake parking lot is located on the east side of Smith-Dorrien/Spray Trail 20 km from the Kananaskis Lakes Trail junction or 40 km from Canmore.

The Sawmill trails are not often groomed but can provide some good skiing. Photo Chic Scott

34. CHESTER LAKE
Ski Touring, ATR 1

Grade Intermediate/advanced
Distance 8 km return
Time 3-4 hours return
Elevation gain 310 m

Max elevation 2220 m
Map Spray Lakes Reservoir
82 J/14

The snow comes early to Chester Lake, making this a very popular early-season ski trail. It gets you up high into beautiful mountain terrain and provides an exciting run on the way back down.

Facilities: There are toilets at the parking lot, and just before you reach the lake there is an outhouse on the left.

Hazards: Be careful of other skiers coming down the steep trail. Ski with caution.

Options: An interesting side trip is to visit Elephant Rocks. Just before Chester Lake a trail climbs steeply up the hill to the left through the trees. After a short climb the route reaches a ridge and levels out. Here there is an impressive area of giant limestone boulders.

Access: There is a parking lot along the east side of Smith Dorrien/Spray Trail 40 km from Canmore or 20 km from the Kananaskis Lakes Trail junction.

The trail starts at the top left-hand corner of the parking lot and follows a wide road, rising gradually for about 100 m to a trail junction. Stay left and continue another 300 m to another junction. Stay left again and continue along the wide trail for about 500 m when it begins to climb more steeply. (It is also possible to take the right-hand fork, which climbs steeply. The two trails eventually join after about 2 km.) The route swings to the right for a ways, then back to the left. It traverses right a second time, then back left again. Finally the wide track swings right for a third time and climbs steeply to a trail sign. At this point you are about 2.5 km from the parking lot (The alternative route joins at this point.)

Beyond here the trail climbs steeply for a short distance, then angles out right. The wide road ends and the trail narrows through the forest. After several hundred metres the route curves left, levels through the

Approaching Chester Lake on a cloudy winter day. Photo Chic Scott

forest for a ways, then climbs steeply over a hill and out into the open. Cross a meadow, then ascend the trail through the forest for about 500 m. Eventually you break out of the trees and ski across open meadows to reach the lake, which is tucked way back in the cirque below Mount Chester.

35. BURSTALL PASS
Ski Touring, ATR 2

Grade Intermediate/advanced
Distance 8 km one way
Time Full-day tour
Elevation gain 500 m

Max elevation 2380 m
Maps Spray Lakes Reservoir
82 J/14, Kananaskis Lakes
82 J/11

This is one of the finest ski tours in the Rockies. The snow comes early (late November) and builds up deep over the winter. There are excellent opportunities for making turns nearby.

Facilities: There are toilets at the parking lot.

Hazards: A large avalanche path crosses the trail near Burstall Pass. Move quickly across this spot. There is avalanche potential in the area if you stray from the trail, so take all safety precautions if you go looking for turns.

Options: You can extend your tour by skiing to South Burstall Pass.

Access: The tour begins at the Burstall Pass parking lot, located on the west side of Smith Dorrien/Spray Trail 40 km from Canmore or 20 km from the Kananaskis Lakes Trail junction.

From the parking lot follow the usually well-packed trail across Mud Lake Dam and up a hill to the French Creek trail junction. Keep right and follow the main Burstall Creek trail for several kilometres until it descends to the right through trees to reach the gravel flats of Burstall Creek.

Angle across the flats to a point just left of West Burstall Creek, where you will find the trail again. Most folks put their skins on here. Climb steeply up through the forest for about 150 vertical metres to where the angle lays back and you ski out into open glades. Ski across meadows (don't linger in the huge avalanche path), then ascend a draw. As you rise above treeline you will see excellent ski slopes off to the right. From Burstall Pass itself (**614500** E **5624500** N) there is an excellent view of Mount Assiniboine to the west.

On the way back down, rather than descend the steep trail through the trees, it is best to descend the drainage of West Burstall Creek. It offers a good ski run. This is not a good choice early in the season, however, as there may not yet be enough snow to cover the many downed trees along the creek.

36. COMMONWEALTH CREEK
Ski Touring, ATR 2

Grade Intermediate
Distance 8 km return from Smith Dorrien/Spray Trail
Time 3–4 hours

Height gain 150 m
Max elevation 2000 m
Map Spray Lakes Reservoir 82 J/14

This is a very popular outing offering a pleasant ski with great views of Kananaskis Country's finest peaks. There are many opportunities for good turns and side trips, enough to keep the well-seasoned adventurer coming back for more.

Hazards: The trail crosses many large avalanche runouts. It is advisable to ski conservatively and avoid the valley entirely when the avalanche hazard is high.

Access: Park along the west side of Smith Dorrien/Spray Trail 4.4 km north of the Burstall Pass parking turnoff and 2.3 km south of the Mount Shark road.

Ski down the bank and head west across open meadows. The route then begins to climb gently as you head into the trees. After a short distance the trail enters a large cutblock, now filled with small, new-growth trees. The trail trends right (north) for a short distance before a junction. At the junction turn left (west) and follow another old logging road through older-growth forests parallel to Commonwealth Creek. (Continuing straight through the junction (northward) follows a logging road that brings you to a parking lot along the Mount Shark road.) Follow this trail until it splits at a small cutblock (short trees). There is often a trail that splits left here and ascends through the forest to Commonwealth Ridge. Turning right, the trail meanders along the south side of Commonwealth Creek, steadily climbing through the trees until it opens out into pleasant meadows. This section beside the creek offers an exhilarating roller-coaster ride on the way back down. It can be tricky when icy.

From the meadows the trail is obvious to follow – just continue up the valley. This section crosses many large avalanche runouts. Use caution. Upon reaching the far end of the valley, the route trends left, following a creek to avoid entering the trees. The terrain opens up into a large amphitheatre threatened by a large avalanche path. Most people turn around here. The more adventurous can continue on to Smuts Pass and to Birdwood Lakes, but this involves skiing on serious avalanche slopes.

37. COMMONWEALTH LAKE
Ski Touring, ATR 1

Grade Easy
Distance 4.6 km from Smith
    Dorrien/Spray Trail, return
Time 2 hours
Height gain 150 m to
    Commonwealth Lake

Max elevation 2025 m at
    Commonwealth Lake
Map Spray Lakes Reservoir
    82 J/14

This is a short tour to a beautiful lake. On a sunny day the views of Commonwealth Peak are stunning.

Options: It is possible to ski up Commonwealth Ridge from the lake. It is also possible to continue skiing up the valley above the lake, but this area is threatened by many avalanche paths.

Access: Most people park along the west side of Smith Dorrien/Spray Trail 4.4 km north of the Burstall Pass parking turnoff and 2.3 km south of the Mount Shark road.

The easiest way to find the lake is to ski along the Commonwealth Creek trail (see page 109). There is a drainage leading south from the trail a couple hundred metres before the route breaks out of the trees into the meadows in the Commonwealth Valley. Following this drainage leads directly to Commonwealth Lake. If you have not been to the lake before, it is easiest to ski all the way to the meadows and then backtrack to the drainage. The drainage offers an enjoyable ski descent.

38. RUMMEL LAKE
Ski Touring,
ATR 1 to lake; ATR 2 to pass

Grade Intermediate
Distance 10 km return to lake
Time 3–4 hours
Height gain 400 m

Max elevation 2200 m
Map Spray Lakes Reservoir
    82 J/14

This route is named after the celebrated mountain woman Lizzie Rummel, who ran Skoki Lodge and Sunburst Lake Camp for many years. The easy terrain and lack of avalanche hazard on the way to the lake makes for a popular destination amongst skiers and snowshoers alike. Route finding can be tricky if there is no evidence of the previous party's tracks. This is rare, however, as the trail is popular.

Facilities: There is an outhouse at the lake.

Hazards: Avoid getting too close to the avalanche slopes on the southern side of the lake. The route from Rummel Lake up to Rummel Pass is threatened by large avalanche paths.

Access: Drive down Smith Dorrien/Spray Trail about 33 km from Canmore or 28 km from Kananaskis Lakes. Park at the turnoff to Mount Shark and Mount Engadine Lodge.

The trail begins on the east side of Smith Dorrien/Spray Trail, opposite the Mount Shark road. The route starts off heading south parallel to Smith Dorrien/Spray Trail, along an ingrown logging road and passes through a small cutblock followed by a larger one. Midway through the larger cutblock the trail ascends, making its way to the northeast corner of the cutblock. Here the trail follows another overgrown logging road for a short distance to an even larger cutblock. The trail ascends through this, heading eastward. The well-spaced trees and gentle angle of this cutblock makes for a good, safe place to practise your telemark turns. The short, new-growth trees also afford exceptional views across to the valley of Commonwealth Peak, Mount Smuts and Tent Ridge. At the top of the cutblock, where the trail enters old-growth forest, a small white arrow on a green metal sign affixed to a tree points out the correct trail. Ambling eastward, the route makes its way through the forest, eventually paralleling Rummel Creek, staying above the creek on top of an embankment. The trail finally descends a short distance and crosses Rummel Creek before continuing on through the forest to the lake. Much of the way through the trees is well-signed by placards on trees but can still be tricky to follow if there is no evidence of previous parties. An outhouse can be found on the left, just before reaching the lake. Stick to the north side of Rummel Lake, as the south is rimmed with many avalanche slopes.

If you want to extend your tour, you can continue past the lake to Rummel Pass. Two and a half kilometres will get you to the true pass, but just skiing to treeline is a delightful option to get some nice views. Ski along the north side of the lake for about 100 m and turn left (north), ascending through a patch of short trees. As the terrain gets steeper, angle towards the northeast. After you've climbed steeply for 50 vertical metres, the trees thin out and the terrain begins to level off. The rest of the way to the pass is a gentle ski with few difficulties, but be warned that several large avalanche paths coming off of The Tower and Mount Galatea threaten this section of trail.

39. MOUNT SHARK TRAILS
Nordic Skiing, ATR 1

Grade Most routes are easy/intermediate.
Distance 18 km of trails
Max elevation 1810 m

Map Spray Lakes Reservoir 82 J/14
Groomed for classic and skate skiing

Due to their high elevation these trails get lots of snow, offering great skiing from late November to May. They were designed and built in 1984 under the direction of Tony Daffern and members of the Foothills Nordic Ski Club. There are outstanding views all around of Tent Ridge, Mount Shark, Cone Mountain, Mount Engadine and even the tip of Mount Assiniboine. It is one of the few places groomed for both classic and skate skiing. All of the routes are one-way, except for Watridge Lake Trail.

Facilities: Toilets are located at the parking lot.

Access: Turn west off Smith Dorrien/Spray Trail about 33 km from Canmore or 28 km from the Kananaskis Lakes Trail junction onto the road signed for Mount Engadine Lodge and Mount Shark. Continue past the turnoff for the lodge and drive about 5 km to the end of the road, where you will find parking for the Mount Shark trail system.

The trails at Mount Shark do not have names. Instead there are multiple variations to the main loop so that skiers can choose a distance they would like to ski. The loops are colour coded and signed at junctions. The various distances you can ski include 15 km (the entire trail system); 10 km; three 5 km loops; and a 2 km loop. The 2 km option sticks to the easiest terrain, while the other loops travel over some of the more challenging track skiing terrain in the Canadian Rockies. Watridge Lake Trail (see next) is a good option for beginner skiers.

40. WATRIDGE LAKE
Nordic Skiing, ATR 1

Grade Easy
Distance 6.5 km to Watridge
   Lake return
Time 2–3 hours return
Elevation gain 50 m

Max elevation 1800 m
Map Spray Lakes Reservoir
   82 J/14
Groomed for classic and skate
   skiing

This is a very pleasant tour along a wide and easy trail that will likely be trackset all the way. There are plenty of trail signs, so it is almost impossible to get lost. Along the way you may see heavily laden skiers heading to or from Mount Assiniboine.

Facilities: There are toilets at the trailhead.

Access: Turn west off Smith Dorrien/Spray Trail about 33 km from Canmore or 28 km from the Kananaskis Lakes Trail junction onto the road signed for Mount Engadine Lodge and Mount Shark. Continue past the turnoff for the lodge and drive about 5 km to the large parking lot for the Mount Shark ski trails.

The Watridge Lake trail is actually a wide road that cuts through the Mount Shark ski trails complex. It starts from the information board in the corner of the parking lot where the access road comes in, then descends 50 m through trees to the right to reach the wide, snow-covered trail. Continue 500 m along the trail through the forest, then descend a short hill to a creek. Ascend the other side and ski out into the open (old cutblocks). Continue along rolling trail for about 1 km, then angle right and enter the forest again. After several

Engadine Lodge. Photo Bow Valley Photography

hundred metres the route crosses a bridge over Watridge Creek and comes out into the open again. Ski along the left (south) edge of the cutblock for about 500 m. The trail then begins to climb, entering the trees again. After gaining about 50 vertical metres the track levels off. Here you will see a trail sign for Watridge Lake, which is located short distance down a steep hill to your left. There are a couple of options available here:

1: Beyond the turnoff to Watridge Lake you can continue for about 1 km to the bridge over the Spray River. The trail is level at first, then descends steeply, losing about 120 vertical metres. Be sure to zip up your jacket for the thrilling descent. Watch for descending skiers on your way back up.

2: You can ski about 1 km, then hike up to Karst Spring, where a natural underground stream flows out of the mountain.

Karst Spring

Ski around the left (east) side of Watridge Lake, then follow a trail through the forest in a southerly direction. After about 300 m the route reaches the stream flowing from the Karst Spring. To see the actual outlet, which is very interesting, ski through the trees along the right side of the stream for about 400 m, then climb steeply on foot for about 75 vertical metres to reach the point where the water rushes from the mountain. The water is warm from its journey within the earth and never freezes. The moss is a vibrant green and stands out beautifully in its snowy-white setting.

41. MARUSHKA (SHARK) LAKE
Ski Touring, ATR 1

Grade Easy

Distance 11 km return

Time 3–5 hours

Height gain 40 m

Height loss 70 m

Max elevation 1920 m

Map Spray Lakes Reservoir 82 J/14

This trail follows an old logging road to beautiful Marushka Lake. There are great views of Mount Nestor and Spray Lakes all along the way.

Options: There are many variations you can take to reach Marushka Lake. The route described here is one of the most popular ways, owing to the good views and easy navigation.

Access: Turn west off Smith Dorrien/Spray Trail about 33 km from Canmore or 28 km from the Kananaskis Lakes Trail junction onto the

Ken Farley skiing along the Watridge Lake trail. Photo Darren Farley

road signed for Mount Engadine Lodge and Mount Shark. Continue past the turnoff for the lodge, follow the road for 1.8 km and park in the pullout on the right.

The trail follows a logging road located on the west side of the Mount Shark road about 100 m from the parking pullout. The logging road ascends steeply for the first few metres before levelling off. Continue to a junction. The path on the left leads towards Tent Ridge, while the one on the right continues on to Marushka Lake. The road remains relatively flat until a second junction is reached. Keeping right, the trail descends gently. Many trees now grow along certain sections of the road but travel is still easy and the route finding is simple. The trail eventually levels off, leading to a large cutblock. This is where the logging road ends. If the trail is not already broken for you, continue through the trees on the west side of the cutblock, trending to the southwest. The lake is a short distance away. Depending on your route you may come across a creek which can be followed to the lake. There are tremendous views of Mount Shark and Mount Smuts from the lake.

> *"I learned this, at least, by my experiment; that if one advances confidently in the direction of his dreams, and endeavors to live the life which he has imagined, he will meet with a success unexpected in common hours. He will put some things behind, will pass an invisible boundary; new, universal, and more liberal laws will begin to establish themselves around and within him; or the old laws will be expanded, and interpreted in his favor in a more liberal sense, and he will live with the license of a higher order of beings. In proportion as he simplifies his life, the laws of the universe will appear less complex, and solitude will not be solitude, nor poverty poverty, nor weakness weakness. If you have built castles in the air, your work need not be lost, that is where they should be. Now put the foundations under them."*

> —*Henry David Thoreau*, Walden

CANMORE TO BANFF

42. **Dead Man's Flat to Skogan Pass**
Intermediate, p. 121

43. **Canmore Nordic Centre**
Easy/Intermediate/Advanced, p. 122

44. **Cascade Fire Road** Easy, p. 125

45. **Tunnel Mountain Trailer Court
and Village I** Easy, p. 126

46. **Spray River Fire Road** Easy, p. 127

47. **Canmore to Banff via Goat Creek** Intermediate, p. 129

48. **Sundance Canyon Road/Old Healy Creek Road/
Sundance Lodge** Easy/Intermediate, p. 130

49. **Sundance Pass** Advanced, p. 135

50. **Forty Mile Creek** Intermediate/Advanced, p. 137

51. **Elk Lake Summit** Intermediate/Advanced, p. 138

52. **Mystic Pass** Advanced, p. 139

The town of Banff is located in Banff National Park along the Trans-Canada Highway (Highway 1) 130 km west of Calgary. It is a town of about 8,000 permanent residents and is the major mountain resort in the Canadian Rockies. Canmore, population about 13,000, is located just outside the park, along the Trans-Canada Highway 20 km to the east of Banff. It has become a major tourist destination and, due to the presence of the Canmore Nordic Centre, is now Canada's premier centre for Nordic ski racing. Canmore was host to the cross-country ski events at the 1988 Olympic Winter Games. Both these towns are located along the Bow River, which flows from Bow Pass through Calgary. There are two major highways along the valley: Highway 1 (Trans-Canada Highway) a major four-lane freeway, and Highway 1A (also known as the Bow Valley Parkway where it runs through Banff National Park), a narrow, two-lane road intended largely for sightseeing.

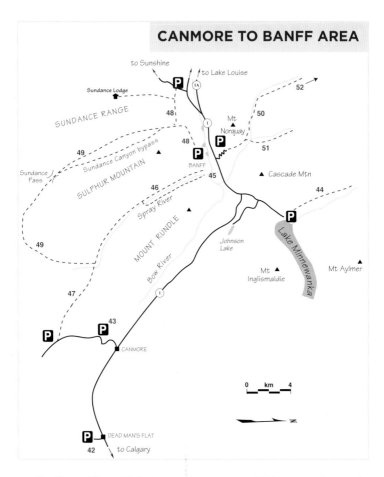

CANMORE TO BANFF AREA

to Sunshine

to Lake Louise

Sundance Lodge

SUNDANCE RANGE

52

48

Mt Norquay

50

49

Sundance Canyon bypass

48

51

Sundance Pass

SULPHUR MOUNTAIN

BANFF

45

Cascade Mtn

46

44

Spray River

MOUNT RUNDLE

Johnson Lake

49

Bow River

Mt Inglismaldie

Mt Aylmer

47

Lake Minnewanka

43

CANMORE

0   km   4

N

42

DEAD MAN'S FLAT

to Calgary

Facilities: You will find everything you are likely to need on a ski trip in Banff. There are many stores and shops with all manner of goods and services and several gas stations. Monod Sports (403-762-4571) is the main mountain equipment provider.

All amenities are also available in Canmore, where there are numerous restaurants, shops and gas stations. For your equipment needs, phone Valhalla Pure Outfitters (403-678-5610), Trail Sports (403-678-6764) or

Gear Up Sports (403-678-1636). In the unlikely event you cannot find what you need in Banff or Canmore, try Mountain Equipment Co-op (403-269-2420) in Calgary.

Accommodation: Banff and Canmore have accommodation to suit all budgets, ranging from small bed and breakfast establishments to grand hotels like the Banff Springs. There is a large, modern hostel in Banff (403-762-4123), and The Alpine Club of Canada runs an inexpensive and comfortable hostel (403-678-3200) in Canmore.

Information/permits: Information about snow conditions, weather and trails, as well as backcountry permits, may be obtained from the Banff Visitor Centre at 224 Banff Ave. (403-762-1550). The centre is open in the winter from 9 am to 5 pm, seven days a week.

42. DEAD MAN'S FLAT TO SKOGAN PASS
Ski Touring, ATR 1

Grade Intermediate
Distance 9.5 km one way
Time Full-day tour
Elevation gain 670 m

Max elevation 2070 m
Maps Canmore 82 O/3, Spray Lakes Reservoir 82 J/14

This is an excellent trail with a great view at the end. It is uphill all the way to the pass but there is a good run back down at the end of the day.

Hazards: Some years there may not be sufficient snow to do this tour.

Options: You can traverse the pass in either direction, between Dead Man's Flats and Kananaskis Village (see page 92). It will be necessary to leave a second car at the other end.

Access: Turn off the Trans-Canada Highway at Dead Man's Flats and drive south up the hill for about 1 km towards Alpine Haven Resort. Just before the resort, turn right to enter a parking lot.

The trail starts at the far end of the parking lot. Ski down a road through the trees for several hundred metres to a power line. Turn left and start up the hill, following the power line. After about 200 m angle left into the trees along a road. Do not attempt to ski directly up the power line, as the way ahead is blocked by a deep canyon. After about 1.5 km the road comes out of the trees onto the power line right-of-way again. Follow the power line for about 1.5 km, then angle left into the trees again. After about 200 m the road comes out onto the power line again. Continue along the power line – almost immediately it drops steeply into a dip, then climbs steadily up the hill. After about 2 km, just before the power line levels off, turn sharply up to the left on a road into the trees.

The road makes three switchbacks up the hill, then a long, rising traverse to the right, eventually breaking out of the trees into meadows at treeline. There is a great view of the four peaks of Mount Lougheed to the southwest at this point. Continue across meadows and open trees, gradually gaining elevation until the trail enters trees again. The angle now lays back and the route continues for a ways through the trees. The way then curves right and begins climbing at a moderate angle, then lays back again. Finally it curves up to the left and climbs at a moderate angle to the pass. About 500 m before you reach the pass, a road cuts to the right. Do not take this; continue straight ahead.

The road crosses the low point in the pass. If you are traversing over to Kananaskis Village you just continue straight ahead down the road. For an excellent viewpoint, turn sharply to the right and climb a short, steep hill up to the power line. From here you will have a great view back down to Dead Man's Flats.

43. CANMORE NORDIC CENTRE
Nordic Skiing, ATR 1

Grade All grades

Distance More than 65 km of trails

Time You can spend all day here or just a few . ours.

Max elevation 1500 m

Map Canmore 82 O/3
Groomed for skate and classic skiing

The Canmore Nordic Centre is a world-class system of ski trails that was created for the XV Olympic Winter Games, held in 1988. There are recreational trails and trails of the most advanced difficulty. All are groomed and trackset.

Facilities: There is a day lodge with toilets, lockers, showers and food and beverage service. The day lodge is open from 9 am to 5:30 pm daily. Trail Sports (403-678-6764) is located on site, providing rentals, lessons and equipment.

Information: At the day lodge you can acquire a map of all the trails and information on which ones are currently in the best condition.

Note: There is an admission fee to ski these trails. An adult day pass costs $10, a season pass $150.

Access: The Nordic Centre is located on a bench above the northwest end of the town of Canmore, under Mount Rundle. From the centre of Canmore drive west along 8th Avenue, cross the bridge over the Bow River and continue for a few blocks along Rundle Drive. Turn left onto Three Sisters Drive, ascend the hill and take the right-hand exit onto Spray Lakes Road. The Nordic Centre is on the right about 1 km along this road (large signs).

There is a very wide range of difficulty in the trails at the Canmore Nordic Centre. The easiest route, as well as the most popular, is Banff Trail, which starts in the main stadium and heads northwest. It is the best option for beginners.

The trails directly west of the day lodge are known as the Olympic Trails. These are arguably some of the most difficult Nordic routes in Canada. It is interesting to ski these trails and imagine Canada's athletes racing on them, sometimes skiing as much as 50 km in only a few hours!

There is a 6.5 km loop that is illuminated every evening until 9. It starts in the main stadium, follows Banff Trail and returns along Lynx Trail.

The Nordic Centre is the earliest place you can ski in the Canadian Rockies. Every winter large piles of snow are covered in sawdust, which protects the snow from the summer sun. In the fall this snow from the previous winter is spread out and groomed into a small loop known as Frozen Thunder. This loop is popular with ski racers wanting to get in some early-season training. Frozen Thunder is usually open by the middle of October.

The Canmore Nordic Centre. Photo courtesy of the Canmore Nordic Centre

A racer on the Canmore Nordic Centre trails. Photo Gill Daffern

Chic Scott on the Cascade fire road. Photo Ken Chow

44. CASCADE FIRE ROAD
Nordic Skiing, ATR 1

Grade Easy
Distance 12 km to Stony Creek warden cabin
Time A few hours or all day
Elevation gain 180 m
Max elevation 1480 m

Maps Banff 82 O/4, Castle Mountain 82 O/5
Groomed for classic and skate for first 6 km, to Cascade River bridge

This is one of the most popular routes in the Rocky Mountains. The snow is usually very good and this is one of the first trails to be track-set. Highly recommended.

Access: Drive east from Banff, pass under the Trans-Canada Highway, and continue up the Lake Minnewanka road. You soon reach a barrier and must turn right. Continue along this road for about 10 km to the large parking lot at Lake Minnewanka.

The trail begins on the left just before you enter the parking lot. Go under or around the road barrier and ski along the snow-covered road for about 500 m. Angle across to the right, crossing an open meadow to reach the Cascade fire road. From here you can ski along the fire road as far as you like. The route climbs for the first couple of kilometres, enough for you to work up a good sweat; then it rolls along through open forest. After about 6 km the road descends and crosses a bridge over the Cascade River. This is a good place to stop and have lunch. You can continue another 6 km to the Stony Creek warden cabin but the trail may not be trackset.

Note: The floods of June 2013 washed away the bridge over the Cascade River, but it is currently being rebuilt and the job should be complete by the time this book reaches the stores in the winter of 2015.

45. TUNNEL MOUNTAIN TRAILER COURT AND VILLAGE Nordic Skiing, ATR 1

Grade Easy

Distance About 4 km of trails

Max elevation 1400 m

Map Banff 82 O/4

Groomed for classic and skate

The gridded roadways of the Tunnel Mountain trailer court and the adjacent Tunnel Mountain Village I are trackset in the winter. These trails are flat, making this a good place for beginners to practise.

Access: If you are arriving from Calgary, turn off the Trans-Canada Highway at the east exit and follow the signs for Banff. At the Banff Rocky Mountain Resort Hotel take the first left onto Tunnel Mountain Drive. Follow the road for 4.5 km. Turn right at the signs for Tunnel Mountain Village II. The Nordic trails are on the right, just past the campground kiosk. If you are coming from Banff, follow Tunnel Mountain Road past the intersection with Tunnel Mountain Drive (there are numerous hotels here: Buffalo Mountain Lodge, Douglas Fir Chalets, Tunnel Mountain Resort and Hidden Ridge Resort) and turn left into Tunnel Mountain Village II.

46. SPRAY RIVER FIRE ROAD
Nordic Skiing, ATR 1

Grade Easy

Distance 10 km return

Time 3-4 hours return

Elevation gain 200 m

Max elevation 1390 m

Map Banff 82 O/4

Groomed for classic and skate

This is one of the most popular ski trails in Banff Park. It is always well groomed, and because it follows an old fire road, it requires little snow to be skiable. This route makes a pleasant outing for all levels of ability.

Facilities: There is a small shelter at kilometre 5.

Options: The Spray River fire road is an integral part of two other routes in this book: Goat Creek trail (see page 129) and Sundance Pass (page 135).

Access: In Banff drive up Spray Avenue to the Banff Springs Hotel. Go past the statue of Cornelius Van Horne, drive under the arch and continue past the parkade into a small parking lot.

The trail sets off from the end of the parking lot along a wide road. There are lovely views of Mount Rundle and the Spray River Valley along the way. There are a few hills but they are all manageable even for novice skiers. After about 5 km the trail reaches an open meadow. On the left is a bridge over the Spray River and, nearby, an open shelter. This is a good spot to have a cup of tea and a sandwich.

From here you can continue another 5 km to reach a second bridge over the Spray River. This leads to Goat Creek. You can also cross the first bridge and ski back along a trail on the east side of the Spray River. This trail is narrower and may not be trackset. It gains some elevation, then continues along a bench with views of Sulphur Mountain and the Banff Springs Hotel. Eventually the trail descends a moderately steep hill to the Banff Springs golf course. To find your way to your car, follow a trail back along the Spray River for about 500 m, cross a bridge to the west bank, then climb a steep little hill to join the Spray River fire road again. Turn right and continue about 500 m to the parking lot.

Karen Kunelius skis along the Spray River fire road. Photo Chic Scott

47. CANMORE TO BANFF VIA GOAT CREEK
Nordic Skiing, ATR 1

Grade Intermediate
Distance 18 km one way
Time 4–5 hours one way
Elevation loss 270 m

Max elevation 1640 m
Maps Canmore 82 O/3,
Banff 82 O/4

The trail is usually skied in one direction as a downhill run from Canmore to Banff. It is necessary to leave a second car at the Spray River Trail parking lot in Banff (see page 127), then drive back to Canmore and up to the Goat Creek trailhead.

Facilities: There are toilets at the Goat Creek trailhead at the Canmore end and an open shelter at the bridge across the Spray River about 5 km from Banff.

Hazards: The descents to Goat Creek and later to the Spray River can be challenging if icy.

Access: There is a large parking lot at the Goat Creek trailhead, which is located on the right (west) side of Smith-Dorrien/Spray Trail about 8 km from Canmore. To reach it, drive through the town of Canmore and follow the signs for the Nordic Centre (see page 122). Do not enter the Nordic Centre but continue up the steep hill to the pass. Follow the road around a little lake and down a short hill. The parking lot is on the right.

From the Goat Creek trailhead ski a few metres down to the creek and cross a small bridge. The trail then angles up onto the right bank and contours around the hillside for about 1.5 km, entering Banff National Park. From here the trail gradually descends towards Banff for another 5 km until it crosses Goat Creek. The track is wide and the skiing is generally easy, though the last descent to Goat Creek is moderately steep.

Cross the creek on a footbridge and climb the hill on the other side. The trail then ascends for about 50 vertical metres, contours around the hillside and, after about 1 km, descends to the Spray River. Cross the

Spray on a small bridge, then climb a short distance to join the Spray River fire road. Turn right on the road and ski up the hill. From the top of the hill you will get a long and gentle downhill run for several kilometres to the Spray River shelter and bridge. Continue along the Spray River road (see page 127) to your car at the parking lot near the Banff Springs Hotel.

Note: The floods of June 2013 washed out the Goat Creek bridge. It has now been replaced.

48. SUNDANCE CANYON ROAD/OLD HEALY CREEK ROAD/SUNDANCE LODGE
Nordic Skiing, ATR 1

Grade Easy/intermediate

Distance You can ski along this trail for a couple of hours or, if you go all the way to Sundance Lodge, make a full day of it. It is 12 km to Sundance Lodge.

Elevation gain There is little elevation gain on Sundance Canyon Road and along Old Healy Creek Road, but up to Sundance Lodge the trail gains about 250 m.

Max elevation 1580 m at Sundance Lodge

Map Banff 82 O/4

Usually groomed for classic skiing

These three trails, which run sequentially, offer a delightful ski. They are located right on the doorstep of Banff and can be accessed without a car. The views across the Bow Valley toward mounts Edith and Norquay and west toward mounts Bourgeau and Brett are superb. The snow is usually reasonable and the trail may be trackset much of the way. Highly recommended.

Facilities: At Sundance Canyon there is a camp shelter and picnic tables.

Options: In the past these trails could also be accessed from a parking lot along the Sunshine Village ski resort road. The parking lot is located 800 m down the road from the Highway 1 turnoff. The bridge over Healy Creek was washed away in the floods of June 2013 but will likely have been replaced by the time this book reaches the stores in winter 2015.

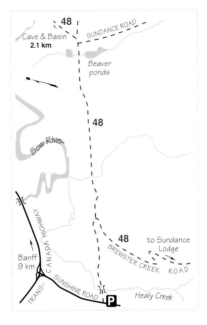

Access: Park at the Cave and Basin parking lot at the end of Cave Avenue. Walk past the Cave and Basin, then put on your skis and head down Sundance Canyon Road. This is a wide trail that is often trackset, but it is subject to wind and frequently the tracks get filled in. After a short distance the trail parallels the Bow River and the view of the surrounding peaks is superb.

If you choose to extend your tour you can follow Old Healy Creek Road for a way. This route branches off to the right from Sundance Canyon Road about 2.5 km from the Cave and Basin. Old Healy Creek Road is a delightful trail that rolls up and down, offering short little climbs and thrilling little downhill runs.

Finally, if you are fit and energetic you can ski another 7.5 km up to Sundance Lodge. This trail branches off left from Old Healy Creek Road about 3 km from its junction with Sundance Canyon Road. The trail to Sundance Lodge, which is wide and sometimes trackset, climbs steadily for several kilometres gaining about 250 vertical metres. It then levels off and continues very pleasantly rolling up and down and turning one way then the other. After several kilometres the trail descends gently for about 100 vertical metres then continues up the valley to the lodge.

Ken Chow admires the rock spire of Mount Edith from the Sundance Canyon trail. Photo Chic Scott

Margaret Gmoser skis the groomed trail to
Sundance Lodge. Photo Chic Scott

Sundance Lodge. Photo Chic Scott

SUNDANCE LODGE

This modern lodge is located on the site of the historic Ten Mile Cabin used by skiers in the 1930s on their way to Mount Assiniboine.

Location Along Brewster Creek 11 km SW of Banff (59**34**00 E 56**61**600 N)

Map Banff 82 O/4

Facilities Sundance Lodge has been completely rebuilt and now has indoor plumbing, hot showers and solar electric power.

Capacity 20 in ten private rooms

Cost About $150/person/night, all meals included

Reservations Banff Trail Riders, Box 2280, Banff, AB, Canada T1L 1C1

Phone 1-800-661-8352 or 403-762-4551

Website www.horseback.com

Old Healy Creek Road can also be accessed from a parking lot along the Sunshine Village access road. Drive west of Banff for 9 km along the Trans-Canada Highway and take the turnoff for Sunshine Village. The parking lot is located 800 m along this road, on the left. The bridge, which was washed away in June 2013, was scheduled to be replaced in the summer of 2015.

From this parking lot, cross Healy Creek on a bridge, then put on your skis and continue along a wide, flat trail (Old Healy Creek Road). About 2 km from the parking lot the trail to Sundance Lodge branches off to the right. Note that there is an earlier turnoff to the right after about 1 km, but this is a steep trail and not recommended. It is best to continue another kilometre to the proper turnoff.

"Take more time, cover less ground."

—*Thomas Merton*

49. SUNDANCE PASS
Ski Touring, ATR 1

Grade Advanced
Distance 28 km loop
Time Very long day

Elevation gain 350 m
Max elevation 1740 m
Map Banff 82 O/4

This is a long and challenging tour that is not often skied, so you may be breaking trail. Although the trail starts at the outskirts of the Banff townsite, it is not long before you feel as though you are really in the wilderness. The route finding from Sundance Pass down to the Spray River road is tricky and the skiing is not easy. There should be at least 60–70 cm of snow to make this tour enjoyable, so wait until later in the season. Due to its north/south orientation, the valley gets lots of sun.

Facilities: There is a camp shelter with picnic tables at Sundance Canyon, near the start of the tour.

Access: Park in the Cave and Basin lot at the end of Cave Avenue. A second car should be left at the Spray River Trail parking lot (near the Banff Springs Hotel: see page 127). Otherwise, it is a long walk back to the Cave and Basin at the end of the day.

From the parking lot, walk past the Cave and Basin to Sundance Road. Put on your skis here and ski along the road. The skiing is easy and the views across the Bow Valley are excellent. There are two options for negotiating the canyon itself.

Option 1: You can ski up Sundance Road and then follow the summer trail directly up Sundance Canyon. This trail starts by crossing a footbridge to the left bank of the creek, then climbs without difficulty for a short distance. The terrain steepens and it is necessary to take your skis off. For the next 50 vertical metres you climb steps with a railing, cross a little bridge, then climb steeply to reach easier ground above. Beyond here, put your skis back on and follow the creek and the trail. Just after the end of the right-hand cliffs, cross to the right side of the creek. The trail climbs a short distance through the trees before it begins to turn right, back towards Banff. At this point, break off from the trail to the left and carry on straight up the valley. The way through the woods is quite open. Carry on, trending slightly left, until you reach the creek again. Follow the creek for 4 or 5 km until near the area of the pass. Following the creek is occasionally difficult and it is necessary to travel through the woods on the right or the left bank for a distance until it is possible to return to the creek. When you are near the pass there is a large meadow off to your right. This is a scenic place to sit in the sun and have lunch. Above you rises the summit of Sulphur Mountain and to the west is the Sundance Range.

Option 2: An excellent alternative route is to follow the canyon bypass trail, which avoids Sundance Canyon completely. It starts on the left side of Sundance Road between the Old Healy Creek Road turnoff and Sundance Canyon itself. After a steep start, this trail climbs gradually through the forest and is easy to follow. It soon levels out and runs back into the valley for several kilometres. Eventually the trail becomes more difficult to follow as the forest opens up. If you lose the trail, traverse out to the right to the creekbed and continue along the valley bottom to the previously described meadow near the pass.

Not far beyond this meadow, the creek peters out and it is necessary to ski through the forest. There is a great deal of deadfall here and it is imperative to work your way to the left (east) side of the valley bottom, where you will locate a trail that runs through the woods. This is the only reasonable way through the forest, so take a little time to search for it. Follow the trail for 2–3 km.

Eventually the trail breaks out into a series of long, narrow clearings trending downhill where you should keep to the left side. At the end of the clearings it is necessary to find the trail again. A creek also appears at this point, and for the next kilometre the trail is never far from the creek. The trail initially starts on the left bank, then soon crosses to the right bank. It climbs high on a ridge, then drops steeply down and swings left again to the creek. The trail crosses the creek one more time to the left bank and climbs very steeply up a hill. From the top of this hill the rest of the descent becomes more reasonable. The trail now stays in the forest and does not return to the creek. The descent begins steeply but soon becomes more moderate. It is a fun glide down the trail to the Spray River road.

Turn left and ski along the Spray River road. It is 2.2 km to the junction with Goat Creek Trail (Canmore to Banff, see page 129) then an additional 9.5 km to the Spray River Trail parking lot (see page 127).

50. FORTY MILE CREEK
Ski Touring, ATR 2

Grade Intermediate/advanced

Distance 8 km to creek and return; 12 km return to Edith Pass turnoff; 36 km return to Mystic warden cabin

Time 4 hours return to creek; 5–6 hours return to Edith Pass turnoff; all day to Mystic warden cabin and back.

Elevation loss 150 m to Forty Mile Creek

Elevation gain 120 m to Edith Pass turnoff; 270 m to Mystic warden cabin

Max elevation 1830 m

Maps Banff 82 O/4, Castle Mountain 82 O/5

This is an interesting and pleasant ski tour. You can go as far as the creek or continue up Forty Mile Creek for many kilometres. The trail down to the creek from the Mount Norquay ski resort is reasonably steep and will be difficult if conditions are icy or the trail is heavily rutted.

Facilities: Food, toilets and telephones are available at the Mount Norquay resort. There is an outhouse at the Mystic warden cabin.

Options: Beyond the Mystic warden cabin you can ski another 3 km to Mystic Lake. You can also carry on over Mystic Pass (see page 139) and down Johnston Creek to the Bow Valley Parkway.

Access: Drive up the road from the Trans-Canada Highway to the Mount Norquay ski resort. Park in the large parking lot on the right.

From the parking lot, ski past the big day lodge, then down and across the ski slopes passing below the lower terminals of the Cascade, Spirit and Mystic chairlifts. From the lower terminal of the Mystic chairlift, ski up the green ski run (called Easy Out) which is the lowest and farthest northwest from the chairlift. Ascend about 50 vertical metres over a distance of several hundred metres up the green run, keeping your eye open for descending skiers. Just before this ski run curves left and joins the major run, the trail to Forty Mile Creek sets off through the trees to the right (there is a Parks Canada trail sign here).

Initially the trail traverses through the trees and even climbs a bit. Then it begins a steady descent for about 4 km down to Forty Mile Creek. Keep your eyes open for deadfall across the trail.

Cross the bridge and continue up the right side of Forty Mile Creek for another 2 km until you reach the Edith Pass turnoff. The very impressive peaks you have been admiring along the trail are mounts Edith, Louis and Fifi, some of the great rock climbs in the area.

Follow the right-hand trail, which continues up Forty Mile Creek for the next 12 km, staying on the right side of the creek and climbing very gradually. It is generally easy to follow. Sometimes it is a few metres above the valley bottom and sometimes it drops down near the creek. The trail crosses some small creeks, which can be a nuisance early in the season. It also crosses some large slide paths – do not linger here. Toward the end the trail descends to the left for a short distance to a fork. Follow the left branch, which descends to the creek. Cross the bridge to the Mystic warden cabin on the far side. The cabin steps are a great place to sit and eat your lunch.

Return the same way to your car at the Mount Norquay resort.

51. ELK LAKE SUMMIT
Ski Touring, ATR 2

Grade Intermediate/advanced
Distance 16 km return
Time Long day
Elevation loss 120 m to Forty Mile Creek
Elevation gain 500 m from Forty Mile Creek to Elk Lake Summit
Max elevation 2060 m
Maps Banff 82 O/4, Castle Mountain 82 O/5

This is a challenging trail, particularly on the return trip. It does, however, offer a varied and entertaining tour without having to drive too far from Banff.

Options: It is possible to visit Elk Lake. To do this, continue through the pass and ski down into the drainage that flows from Elk Lake, then climb up the drainage to the lake.

Access: This tour begins at the Mount Norquay ski resort. Drive up the road from the Trans-Canada Highway to the resort and park in the large parking lot on the right.

From the parking lot, ski past the big day lodge, then down and across the ski slopes, passing below the lower terminals of the Cascade, Spirit and Mystic chairlifts. The trail begins just below the lower terminal of the Mystic chairlift.

After about 100 m a steep trail branches down to the right. Do not take this trail. Instead take the left-hand branch which climbs uphill for a ways. Then the trail descends gradually for about 2 km to Forty Mile Creek, losing about 120 m in elevation. It is generally wide and has no sharp corners but steepens just before it reaches the valley.

Cross the creek on a footbridge in an easterly direction toward Cascade Mountain. On the far side of the bridge the trail goes to the right for about 50 metres, then turns back to the left and soon begins climbing in steep switchbacks. After several hundred metres you reach a junction – follow the branch that heads left, up the valley. The trail now climbs at a much more moderate angle and is very enjoyable. It continues along the hillside without difficulty for 6 km to Elk Lake Summit.

52. MYSTIC PASS
Ski Touring, ATR 3

Grade Advanced

Distance 13 km from Forty Mile Creek over the pass to Johnston Creek. The circuit from the Mount Norquay ski resort to the Bow Valley Parkway, near Johnston Canyon, is 31 km.

Time Most parties will need two days to do the circuit but it can be done in one day.

Elevation gain 430 m from Forty Mile Creek to Mystic Pass

Elevation loss 730 m from Mystic Pass to Johnston Creek

Max elevation 2250 m

Map Castle Mountain 82 O/5

This tour begins at the Mystic warden cabin and connects Forty Mile Creek with Johnston Creek. It is a long adventure and it is likely you will be breaking trail most of the way. Only very strong parties will do this tour in one day. If visibility is poor, it will be tricky to find your way over the pass, so be sure to bring your map, compass and GPS receiver.

Hazards: Much of this tour is threatened by avalanche slopes. It is recommended that you only undertake this when the hazard is low.

Access: This tour starts at the Mystic warden cabin (see the Forty Mile Creek tour on page 137).

The trail begins on the north side of the cabin. After a short flat section through the woods, it climbs steeply for about 75 vertical metres, then levels off and heads left into the valley. The route runs along horizontally for several kilometres, crossing some large avalanche slopes. Eventually, at a huge avalanche slope, you angle down left to the creek, where you will find a camping area and some picnic tables. It is also possible to ski along the creek for much of this section and avoid the avalanche hazard.

From here the way to the pass is tricky. It is possible to follow the trail most of the way if you have sharp eyes. The trail begins straight up the hill above the campsite. It is also possible to work your way up the drainage coming down from the pass. Either way, it is not easy and requires good route finding skills.

From Mystic Pass descend a groove which soon steepens into a creek drainage. The slope continues to steepen and it is best to traverse left and descend open timber to the valley below. Once you are in the valley, work your way along as best you can, following the creek at times, through the open woods and even skirting the forest on the right or left flank.

After 1.5 km the valley bottom opens up beneath a large rock tower high on your right. After another kilometre the trees begin again but the way is easy down the creek or through open timber on either side of the creek. At the point where a large avalanche path descends from the left (south) side of the valley, the summer trail climbs up on the right bank of the creek and traverses along about 60 m above the creek. It is possible to follow the trail or you can also carry on down the creekbed. The last kilometre of descent downstream to reach Johnston Creek is easy, either along the creek itself or following the trail along the right bank. Continue past the junction with the Johnston Creek trail, following the creek for several hundred metres, to reach Johnston Creek. Turn left and continue to the Ink Pots (see the Johnston Creek trail on page 170).

> *"The true harvest of my daily life is somewhat as intangible and indescribable as the tints of morning or evening. It is a little star-dust caught, a segment of the rainbow which I have clutched."*
>
> —*Henry David Thoreau,* Walden

BANFF TO CASTLE JUNCTION

53. **Rock Isle Lake** Easy, p. 145

54. **Quartz Ridge** Intermediate, p. 146

55. **Citadel Pass** Easy/Intermediate, p. 148

56. **Healy Creek Trail from Sunshine Village Ski Resort** Intermediate/Advanced, p. 149

57. **Egypt Lake via Healy Pass** Intermediate/Advanced, p. 150

58. **Monarch Ramparts** Advanced, p. 153

59. **Redearth Creek** Easy/Intermediate, p. 155

60. **Haiduk Lake** Intermediate, p. 160

61. **Ball Pass** Advanced, p. 161

62. **Twin Lakes** Advanced, p. 162

63. **Gibbon Pass** Advanced, p. 163

64. **Boom Lake** Easy/Intermediate, p. 164

65. **Trails near Castle Junction** Easy, p. 165

66. **Loppet Trail** Easy/Intermediate, p. 166

67. **Tower Lake and Rockbound Lake** Intermediate/Advanced, p. 169

68. **Johnston Creek** Intermediate/Advanced, p. 170

The section of the Bow Valley between Banff and Castle Junction offers some excellent skiing. Trailheads are located along the two highways that run parallel along the valley: the Trans-Canada Highway (Highway 1) and the Bow Valley Parkway (Highway 1A). Trailheads are also located along the Kootenay Highway (Highway 93) and at Sunshine Village Ski Resort. The turnoff for Sunshine Village is along the Trans-Canada about 9 km west of Banff.

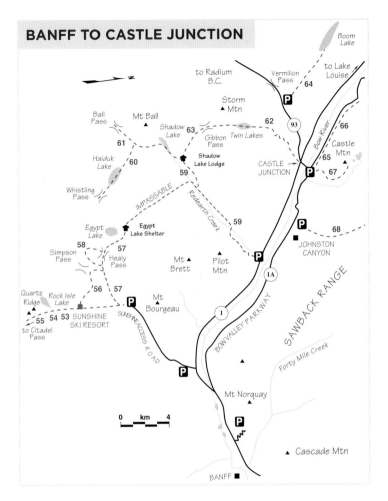

BANFF TO CASTLE JUNCTION

Boom Lake

to Radium B.C.

Vermilion Pass 64

to Lake Louise

Storm ▲ Mtn

Ball Pass

Mt Ball ▲

Shadow Lake 63

Gibbon Pass

Twin Lakes

62

93

66

61

Haiduk Lake 60

Shadow Lake Lodge

59

CASTLE JUNCTION ←

Castle Mtn ▲

65

67

Whistling Pass

IMPASSABLE

Redearth Creek

59

68

Egypt Lake

Egypt Lake Shelter

JOHNSTON CANYON

58

57

59

Simpson Pass

Healy Pass

Mt ▲ Brett

Pilot Mtn ▲

57

1A

56

57

Quartz Ridge

Rock Isle Lake

Mt Bourgeau ▲

55 54 53 SUNSHINE SKI RESORT

to Citadel Pass

SUNSHINE ACCESS ROAD

1

BOW VALLEY PARKWAY

SAWBACK RANGE

Forty Mile Creek

0   km   4

Mt Norquay ▲

▲ Cascade Mtn

BANFF ■

Bow Valley Parkway

This is the "old highway" along the Bow Valley and is perfect for sightseeing. The road is narrow and curvy and a 60 km/h speed limit is in effect. It is well maintained but during storms it is advisable to drive the Trans-Canada Highway, as it will be plowed and sanded more promptly.

The only facilities along this road in winter are at Castle Junction and Baker Creek. To protect wildlife the section of the road between the Trans-Canada Highway intersection 5 km west of Banff and the Johnston Canyon campground is closed overnight between 8:00 pm and 8:00 am from March 1 to June 25.

Facilities: Castle Mountain Chalets (www.castlemountain.com, 403-762-3868) is a resort located at Castle Junction along the Bow Valley Parkway that offers accommodation, a gas station and a general store. Just across the road is the Castle Mountain Hostel (www.hihostels.ca, 1.866.762.4122), which offers more-rustic accommodation. Ski trails start nearby. Farther west along the Parkway is Baker Creek Mountain Resort (www.bakercreek.com, 403-522-3761), which offers cozy cabins, a fine restaurant and lounge and ski trails just across the road.

Backcountry accommodation: There are two possibilities for backcountry accommodation in this area: the Egypt Lake shelter, which is primitive with no equipment apart from a heating stove and axe; and Shadow Lake Lodge, which offers fine food and deluxe accommodation in 12 heated cabins.

Sunshine Village Ski Resort

The meadows near Sunshine Village provide a wonderful opportunity for ski touring. They stretch 10 km out to Citadel Pass, and on a sunny day it is paradise up there. The terrain is open and rolling, perfect for ski touring. However, when the clouds roll in and visibility becomes poor, navigation can be difficult. So save this area for that beautiful spring day when you can sit in the sunshine and marvel at the tower of Mount Assiniboine in the distance.

Access to Sunshine Meadows is now difficult. It is no longer possible to purchase a one-ride ticket for the gondola up to the ski resort. The only alternatives are to go up the ski-out or purchase a full-day lift ticket for about $85.

Sunshine Village cannot stop you from crossing their territory to reach the meadows beyond, however. The pertinent section from their lease reads:

The Lessee will not unreasonably impede any residents and/or visitors to the National Park from passing freely over the land; PROVIDED, HOWEVER, THAT the Lessee shall have the right to make reasonable restrictions as to such access, such restrictions to be consistent with the safety requirements of a first-class downhill skiing resort.

To reach Sunshine Village Ski Resort, turn off the Trans-Canada Highway about 9 km west of Banff and drive up the Sunshine Village access road for about 8 km to the Bourgeau parking lot. If you choose to go up the ski-out, the trail begins just in front of the gondola terminal building. The climb takes about two hours and gains 480 vertical metres over a distance of 6 km.

53. ROCK ISLE LAKE
Ski Touring, ATR 1, 2

Grade Easy   **Elevation gain** 110 m
Distance 4 km return   **Max elevation** 2290 m
Time 2 hours return   **Map** Banff 82 O/4

The tour to Rock Isle Lake is a perfect introduction to the joys of ski touring. It is hard not to notice the change – leaving the hectic pace of the resort behind and skiing out into the solitude and peace. Many people have discovered the mountains and themselves at Sunshine Meadows.

Facilities: There are toilets, telephones and restaurants at both the resort and the lower terminal of the gondola.

Hazards: Skiing in the meadows is not recommended when visibility is poor, unless you are an expert at navigation with a map, compass and GPS. The hillside just to the south of Rock Isle Lake offers good turns but the slopes present avalanche potential. Ski with caution.

Options: From Rock Isle Lake you can carry on to Quartz Hill (see page 146) or to Citadel Pass (see page 148).

Access: See page 144 for access to Sunshine Village Ski Resort.

Looking out over Rock Isle Lake towards Quartz Ridge and in the distance Mount Assiniboine. Photo Gill Daffern

The trail to Rock Isle Lake begins at the bottom of the Strawberry chairlift. Ski up the run to the left of the chairlift (Rock Isle Road), then continue through the broad pass out into the meadows. There is a good view of Mount Assiniboine from here. The lake is about 500 m ahead and down to the right.

54. QUARTZ RIDGE
Ski Touring, ATR 2

Grade Intermediate
Distance 10 km return
Time 5 hours return

Elevation gain 350 m
Max elevation 2530 m
Map Banff 82 O/4

The tour to Quartz Ridge is a classic and highly recommended. The view from the top is outstanding and good visibility is required to do this tour safely. This route description takes you up the lower peak only. The higher one is a more challenging ascent.

Setting off up the wind-blasted slopes of Quartz Ridge. Photo Gill Daffern

Access: See page 144 for access to Sunshine Village Ski Resort.

The first part of the trail to Quartz Ridge is identical to the tour to Rock Isle Lake (see page 145). When the trail turns to the right to Rock Isle Lake, continue south towards the twin summits of Quartz Ridge, which can be seen clearly ahead. From this point you can reach Quartz Ridge by two routes.

1: You can ascend the small hill on the right, above Rock Isle Lake, then continue along the crest of the ridge to the base of Quartz Ridge, rounding any difficulties on the left.

2: Alternatively, you can follow a groove on the left side of this ridge until near Quartz Ridge and then turn up to the right to gain the start of the hill.

Either way, you end up at the base of a broad, open slope on the north side of Quartz Ridge. From here work your way up easily, gaining about 200 vertical metres, to reach the top of the hill. Skis can be worn right to the top.

To return to Sunshine Village you can head back down the same trail you came up, or if you feel adventurous you can descend carefully down the other side of the peak into the notch between the two summits of Quartz Ridge. It may be easiest to take your skis off and walk the short distance into the notch. The climb to the higher summit of Quartz Ridge is steep, with large drops down the west face, and step-kicking is required. This climb is real mountaineering and is recommended only for those with some climbing experience. The descent from the notch down the northeast side of Quartz Ridge, however, is fun and not too steep. Stay right to avoid steeper slopes lower down. From the bottom of this descent you can work your way back north across the meadows to rejoin your track from earlier in the day. This necessitates a short climb through a notch where you may have to wax your skis or herringbone up the slope.

55. CITADEL PASS
Ski Touring, ATR 2

Grade Easy/intermediate
Distance 20 km return
Time Full day

Elevation gain 430 m
Max elevation 2390 m
Map Banff 82 O/4

This tour is a perennial favourite with local skiers. On a sunny day, the tour across the meadows to Citadel Pass with the summit of Mount Assiniboine on the horizon can't be beat.

Options: From Citadel Pass it is possible to continue to Mount Assiniboine (see page 67)

Hazards: If visibility is poor, route finding can be very difficult.

Access: See page 144 for access to Sunshine Village Ski Resort.

Ski up the run to the left of the Strawberry chairlift (Rock Isle Road). At the top the angle lays back and you ski through a broad, gentle pass. Far to the south Mount Assiniboine can be seen on the horizon. Beyond the pass the tour continues south across the meadow. The route most skiers follow stays on the right side of the meadow, passes under lower Quartz Hill, then climbs for about 100 vertical metres

Skiing across Sunshine Meadows towards
Quartz Ridge. Photo Clive Cordery

to cross a ridge that runs out from the higher Quartz Hill. This is
the high point of the tour. Descend the other side of the ridge for
about 2 km, losing about 150 m in elevation and passing by a small lake.
The trail then levels out, crosses a drainage and begins to climb again,
gaining about 120 vertical metres over the next 1.5 km to Citadel Pass
(590400 E 5652800 N).

56. HEALY CREEK TRAIL FROM SUNSHINE VILLAGE SKI RESORT
Ski Touring, ATR 2

Grade Intermediate/advanced
Distance 10 km
Time Easy day trip
Elevation gain 170 m

Elevation loss 650 m
Max elevation 2360 m
Map Banff 82 O/4

This is a very enjoyable tour which is almost completely downhill

    Options: You can combine this tour with the one to Healy Pass

Hazards: There is a cliff band that partially blocks the descent to Simpson Pass. Scout around until you find a safe route down.

Access: See page 144 for access to Sunshine Village Ski Resort.

From Sunshine Village ski to the top of the Wa Wa chairlift. Angle off northeast to a notch in Wa Wa Ridge, north of a small peak called Twin Cairns. From the notch, curve around left, heading west across open meadows. Soon you encounter a steep escarpment, which you can bypass by staying well to the left. The meadows roll up and down with short little hills, and after 1.5 km they lead you to the top of a long descent to the valley, just north of Simpson Pass. This descent is generally straightforward and much of it is through open forest, but there is one cliff band and you should scout around to find a safe way through it. Even at the most reasonable point, the descent is steep and offers some avalanche risk. If you stay far enough to the left, however, you can avoid the cliff altogether.

Once through the cliff band, descend into the valley and angle to the right to locate the Healy Creek drainage. The trail along here will be difficult to follow, but eventually you should reach the well-packed Healy Pass trail, which you can follow down to the Bourgeau parking lot. See the Egypt Lake via Healy Pass trail description just below for more information.

57. EGYPT LAKE VIA HEALY PASS
Ski Touring, ATR 2

Grade Intermediate/advanced

Distance About 7 km to Healy Pass one way plus 3 km down to Egypt Lake shelter

Time For most people the tour to Healy Pass is a full-day. With a packed trail, however, it is possible to reach the pass in as little as two hours. It is an additional hour down the hillside to the Egypt Lake shelter.

Elevation gain 620 m to pass

Elevation loss 340 m to shelter

Max elevation 2320 m

Map Banff 82 O/4

The ski tour to Healy Pass is very popular and for good reason: it is accessible and gets you up high without too much difficulty. The views from the pass are outstanding – Mount Assiniboine can be seen clearly to the south; Monarch Mountain to the west is very imposing; and the view of the Egypt Lake group of peaks and Mount Ball to the northwest is impressive. Some good skiing can be found in the vicinity of the pass. If you want to continue down the west side of the pass to the Egypt Lake shelter, you can treat yourself to a marvellous Canadian Rockies night, complete with stars and the smell of wood smoke.

Facilities: There are toilets, telephones and restaurants at the bottom terminal of the gondola at the Bourgeau parking lot. There is a camping area with picnic tables and an outhouse about halfway along the trail to the pass.

Hazards: This route crosses several major avalanche paths. Take note of the steepness of the trail as you ski to Healy Pass and be sure you will be able to ski back down.

Access: Take the turnoff for Sunshine Village Ski Resort, located about 9 km west of Banff along the Trans-Canada Highway. Drive another 9 km to the Bourgeau parking lot and park with the crowd of downhill skiers. Walk to the far side of the gondola terminal building and locate the trail, which is the bottom of the old ski-out (there is a large trail sign with a map here).

Begin by skiing up the old ski-out from the gondola terminal. Be sure you have good grip wax on your skis, because it is pretty much uphill all the way to the pass. Some people use climbing skins to make it easier. The trail ascends the broad ski-out for about 500 m, then turns off on a smaller trail to the right. Along this section of trail you can admire the frozen waterfall on the cliff face across the valley. It is called Bourgeau Left-Hand and is a well-known and popular ice climb.

The trail descends a short distance and crosses a creek. It now climbs steadily for several kilometres to reach Healy Creek. This section of the trail is narrow, fast and tricky to negotiate on the way down.

Cross the creek and continue along the north bank through the woods, gradually gaining height. The trail crosses several large avalanche paths where it is not advisable to stop. After about 4 km there is a camping area on the left with some picnic tables and an outhouse. A

Margaret Gmoser and Lynne Grillmair near Healy Pass, with Mount Assiniboine in the distance and The Ramparts and Monarch Mountain on the right. Photo Chic Scott

Lynne Grillmair at Healy Pass. In the distance the Pharaoh Peaks tower over Egypt Lake. Photo Chic Scott

EGYPT LAKE SHELTER

This is a rustic cabin in a delightful setting near Egypt Lake, at the base of the Pharaoh Peaks.

Location In a meadow just above the right bank (true left bank) of Pharaoh Creek, 500 m NE of Egypt Lake (**577**100 E 56**623**00 N)

Map Banff 82 O/4

Facilities Wood heating stove, axe and woodpile. There are no cooking stoves, pots or utensils. Bare wooden bunks with no foamies.

Capacity 18

Water Snowmelt and Pharaoh Creek

Reservations Banff National Park Information Centre, 403-762-1550

short distance farther along, the trail branches, the left fork heading up to Simpson Pass, the right fork to Healy Pass. Beyond this point the trail climbs steeply again and after some distance goes almost straight up the hill. Just as the route reaches treeline it begins to level off, making a traverse to the left out into the open where the drainage comes down from the pass.

If it is a cold, blustery day this is your last point for shelter, so it is a good place to have a drink and a bite to eat before heading up to the pass. Once into the drainage you can follow it straight west to the pass. On a sunny day, this section of the tour in the meadow, high above the valley, is very beautiful. Looking back you can see the striking tower of Mount Assiniboine on the horizon. The view from the pass is outstanding.

The descent back down the trail is steep and tricky. Stay in control and watch for skiers on their way up.

If you are continuing to Egypt Lake it is best to head directly down the meadows ahead of you and through the trees until you gain the valley. It is likely you will reach Pharaoh Creek upstream from the shelter. Turn right and ski down the creekbed for a short distance until the creek opens up dramatically into a broad meadow where you will see a very obvious bridge crossing the creek, sticking out of the snow. The shelter is on a bench on the left (west) bank, about 20 m above the creek.

58. MONARCH RAMPARTS
Ski Touring, ATR 2

Grade Advanced
Distance 25 km return
Time Full day

Height gain 735 m
Max elevation 2410 m
Map Banff 82 O/4

Monarch Ramparts is a broad ridge that makes for a wonderful ski tour with exceptional views. Save it for a sunny day.

Hazards: Route finding on this tour can be difficult in poor visibility. Avoid the temptation to get too close to the edge of the ridge, as it is rimmed with very large cornices. Good route finding can minimize most of the avalanche hazard on this tour, but there is potential to get into some serious avalanche terrain if you are not cautious.

Access: Follow the trail to Healy Pass from the Sunshine Village parking lot (see page 150).

Option 1: From Healy Pass the Monarch Ramparts can be gained by skiing westward, sticking to high ground, until you have made it around onto the ridge.

Option 2: There is a shortcut that avoids going all the way to Healy Pass. When the Healy Pass trail opens up into the meadows shortly before the pass, angle westward, heading towards Healy Lake. From the lake continue westward and ascend to the low point between the ridge and the small hump to the north. Be careful here to stick to the lowest-angled terrain. After the angle levels off, continue skiing towards the low point along the ridge, staying well away of the corniced slopes of The Ramparts to the left.

Once on the ridge, the route finding is simple, leaving you free to enjoy the views along this sidewalk in the sky. On a clear day the prominent silhouette of Mount Assiniboine dominates the horizon to the southeast, while Mount Hector can be seen in the distance to the northwest. Towards the southernmost end of the ridge, densely packed small trees begin to impede further progress and it is best to turn around and return to Healy Pass the same way you came.

Looking across at Monarch Ramparts from Twin Cairns. Monarch Mountain is at left, with Eohippus Lake directly below and Healy Pass at far right. Photo Travis Rousseau

However, from the southernmost part of the ridge, it is possible to descend to Eohippus Lake on moderate-angled slopes. Avoid the temptation to ski down to the east too quickly, as there are cliffs. Instead, ski south until quite near Monarch Mountain, then descend along the top of a sub-ridge down to the lake. From the lake there are many variations to get back to the Healy Pass trail. It is possible to skirt along the base of The Ramparts or meander through the meadows. It is a good idea to get an overview of your planned way back while you are still on top of the ridge.

59. REDEARTH CREEK
Nordic Skiing/Ski Touring, ATR 1

Grade The trail along the Redearth Creek fire road, as far as the turnoff to Shadow Lake, is easy. The route from there to Shadow Lake, however, begins with a very steep section. Some people take off their skis and walk up and back down. The bridges on the trail up Pharaoh Creek, from the warden cabin to Egypt Lake, were all washed away in the floods of June 2013 and have not been replaced. This trail is now impassable. There is another one that climbs steeply on the east flank of Pharaoh Creek but it is not recommended for skiers.

Distance 11 km to the Shadow Lake turnoff and another 2.5 km from the turnoff to Shadow Lake

Time Most people can ski to Shadow Lake and back out in one long day. If you are looking for a shorter tour, you can ski 6 km to the picnic area, where the Redearth Creek road crosses the creek, and back in a few hours.

Elevation gain 425 m to Shadow Lake

Max elevation 1820 m at Shadow Lake

Map Banff 82 O/4

The Redearth Creek fire road is a very popular ski trail. The first part, along the road, is often trackset and is a good place to practise your skills in a safe environment. The tour all the way to Shadow Lake is popular as well.

Options: You can ski from Shadow Lake over Gibbon Pass and exit via Twin Lakes (see page 162).

Facilities: There are toilets at the Redearth Creek parking lot. Picnic tables and an outhouse can be found at the 6 km bridge, where the fire road crosses Redearth Creek. There is a deluxe, full-service lodge at Shadow Lake.

Access: There is a large parking lot on the south side of the Trans-Canada Highway about 20 km west of Banff. It is located 200 m west of the second animal overpass that crosses the highway. When approaching from the east use caution, as you must turn left across two lanes of oncoming traffic.

Cross through the metal animal fence by using the gate provided and ski west up the hillside. After about 200 m the trail swings left through the forest and soon joins the fire road. From here the road is wide and the skiing is easy but climbs steadily. After 6 km the road descends gently to the creek and crosses it on a bridge. There are picnic tables and an outhouse on the far side.

The road continues up the right bank of the creek for another 5 km to the Shadow Lake turnoff. To reach Shadow Lake, climb steeply to the right for about 100 vertical metres, and when it levels off, continue

SHADOW LAKE LODGE

This is a modern, comfortable log lodge in a beautiful setting.

Location About 500 m NE of Shadow Lake

(573500 E 5668900 N)

Map Banff 82 O/4

Facilities There are two central lodges surrounded by 12 guest cabins. There are outdoor toilets.

Capacity 32

Hosts Brian Nieuhaus and Alison Brewster

Season January 31 through March 16, Thursday to Saturday nights only

Cost About $225/person, all meals included

Reservations Shadow Lake Lodge and Cabins, Box 2606, Banff, AB T1L 1C3

403-762-0116; fax 403-760-2866

www.shadowlakelodge.com

Relaxing in the sun on the porch at Shadow Lake Lodge. Photo Chic Scott

Alison Brewster, Brian Nieuhaus, their daughter Joleen and dog Sandy in front of Shadow Lake Lodge. Photo Chic Scott

Kathy Madill admires Mount Ball above Shadow Lake. Photo Chic Scott

another 2 km up the valley to Shadow Lake Lodge. A few hundred metres before you reach the lodge, the trees begin to open up into a meadow. The lodge is on the right at the edge of the trees.

Karen Kunelius skis the Redearth Creek fire road. Photo Chic Scott

60. HAIDUK LAKE
Ski Touring, ATR 2

Grade Intermediate
Distance 14 km return from Shadow Lake Lodge
Time Moderate day trip

Elevation gain 250 m
Max elevation 2060 m
Map Banff 82 O/4

This is a popular tour with guests at Shadow Lake Lodge. The tour takes you to a lovely lake tucked away high in the mountains.

Options: If you wish to continue to Whistling Pass, ski across Haiduk Lake and then climb steeply, gaining about 100 vertical metres, to reach a higher bench. Soon the trees disappear and you can ski straight up the valley to the pass, avoiding a small band of cliffs on the left. From the pass it is possible to descend a short distance to Scarab Lake.

The descent to Egypt Lake is steep and difficult and is not recommended.

Access: This tour begins at Shadow Lake Lodge.

From the lodge follow the right bank of the creek up to Shadow Lake. Ski along the left side of the lake to the point where Haiduk Creek enters the lake (this point is usually obvious because the incoming stream creates a pool of open water out into the lake).

From here the route follows Haiduk Creek upstream for about 2.5 km. At the start the ascent is steep and forested but it soon opens up into meadows. After about 1 km you reach a large meadow. Angle out to the right corner, where the way continues up the drainage of the creek.

After another 2 km you cross a second large meadow to its end, where a huge avalanche path can be seen sweeping down. Just before reaching the end of the meadow, look for a trail on the left (572300 E 5665600 N), normally marked with flagging, which climbs to Haiduk Lake.

The trail now climbs steeply for about 150 vertical metres and then meanders through forest for a short distance until it breaks out into more open country. Continue skiing along the right side of the creek. It is sometimes hard to stay on the trail as it makes its way through meadows, glades and open forest. The way is often marked with flagging.

Eventually you arrive at a large open meadow which is crossed to reach the lake about halfway along its left shore.

Note: Many people turn up left from Shadow Lake before they reach the true creekbed. They follow a false creekbed which appears to be the obvious way. However, the forest soon pinches in and the way becomes very narrow. After about 1 km this route pops over a hill and descends to the meadow mentioned above.

61. BALL PASS
Ski Touring, ATR 3

Grade Advanced
Distance 12 km return from
   Shadow Lake Lodge
Time Easy day trip

Elevation gain 380 m
Max elevation 2200 m
Map Banff 82 O/4

This is an adventurous ski tour that takes you to a high and remote pass.

Hazards: The final part of the climb up to the pass is subject to avalanche risk. You should turn back if you doubt the stability of the snowpack.

Access: This tour begins at Shadow Lake Lodge.

Follow the Haiduk Lake trail to campground RE21 (572300 E 5665600 N) along the west fork of Haiduk Creek (where the Haiduk Lake trail leaves the creek and begins to climb steeply through the trees (see page 160). To ski to Ball Pass, continue southwest along the right bank of the creek. At times the route follows the creek itself. After about 500 m the angle eases and after 1.5 km a band of cliffs looms straight ahead. Ski along the creek, which curves to the right under the cliffs. Gradually the cliffs peter out and after 500 m disappear completely. Swing left and begin climbing the treed slope above the creek. Soon another set of cliffs will appear straight ahead. Climb diagonally up and to the left under the base of the cliffs to the highest larch trees, then climb the slopes above, angling to the right into the pass. This last section of about 75 vertical metres, above the final larch trees, is steep and potentially dangerous. Use caution!

62. TWIN LAKES
Ski Touring, ATR 1

Grade Advanced
Distance 15 km return
Time Full day
Elevation gain 630 m

Max elevation 2060 m
Maps Banff 82 O/4,
       Castle Mountain 82 O/5

This is a very steep and challenging trail that can often be icy

    Hazards: The descent from Twin Lakes can be difficult. Ski carefully.

    Options: This make a good, long day tour when combined with a crossing of Gibbon Pass (see page 163) and the descent of Redearth Creek (see page 155).

    Access: There is a small parking area along the off ramp from Kootenay Highway 93 onto the Trans-Canada Highway eastbound. Climb through the gate in the fence and put your skis on.

Ski a short distance down a wide road to a clear area with a trail bulletin board on the left. Continue straight ahead for about 50 m, cross a bridge over the creek, then continue ahead for 50 m to a junction. Turn right and ski about 1 km along a wide trail through the trees, parallel to the creek. Go through an open meadow with a cliff above on the left and then enter the trees. Continue another 300–400 m along a narrow trail, then cross a bridge over the creek.

    From the bridge make several switchbacks up the steep hillside above, then continue along over rolling terrain high above the right bank of the creek. The trail is hard to follow as it climbs and descends and meanders along. After about 500 m the route begins to climb steeply. It does not switchback much but just climbs straight up the hillside. Over the next few kilometres the trail gains 400 vertical metres.

    At the 2000 m level the angle lays back and over the next 2 km the trail traverses left (south), climbing gradually into the Twin Lakes drainage. Ski up the creekbed for another 2 km to reach the lower (south) Twin Lake.

63. GIBBON PASS
Ski Touring, ATR 2

Grade Advanced
Distance 5 km from Twin Lakes
    to Shadow Lake
Time 3–4 hours one way

Elevation gain 230 m
Max elevation 2290 m
Map Banff 82 O/4

The route over Gibbon Pass can be skied in either direction. The Shadow Lake side is easy to ascend, as the trail is easy to follow through the trees, but it can be difficult to find your way down if you are going in the opposite direction.

Hazards: There is some avalanche hazard off the slopes of Storm Mountain.

Access: This trail connects the Twin Lakes Tour (see page 162) and the Redearth Creek/Shadow Lake tour (see page 155).

Ski south across south Twin Lake to the far end, then work your way up through the trees to the southeast. There is an open draw to the right but this is exposed to avalanches and is not recommended. Going through the forest is not too difficult, as the trees are far apart. After about 100 vertical metres the angle lays back and the trees open up into meadows. Then the terrain steepens again for about 100 vertical metres through open trees (this is a very nice ski slope). Eventually you break out into open meadows which lead to the pass. From here there are great views of Mount Assiniboine to the south.

From the pass, ski southeast across open meadows. The trees begin very quickly and you must follow the best line possible, dropping 460 vertical metres straight down the hillside to Shadow Lake Lodge. The hill is steep and the skiing is tricky. Many switchbacks will be necessary. At times it may be possible to follow the summer trail, but most of the

Marg Gmoser leads Lynne Grillmair, Mireille Delesalle and
Hans Gmoser across Gibbon Pass. Photo Chic Scott

time it will be hard to find. The lodge is located on the edge of a meadow, right at the bottom of the hill.

If you are doing this tour from Shadow Lake the trail up the hill to
Gibbon Pass will be found behind the cabins at Shadow Lake Lodge.
Put on your climbing skins for the ascent to the pass.

64. BOOM LAKE
Ski Touring, ATR 2

Grade Easy/intermediate
Distance 10 km return
Time 3–4 hours return

Elevation gain 180 m
Max elevation 1890 m
Map Lake Louise 82 N/8

The Boom Lake trail is one of the most popular ski tours in the
Canadian Rockies. Due to its high location near Vermilion Pass, it gets
snow early in the season and keeps it well into the spring. It takes little
snow to make the trail skiable and you can often find keen skiers here

in November. This tour is a very pleasant outing.

Facilities: Toilets are located at the trailhead.

Hazards: The steep hill at the beginning of this trail can prove difficult for beginner skiers on the way back down. Beware!

Access: A large parking lot is located on the north side of Kootenay Highway 93, near Vermilion Pass, 6 km southwest of Castle Junction.

Skiers on Boom Lake.
Photo Alan Kane

The trail starts at the north end of the parking lot, immediately crosses a bridge and then starts to climb. For the next 500 m the trail climbs steeply, then for another kilometre it continues to climb but at a lesser angle. For the next 3 km, until just short of the lake, the trail rolls up and down through mature forest. The last several hundred metres is a downhill run to the lake, reaching the shore about one quarter of the way along the north bank. This trail is usually well packed.

65. TRAILS NEAR CASTLE JUNCTION
Nordic Skiing, ATR 1

Grade Easy
Distance About 9 km of trails.
Time From a few hours to all day
Elevation gain Nil

Max elevation 1450 m
Map Castle Mountain 82 O/5
Often groomed for classic skiing

This is a good place to spend a few pleasant hours.

Options: You can also ski the trail to Tower Lake and Rockbound Lake from here (see page 168).

Facilities: Castle Mountain Chalets are located at the junction where the connector road (a short continuation of Highway 93 South) from the Trans-Canada Highway intersects with the Bow Valley Parkway. Here you can find deluxe accommodation, gas pumps, a general store and telephones. The Castle Mountain Hostel is located just across the connector road.

Access: All three trails begin at Castle Mountain Junction. Just east of the junction on the north side of the Bow Valley Parkway you will find a parking lot. You can leave your car here and make your way to the trails either on skis or on foot. Maps are available from the store at Castle Mountain Chalets.

Trail #1 starts just across the Bow Valley Parkway from Castle Mountain Chalets and runs west along the north side of the highway. Just beyond Castle Mountain Chalets the route angles right and gets away from the road. You can follow this trail for 5 km to Castle Lookout or almost 15 km to Baker Creek (see Loppet Trail just below).

Trail #2 is 1.5 km and easy. From Castle Mountain Chalets parking lot, cross the Bow Valley Parkway and head northeast through the woods for a short distance and then cross a bridge over Silverton Creek. The trail continues east, reaching a campground where it does a loop, then returns to the start.

Trail #3 makes a 2.2 km loop on the south side of the Bow Valley Parkway. It begins near the access road to the hostel and heads south until it reaches a power line which it then follows to the east for about 1 km. The trail then turns north and works its way back to Castle Junction.

66. LOPPET TRAIL
Nordic Skiing, ATR 1

Grade Easy/intermediate
Distance 9.7 km from Baker Creek to Castle Lookout; 5 km from Castle Lookout to Castle Junction
Time About 3–4 hours

Elevation gain Minimal
Max elevation 1500 m
Maps Lake Louise 82 N/8, Castle Mountain 82 O/5
Likely groomed for classic skiing.

Every year in February a loppet ski race is held along the Bow Valley from Lake Louise to Banff. Sections of this trail are now maintained and trackset all winter. The section of Loppet Trail from Baker Creek to Castle Junction makes for an excellent ski tour.

Facilities: At Baker Creek there is a toilet and at Castle Junction a store and service station.

Hazards: Be very careful crossing the Bow Valley Parkway.

Access: This trail can be accessed from Baker Creek or from Castle Junction and skied in either direction. Park across the Bow Valley Parkway from Baker Creek Mountain Resort about 14 km west of Castle Junction. The parking lot is on the northeast side of the bridge.

Follow the Baker Creek Power Line trail (see page 222) for 3.5 km as far as Protection Mountain campground. From the far southeast corner of the campground, ski 50 metres south through the woods to the Bow Valley Parkway. Walk across the road and ski another 50 m south through the woods to reach a power line beside the railway. Turn left and ski east beside the railway for about 1.5 km, then continue east for another 1.5 km along a straight road through the forest. Ascend a long, gentle hill that takes you high above the rail line and the river, where there are excellent views across the valley. The trail descends after another 1.5 km and crosses a clearing. The route now climbs gradually and for the next 2 km winds its way through clearings and forests between the Bow Valley Parkway and

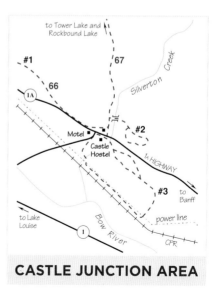

CASTLE JUNCTION AREA

167

Dave Millard and Chris MacDonald along Loppet Trail. Photo Jo Lunn

the railway tracks, eventually reaching the Bow Valley Parkway about 100 m west of Castle Lookout. You can either take off your skis and walk to the Castle Lookout parking lot or cross the road and ski a short distance along a trail to the parking lot.

Pick up the trail again at the far northeast end of the Castle Lookout parking lot. Almost immediately the route reaches the power line and follows it for almost 3 km. When the power line angles down to the right, the trail climbs up left into the trees, then meanders through the forest for about 500 m, descending a gentle hill to reach the Bow Valley Parkway. The trail now travels though the forest, not far from the highway, for another half kilometre, then climbs a steep little hill up left to reach a wide cutline. Follow this broad, open path through the trees for another 500 m to Castle Junction. There are numerous yellow markers reading "#1" along this trail.

67. TOWER LAKE AND ROCKBOUND LAKE
Ski Touring, ATR 1

Grade Intermediate/advanced
Distance 17 km return
Time Full day

Elevation gain 760 m
Max elevation 2200 m
Map Castle Junction 82 O/5

This tour is a steep climb much of the way but you are rewarded at the top with a beautiful valley tucked in behind Castle Mountain. The two lakes are in a lovely setting and the views are exceptional. The ski back down at the end of the day can be hard on the legs, particularly if the trail is icy.

Access: The parking lot is located on the north side of the Bow Valley Parkway, just a few metres east of Castle Junction.

The trail heads straight into the woods from the parking lot and soon begins climbing, so it is best to either wear skins or have good climbing wax on your skis. As you work your way up through the trees there are occasional views over the Bow Valley. Over the next 4 km the trail climbs 500 vertical metres. About halfway up, the route splits – follow the branch that swings steeply up to the right. Eventually the trail reaches the shoulder of Castle Mountain and begins to lay back. It swings to the left sharply and heads northwest into the valley behind the mountain. For another 3 km, as far as Tower Lake, the track rolls pleasantly up and down, gradually gaining elevation. On your left are very impressive views of Eisenhower Tower looming high above. The open meadow near Tower Lake is a good spot to stop and have lunch. The sun leaves this valley early, however, so bundle up.

If you want to continue to Rockbound Lake, the way is not too difficult. Skins will be a real asset. The route climbs treed slopes through the cliffs directly across from you on the other side of Tower Lake. Although the route looks unlikely, it is actually reasonable and there is only about 100 vertical metres of steep climbing. Just over the top of the hill, the route descends a short distance to Rockbound Lake, where you will be surrounded by impressive scenery. An outstanding viewpoint can be found to the right, where the stream leaves the lake and plunges over a cliff. From the edge of the chasm cut by the stream there is a great view down the Bow Valley, all the way to Banff.

The return trip to your car can be a challenge. It follows the same route you took on the way up but is now almost all downhill. Keep your speed under control. The trail down from the shoulder is wide but can be difficult in icy or crusty conditions.

68. JOHNSTON CREEK
Ski Touring, ATR 1

Grade Intermediate/advanced
Distance 10 km to Ink Pots return; 34 km to Luellen Lake return
Time 4-5 hours to Ink Pots return; full day to Luellen Lake return
Elevation gain 200 m to Ink Pots; 520 m to Luellen lake
Map Castle Mountain 82 O/5

This trail offers a moderately steep ascent, then crosses a high shoulder before descending steeply to the Ink Pots. If conditions are icy or crusty the skiing will be challenging. The Ink Pots are a lovely destination. The continuation up Johnston Creek to Luellen Lake is not a difficult tour but is very long, so leave yourself lots of time for the return journey.

Access: There is a parking lot at Moose Meadow, on the north side of the Bow Valley Parkway, 2 km west of Johnston Canyon Resort. (**Note:** There is another parking lot on the south side of the road, 1 km farther west, and it too is called Moose Meadow.)

The trail climbs up and right from the parking lot (do not take the trail that heads off left along the valley floor). It climbs very gradually through the trees for the first 2 km, working its way back to the east towards Johnston Canyon to eventually join the summer trail. From this point the grade begins to steepen, and after another kilometre it climbs at an even steeper angle up to the shoulder. You are now high above the creek and there is an excellent view down the Bow Valley. Up to this point the trail is very wide but beyond here it narrows.

The route now descends, sometimes steeply, down to the valley bottom. When it emerges from the trees, the Ink Pots are right there. On a sunny day this is a lovely spot to sit and contemplate.

If you choose to continue farther up the valley, ski a short distance and you will see a bridge over the creek. You can either cross the creek and ski through the meadow along the right bank or just follow the creek itself (if it is frozen and snow covered). After a kilometre both trails join and the route now follows the creekbed. Continue along the creekbed for another kilometre to where a small creek enters from the right (east). This is where you turn off if you wish to ski to Mystic Pass (see page 139).

To continue up to Luellen Lake you have two choices. You can turn up the small side creek for several hundred metres until you see a trail sign on the left bank. At this point you join the summer trail, which continues up the valley through the forest. Alternatively, it is possible to continue up Johnston Creek for 2 km, then at some clearings on the right side of the creek, work your way several hundred metres through the forest to the right to join the summer trail. From here just follow the summer trail, which climbs steadily but is never very steep. After a few kilometres it passes a warden cabin. Carry on up the trail beyond the warden cabin for another 4–5 km to the cutoff for Luellen Lake.

To reach Luellen Lake, turn left at the cutoff and ski downhill for a short distance, following a trail, to reach the creek. Cross the creek and climb the steep bank on the far side. Find the summer trail again, which climbs the hillside above. There are many blazes. The route climbs steeply up the hill for about 500 m, angles left, pops over a ridge and then descends a short distance to the lake.

An alternative way to begin the trail to the Ink Pots is from Johnston Canyon Resort. Behind the resort there are a number of cabins. At the far uphill end of the cabins a road ascends through the forest, parallel to Johnston Canyon. The road is wide and climbs gradually. After about 2 km it joins the trail that comes from Moose Meadows. This route is an easy ski and it is lots of fun on the way down.

KOOTENAY NATIONAL PARK

69. **Chickadee Valley** Intermediate, p. 174
70. **Stanley Glacier Valley** Intermediate, p. 175
71. **Tokumm Creek (Prospector's Valley)** Easy/Intermediate, p. 176
72. **Simpson River** Easy, p. 177
73. **Dog Lake** Intermediate/Advanced, p. 179
74. **Nipika Mountain Resort** Easy, p. 180

Kootenay National Park is the forgotten treasure amongst our wonderful Rocky Mountain parks.

Access: Kootenay National Park is traversed from northeast to southwest by the Kootenay Highway (Highway 93). There are no commercial establishments along this road that are open in winter. There is an emergency telephone at Kootenay Crossing. The highway sees a fair amount of traffic but it is all headed for the Columbia Valley, the Panorama ski resort and other destinations in BC. The road is well maintained and rarely closed in winter due to avalanches.

Facilities: Radium Hot Springs, just a few kilometres west of the west park gate, is a bustling little town where it is possible to find almost anything you might need. There are service stations, restaurants, grocery stores, motels, a liquor store and a post office. The actual Radium Hot Springs are located along the Kootenay Highway east of town, just inside the park gates.

For information stop by the Radium Hot Springs Visitor Centre at 7556 Main Street East (250-347-9331, http://is.gd/p5tVxb).

Note: In 2003 some 17,000 hectares of forest burned in one of the biggest fires ever in the Canadian Rockies. The northern section of Kootenay National Park was greatly affected, with little old-growth forest remaining. The burnt trees have helped open up the forest, making for good ski runs, but beware: there are many downed trees ready to snag a ski. It is best to wait until later in the season when most of the deadfall is covered with snow.

"The stars are the apexes of what wonderful triangles! What distant and different beings in the various mansions of the universe are contemplating the same one at the same moment!"

—*Henry David Thoreau,* Walden

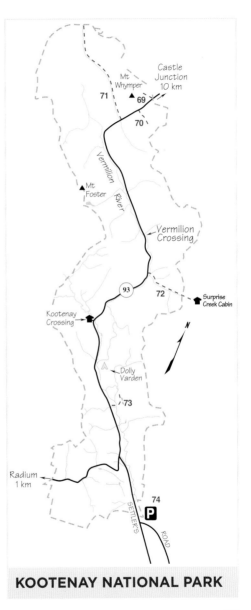

KOOTENAY NATIONAL PARK

69. CHICKADEE VALLEY
Ski Touring, ATR 1

Grade Intermediate
Distance About 6–8 km return
Time 3–4 hours return
Elevation gain 200 m

Max elevation 1860 m
Map Mount Goodsir 82 N/1;
    Adventure Map "The Rockwall"

This tour is a pleasant half-day outing. Good snow cover is required in the creekbed, so wait until after Christmas. The scenery at the head of the valley is alpine and very impressive. For those interested in making a few turns there are opportunities in this valley.

Hazards: There are several large avalanche paths that reach the valley bottom.

Access: Park at the Great Divide parking lot located on the south side of Kootenay Highway 93, 10 km southwest of Castle Junction.

From the parking lot cross the highway and walk a short distance west until just level with the end of the parking lot. Put on your skis and

Dan Verrall skiing in Chickadee Valley. Photo Chic Scott

head northwest into the woods. There is an opening in the trees here. Follow glades for several hundred metres, angling left, until you reach the open area of the creekbed. Ascend the creekbed for about 1 km up into Chickadee Valley. The creekbed has lots of deadfall, so wait until after Christmas when the snow is deep enough to make travel easier. When the angle lays back it is possible to ski another 2–3 km to the end of the valley.

There are excellent opportunities for making turns on the avalanche slopes above the valley, but to do this you should be familiar with snow stability evaluation and avalanche rescue techniques. Use caution!

70. STANLEY GLACIER VALLEY Ski Touring, ATR 3

Grade Intermediate
Distance 10 km return
Time 4 hours return

Elevation gain 275 m
Max elevation 1850 m
Map Mount Goodsir 82 N/1

This tour is better later in the season when there is a good snow base. The steep switchbacks at the start are a little daunting, so you should have a good grip wax or wear climbing skins. The run back down to the car, following the creekbed rather than the trail, is excellent. Since the fire in 2003 many other good ski descents have opened up. Be wary of deadfall.

Hazards: A number of large avalanche paths descend to the valley. You should not stop where you are exposed to the threat from above. There are a lot of downed trees in the area, so ski with caution.

Access: Park in the lot on the south side of Kootenay Highway 93, 13 km from Castle Junction.

Immediately after leaving the parking lot, the trail crosses the Vermilion River on a footbridge. From here it switchbacks steeply up the hillside. Usually the route is not too hard to follow, but often it can have deadfall lying across it (old burned trees) which can be a nuisance on the way up and a real danger on the way down. Later in the season the deadfall should be well covered. After you've gained about 180 vertical metres the angle eases off and the trail meanders for about 500 m across the flats, then dips down left to reach Stanley Creek.

Cross the creek on a small footbridge, then head into the valley on the left side of the drainage. Toward the end of the trees the trail climbs a few metres up onto the left (northeast) flank of the valley and can be hard to follow. Continue up the valley to the end of the forest. For those interested in making some turns there are good slopes nearby.

On your return journey follow the trail back down as far as the crossing over Stanley Creek. From here there is an excellent descent straight down the creekbed. This should be done later in the season, however, when there is good snow cover and the creek is well frozen. Follow the creek down until almost at the valley bottom, then cut over to the left bank and follow the hillside down to the junction with the upward trail.

71. TOKUMM CREEK (PROSPECTOR'S VALLEY) Ski Touring, ATR 3

Grade Easy/intermediate
Distance 28 km to Kaufmann Lake junction return
Time It normally takes a full day to ski to the Kaufmann Lake junction and return to your car.

Elevation gain 340 m to Kaufmann Lake junction
Max elevation 1830 m at Kaufmann Lake junction
Maps Mount Goodsir 82 N/1, Lake Louise 82 N/8

This is a long tour up a wild valley. You can make a short day of it or ski as far as you like. Many of the bridges were destroyed in the flood of 2013 and will not be replaced. The trail to Kaufmann Lake is no longer maintained and the trail sign may be gone.

Facilities: There are toilets at the parking lot.

Hazards: There are many avalanche paths which descend to the valley floor. Do not linger in these areas. Due to the forest fire there may be lots of deadfall across the trail.

Options: The adventurous can continue up the valley, beyond the Kaufmann Lake junction, to Eagle Eyrie near Opabin Pass. There is no trail for much of the way and you should follow the creekbed whenever possible. Travel is not too difficult if you wait until later in the season when the creek is well frozen and there is good snow cover.

This tour is sometimes done in reverse by strong skiers in a long, hard day. You begin by skiing up the road to Lake O'Hara (see page 261). Then continue to Opabin Pass (see page 267) and finally complete the tour by skiing down Tokumm Creek to the Kootenay Highway. Get an early start and bring your headlamp!

Note that Fay Hut burned in the forest fire of 2003. It was rebuilt in 2005 but burned down again in 2009. It will not be rebuilt again.

Access: Park in the Marble Canyon lot, located on the north side of Kootenay Highway 93, 7 km west of the Alberta/BC boundary.

Begin by skiing east, parallel to the highway, through a large swath in the trees, for about 150 m, to gain the Tokumm Creek trail, which is found up on the left bank. This route bypasses the Marble Canyon portion of the route. Follow the trail through thick forest with a few short climbs, and after about 3 km emerge from the trees onto the open flats beside Tokumm Creek. For the rest of the way, follow the trail that runs along the right bank of the creek.

72. SIMPSON RIVER
Ski Touring, ATR 1

Grade Easy
Distance 10 km one way to
   Surprise Creek cabin
Time Full day

Elevation gain 120 m
Max elevation 1370 m
Map Mount Assiniboine 82 J/13

Facilities: The Surprise Creek cabin (582500 E 5647000 N) in Mount Assiniboine Provincial Park is located 2 km beyond the Kootenay National Park boundary.

   Options: The Simpson River can be followed all the way to

Simpson Pass, then down Healy Creek to the parking lot for Sunshine Village Ski Resort.

Access: There is a parking lot on the east side of Kootenay Highway 93 some 700 m north of the Sir George Simpson monument and 6 km south of Vermilion River Crossing.

SURPRISE CREEK CABIN

This is a simple, rustic cabin in a lovely wilderness setting.

Location At the confluence of Surprise Creek and the Simpson River, 10 km from Highway 93 South (582500 E 5647000 N)

Map Mount Assiniboine 82 J/13

Facilities Equipped with a small wood stove, axe, saw, bowls, cutlery and a couple of cooking pots. Bring your own sleeping bags and pads.

Capacity 8

Water From a hole in the ice in Surprise Creek or the Simpson River

Stephanie Vetsch in front of Surprise Creek Cabin. Photo Darren Farley

From the parking lot, cross a footbridge over the Vermilion River. Ski into the forest straight ahead for about 200 m, then turn right and continue for about 1 km through the forest to the Simpson River. Beyond here the route follows the left bank of the river. At the time of publication the trail was in disrepair, with many blowdowns lying across it. The river (if well frozen) offers a good alternative. Two kilometres after the Kootenay/Assiniboine park boundary there is a suspension bridge that crosses the Simpson River. The Surprise Creek cabin is on the east side of the bridge.

Note: At the time of publication the bridge over the Simpson River was closed due to damage from flooding in spring 2015. Check with Mount Assiniboine Provincial Park for up-to-date information: www.env.gov.bc.ca/bcparks/explore/parkpgs/mt_assiniboine.

73. DOG LAKE
Ski Touring, ATR 1

Grade Intermediate/advanced
Distance 6 km return
Time 3 hours return
Elevation gain 75 m

Max elevation 1210 m
Maps Mount Assiniboine 82 J/13,
Tangle Peak 82 J/12

This is a delightful and interesting tour. The trail is a little steep and could be tricky in icy conditions. It is possible to ski this tour as a loop, ascending to the lake via route #1 and descending via route #2.

Access: Park at the McLeod Meadows picnic area on the east side of Kootenay Highway 93, 16 km south of Kootenay Crossing.

Start skiing from the north end of the parking lot where the lot loops around. Skirt along the edge of a meadow next to the trees for about 50 m. Just after a small wooden bridge turn right, into the trees. Follow the trail through the trees for about 300 m. On your left you will see a big building (McLeod Meadows Theatre). Cross the campground road and continue another 300 m to the Kootenay River. Cross two large footbridges in succession to the far shore. The trail now angles steeply up left for about 200 m to reach the East Kootenay fire road. From here there are two ways to reach Dog Lake.

1. Cross the East Kootenay fire road and take the Dog Lake trail that climbs into the forest straight ahead. The trail ascends steeply for the first 500 m, so be sure you have a good grip wax on your skis. It then lays back but continues to gain elevation for another 500 m. The last 500 m is a steep downhill run to the lake. The trail reaches the lake midway along the south shore.

2. A more moderate way to reach Dog Lake is to turn left and ski along the East Kootenay fire road for 2 km. At a trail sign, turn to the right. From here the route climbs gradually for about 1.2 km to reach the lake at its outlet. Much of the way this trail follows along the right bank (true left bank) of the stream that drains Dog Lake.

74. NIPIKA MOUNTAIN RESORT
Nordic Skiing, ATR 1

Grade Most routes are easy **Map** Tangle Peak 82 J/12
Distance 50 km of trails Groomed for classic and skate
Max elevation 1250 m skiing

Nipika is one of the Rockies' finest Nordic ski locations. It boasts an impressive collection of natural sights that are easily accessed on skis, from sculpted waterfalls to postcard-worthy mountain vistas.

Access: Turn onto Settlers Road (well signed), 20 km along Kootenay Highway 93 from Radium Hot Springs and 83 km from Castle Junction. Continue along Settlers Road for 13 km (watch for truck traffic), descend a hill, cross a bridge, ascend the hill for about 500 m and then turn left into the Nipika Mountain Resort.

Facilities: There is a waxing hut (called the Nipika Barn) located at the day-use parking area. It includes washrooms, waxing area, sitting area, ski/snowshoe rentals and hot drinks. You can also find maps of the trails here.

There are nine beautiful guest cabins providing deluxe accommodation for 4–13 guests. All cabins are outfitted with kitchens and are self-catering. There are flush toilets and hot and cold running water.

At Canyon Falls warming hut, located at Junction 9, there is an outhouse, outdoor picnic bench, indoor seating and a wood stove. The walls of the hut are covered in witty and inspirational quotes left by previous visitors.

An unnamed warming hut is located in the meadows at Junction 16. Here there is an outhouse, outdoor picnic bench, indoor seating and a wood stove.

Note: Trail fees are $12 for adults and $6 for children aged 6–12 (free for under 6). Fees can be paid at the wax hut. Nipika also offers rentals and lessons. Dogs are welcome on the trails.

North Trails

Canyons, waterfalls and even a natural bridge make Nipika's north trails some of the most scenic in the Rockies. The routes closest to the Kootenay and Cross rivers are truly spectacular and should not be missed. The north trails are hillier and slightly more challenging than the south routes but are still suitable for most abilities. Below is an overview of some of Nipika's finest sights and trails. The trails are not

Chic Scott enjoys the view along the immaculately groomed Nipika trails. Photo Kathy Madill

T.J. Neault skates on the North Trails at Nipika. Photo Tomasz Gehrke

named but instead connect various numbered junctions. Maps can be found at the waxing hut beside the parking lot.

Junction 18-15 Trail closest to river. A steep, exhilarating downhill leads to the bank of the Kootenay River. On the far side stands an impressive conglomerate wall, slowly being worn away by the river. When temperatures rise in the spring, you can often see rocks break off the wall and tumble into the river.

Junction 15-36 Shortly before Junction 36, you reach two short, steep hills known as "Double Hump Hill." In between the two hills there is a sign that points towards a stunning viewpoint overlooking a steep-walled section of the Cross River.

Junction 13-4 The Waterfall Loop is a short trail that descends steeply down to the river and then steeply ascends back up to the main Junction 13-4 trail. At the bottom of the loop there is a sign for the waterfall. It is advisable to take your skis off and walk down to the falls.

Junction 32-12 The trail skirts alongside the Cross River before entering the forest. There is a nice view of the same waterfall seen from Waterfall Loop, just before entering the forest.

Junction 32 Canyon Bridge A photogenic spot along the Cross River.

Junction 9 Canyon Falls Warming Hut Here there is an outhouse, outdoor picnic bench, indoor seating and a wood stove. As mentioned, the walls of the hut are covered with quotes left by previous visitors. From the hut it is possible to walk down to a waterfall along the Cross River.

Junction 11 Convergence of the Two Rivers A steady downhill leads down the one-way trail to the confluence of the Kootenay and Cross rivers. Definitely worth the return ascent.

Junction 26-5 Natural Bridge The natural bridge is one of Nipika's most unique attractions. There is a wooden bridge in place that overlooks the natural bridge and the river that pours through a slot canyon and into a pool below.

Junction 16 Unnamed Warming Hut Here there is an outhouse, outdoor picnic bench, indoor seating and a wood stove.

NIPIKA MOUNTAIN RESORT

Nipika has nine cozy log cabins at the heart of its ski terrain. They have all been hand built by the Wilson family. Lyle Wilson is proud to note that the entire complex relies on less than one-third of the electricity used by a standard family home. Dogs are welcome.

Location In a large meadow a short distance from the Kootenay River (585500 E 5607800 N)

Map Tangle Peak 82 J/12

Facilities Nine private cabins form a ring around an open meadow. Each one has running water, indoor toilets, a full kitchen and a barbecue. Meals are not included. There is also a communal wood-fired sauna and hot tub. Beside the hot tub is a small skating rink.

Capacity 71

Hosts Lyle, Dianne and Steve Wilson

Cost $290/night for two; includes trail fees

Reservations Nipika Mountain Resort, RR3,
4968 Timbervale Place, Invermere, BC V0A 1K3
250-342-6516
info@nipika.com
www.nipika.com

Rich Petite at Nipika Mountain Resort. Photo Brad Kitching

South Trails

The south trails meander through sparse forests, allowing for plenty of views of the surrounding mountains. Most of the southern trails are flat and do not provide the variation in terrain that is found on the northern routes.

Junction 37-38 One of the more interesting of the southern trails, with a nice viewpoint overlooking the Kootenay River near Junction 38.

A little history

Nipika has a long history. Originally the region was inhabited by the Ktunaxa people, who roamed the area for thousands of years. For five years, until 1925, the land was occupied by the trapper Bill Yearling, whose cabin still stands today. Since then the land has been used by homesteaders and horse outfitters. In 1979 Lyle Wilson discovered it and began developing what we know today as "Nipika." Before starting Nipika, Lyle founded Fresh Air Experience, a ski shop that in its heyday grew to 13 stores across the country. This organization was responsible for teaching an astonishing 70,000 individuals in learn to ski programs. Lyle later went on to coach Nordic skiing for 16 years, during which he attended eight World Championships and two Olympics. He definitely knows a thing or two about skiing, which is more than evident in what he, his wife Dianne, son Steve and daughter Marni, have created at Nipika.

> *"I would rather sit on a pumpkin and have it all to myself than be crowded on a velvet cushion."*
>
> *—Henry David Thoreau,* Walden

COLUMBIA VALLEY

75. **Panorama Nordic Centre** Easy/Intermediate, p. 188

76. **Whiteway (Lake Windermere)** Easy, p. 190

77. **Radium Resort Nordic Trails** Easy, p. 191

78. **Dawn Mountain Nordic Trails**
Easy/Intermediate, p. 192

79. **Cedar Lake** Easy, p. 196

80. **Golden Golf Course Nordic Trails** Easy, p. 197

81. **Columbia Valley Nordic Trails (Baptiste Lake)**
Easy, p. 198

The Columbia Valley runs northwest to southeast separating the Canadian Rockies and the Columbia Mountains. Golden and Invermere are the two largest towns in the area and both have all the amenities a skier could desire. In between Golden and Invermere is the small town of Radium Hot Springs. The hot springs are open year round and make for a great place to relax after a day of skiing. Most of the valley's visitors come for the alpine skiing at Golden's Kicking Horse Mountain Resort and Invermere's Panorama Mountain Village. As well as these alpine resorts, the valley has a wonderful array of Nordic skiing facilities.

Access: Highway 95 (Columbia Highway) runs along the bank of the Columbia River, connecting Golden with Radium and Invermere. Highway 1 (Trans-Canada Highway) passes through Golden, while Highway 93 South (Kootenay Highway) connects with Highway 95 in Radium Hot Springs and continues south, passing near Invermere.

Facilities: Both Invermere and Golden have gas stations, restaurants, hotels and supermarkets. Cross-country skis can be rented at Greywolf Clubhouse at the Panorama Nordic Centre and in Invermere at Inside Edge Boutique and Sports (250-342-0402, www.insideedgeboutiqueandsports.com) as well as Columbia Cycle and Ski (250-342-6164, www.columbiacycleandski.ca). Nordic rentals

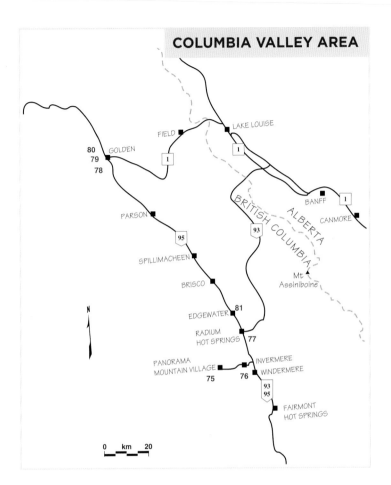

COLUMBIA VALLEY AREA

can be found in Golden at Summit Cycle (1007 11 Ave. S., Golden, BC V0A 1H0, 250-344-6600) and at Kicking Horse Mountain Resort (1.866. SKI.KICK [754.5425], www.kickinghorseresort.com).

Accommodation: The best bargain for accommodation in Invermere is the Invermere Hostel (380 Laurier St., Invermere, BC V0A 1K7, 1-866-222-0325 or 778-776-1744, booking@invermerehostel.net, www.invermerehostel.net).

In Golden the best options for budget accommodation are the Dream Catcher Hostel (528 9 Ave. North, Golden, BC V0A 1H0, 250-439-1090 or 1-877-439-1090, info@dreamcatcherhostel.com, www.dreamcatcherhostel.com) and the Kicking Horse Hostel (250-344-5071, tanya@kickinghorsehostel.com, www.kickinghorsehostel.com).

75. PANORAMA NORDIC CENTRE
Nordic Skiing, ATR 1

Grade Most routes are easy/intermediate

Distance 20 km of trails

Max elevation 1200 m

Map Toby Creek 82 K/8 Groomed for classic and skate skiing

The Panorama Nordic Centre is located at Panorama Mountain Village, a short drive west of Invermere. The trail system is technically in the Purcell Mountains, a region that generally has a deeper snowpack than most of the Rockies. The trails provide for ample views of the surrounding peaks and of Toby Creek, making for a great cross-country skiing destination.

Facilities: Located beside the parking lot is a Nordic day lodge which acts as the golf course clubhouse in the summer. Inside are washrooms, snowshoe and cross-country ski rentals and a restaurant.

Located on top of a ridge, along the Delphine Loop, sits Hale Hut, which has a propane heater, a table and some seating, an outdoor firepit, a small first aid kit and some very nice views. The hut is a 4 km ski from the Nordic day lodge.

Note: Adult passes can be bought at the Nordic day lodge for $10. Children under 6 ski free. Information regarding trails, lodging, shuttle services and other amenities can be found at www.panoramaresort.com.

Access: The Panorama Nordic Centre trails are located beside Panorama Mountain Village, near Invermere. From the main road entering Invermere (Athalmer Road) turn right onto Panorama Drive and follow it for 18 km to Panorama Mountain Village. Continue along Panorama Drive, which turns into Greywolf Drive as it passes

Hale Hut. Photo Darren Farley

Vincent Prenioslo skis along Barbour Trail. Photo Darren Farley

the alpine resort day lodge. The parking lot and day lodge for Nordic skiing are on your left a short ways past the alpine skiing area.

The trails start from behind the Nordic day lodge. Heading east along a 2 m wide track is Tranquility Loop, while heading west leads to the start of the Toby-Barbour and Greywolf trails. These routes have two classic tracks and a large skate lane. Most of the trails at the Panorama Nordic Centre have gentle hills, making it a suitable spot for beginners.

76. WHITEWAY (LAKE WINDERMERE) Nordic Skiing, ATR 1

Grade Easy
Distance 15 km
Max elevation 800 m

Maps Toby Creek 82 K/8, Fairmont Hot Springs 82 J/5 Groomed for classic and skate skiing

The Whiteway forms a loop which stays close to the shore of Lake Windermere and connects the towns of Invermere and Windermere. Beside the Whiteway an ice skating track is often cleared, so that it is possible to enjoy the day with your non-skier friends. The skating lane is touted as the longest skating track in the world! Trail conditions can be found at www.tobycreeknordic.ca.

Note: A map and donation box are located at all three of the Whiteway's main entry points. Toby Nordic Ski Club asks that you pay an individual day-use fee of $5 for use of the trail or that you purchase a club membership.

Access: The Whiteway can be accessed from almost any spot along the lake. The three official access points are at:

Kinsmen Beach, south of downtown Invermere. Head south on 7 Avenue, then turn left onto 7A Avenue. Kinsmen Beach is near the end of the road.

Invermere Bay Condos, located east of downtown.

Windermere Beach: From Highway 95 turn onto The Bench Road,

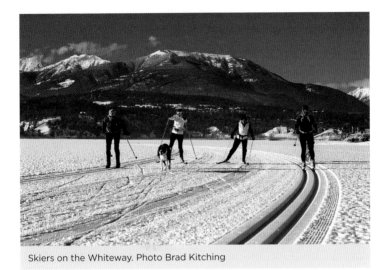
Skiers on the Whiteway. Photo Brad Kitching

which becomes Fairmont Street and then turns into Columbia Avenue. There is a parking area along the west side of Columbia Avenue.

77. RADIUM RESORT NORDIC TRAILS Nordic Skiing, ATR 1

Grade Easy
Distance 3 km of trails
Max elevation 810 m

Map Radium Hot Springs 82 K/9
Groomed for classic skiing

The Radium Resort golf course is a good spot for beginners and for individuals who may want a quick workout. There is no fee for the trails, and dogs are welcome.

Access: To get to the golf course follow Highway 93/95 south from Radium for roughly 3 km. Turn left onto Radium Hill Road, then right onto Golf Course Road. There is a large parking lot in front of the main lodge.

Note: The Radium Resort golf course should not be confused with

Vincent Prenioslo looks over the Columbia wetlands from the Radium Springs golf course. Photo Darren Farley

the Radium Springs golf course located within the town of Radium. It is also possible to ski at the Radium Springs course, but it will not be trackset.

78. DAWN MOUNTAIN NORDIC TRAILS Nordic Skiing, ATR 1

Grade Most routes are easy/ intermediate
Distance 30 km of trails
Max elevation 1200 m

Maps Blaeberry 82 N/6, Golden 82 N/7
Groomed for skate and classic skiing

This is one of the finest Nordic trail systems in the Rocky Mountains. The routes vary from mellow skiing beside beautiful meadows, to steep ridges with panoramic views of the entire valley. The trails are frequently groomed and always in good shape.

Facilities: There is a beautiful new day lodge beside the parking lot. Toilets are on the lower level. The main level has a seating area and a small kitchenette where there is complimentary tea and coffee. There is also a yurt across the stadium with a woodstove and seating. Along Beaver Trail, about 1 km from the trailhead, is Dawn Mountain Cabin, which has a wood stove and seating. An outhouse is located beside it.

Note: There is a small kiosk beside the parking lot where you can sign in and deposit your trail fees. Fees are $10 for adults, $5 for children under 17 and $25 for families. Joining the Golden Nordic Ski Club covers these fees. Up-to-date trail information and membership details can be found at www.goldennordicclub.ca.

Access: From the town of Golden follow signs for Dawn Mountain Nordic Trails. Head up Kicking Horse Drive for 13 km, passing Kicking Horse Mountain Resort. A short ways past the resort turn right onto Hector Trail. Follow this to the parking area.

BEAVER

2.4 km   Easy

Starting at the south end of the stadium, this trail climbs gently until it comes to a right turn. Rolling terrain follows, then a nice long downhill to the Supercharger junction. From here to Beaver Run is mellow terrain, skirting along many large bushes.

SUPERCHARGER

600 m   Difficult

A short diversion from Beaver. It's a steep, one-way trail, heading aggressively uphill before a quick, exhilarating run back down to Beaver.

HAWK OWL

3.1 km   Easy

From Beaver this trail gently descends with many rolls and bumps before reaching a hairpin turn. Be careful here. It then continues downhill, crossing a bridge leading to the Pegasus turnoff. From the turnoff, Hawk Owl gently meanders through the forest, staying relatively flat.

PEGASUS

500 m   Easy

A short connector trail between Hawk Owl and Moose.

UPPER RAVEN

4.0 km   Intermediate

This is one of the finest trails at Dawn Mountain. The route starts in a meadow, ascends a short ridge, then descends quickly to the bottom of a small valley. There is a tight hairpin turn on this section. Use caution. The trail then ascends a ridge and follows its crest. There are great views of the surrounding mountains along this section. There are also a few very steep descents and ascents along here that can be intimidating to beginners. The trail trends downhill, then flattens out before reaching the Lower Raven junction.

MARTEN LOOP

2.1 km   Intermediate

This is a one-way trail only groomed for classic skiing. In a counter-clockwise direction the trail begins heading downhill as it skirts along the top of a drainage. The route begins to steepen farther down, with many corners. At the bottom of the downhill is a very sharp corner. Be careful. The trail ascends the rest of the way back to the starting point.

LOWER RAVEN

1.1 km   Intermediate

From Marten Loop this trail ascends steeply up a ridge before the angle begins to ease off. The ridge has fantastic views of the Dogtooth Range and the Rocky Mountains across the valley.

CARIBOU

2.7 km   Easy

An easy and relatively flat trail. The route skirts along pleasant meadows for much of its length. A good spot for beginners.

The day lodge at the Dawn Mountain trails. Photo Kathy Madill

MOOSE

3.2 km   Easy with an intermediate section

From Chickadee, Moose Trail descends a long, steep downhill to the Pegasus junction. The rest of Moose sticks to mellower terrain, skirting beside many meadows and offering nice views across the valley.

CHICKADEE

2.3 km   Easy with an intermediate section

When heading east from the day lodge, this trail descends quickly down to Moose Meat. There is a sharp hairpin turn in the middle, so be careful. The rest of the trail consists of gentle, moderate terrain that is very good for beginners. At the northern tip of Chickadee there is a pleasant viewpoint. A fantastic place for a snack.

Note: Beginners can avoid the initial steep section of Chickadee by using the Chickadee Connector from the day lodge.

MOOSE MEAT

600 m
Intermediate
   A moderate uphill to Chickadee.

COUGAR

700 m
Difficult
   Steep connector trail. Use caution.

HUFF-N-PUFF

800 m
Difficult
   Steep connector trail. Use caution.

Chic Scott skis along the Dawn Mountain trails.
Photo Kathy Madill

79. CEDAR LAKE
Nordic Skiing, ATR 1

Grade Easy
Distance 4 km return from Cedar
   Lake 2

Max elevation 1100 m
Maps Blaeberry 82 N/6, Golden
   82 N/7

A brief, easy ski that is great for beginners. Despite the short distance, the views and setting are spectacular.

Facilities: There are toilets at the parking lot.

Hazards: Make sure the ice on the lake is well frozen.

Note: A trail map of the area is on the back side of the Moonraker sign.

Access: Follow signs in town for Kicking Horse Mountain Resort. After crossing the Columbia River bridge, travel 6.4 km along Kicking Horse Drive until you reach a sign for Cedar Lake/Moonraker Trails. Turn here and continue along the road for 1.8 km. Turn left at the sign for Cedar Lake. Park in front of the large Moonraker sign.

From the parking area, the trail follows the closed summer road for a few hundred metres to Cedar Lake. Upon reaching the lake, ski along the east bank (left), passing the infamous rope swing about halfway across the lake. At the far end of the lake the trail continues south along the obvious drainage. After a few hundred metres you reach Cedar Lake. You can ski a nice loop around the lake before returning the way you came. There are many more possible ski options in this area. The Moonraker trail system is comprised of over 45 km of mountain bike trails that can also be explored on skis.

80. GOLDEN GOLF CLUB NORDIC TRAILS
Nordic Skiing, ATR 1

Grade Most trails are easy
Distance 6 km
Max elevation 800 m

Maps Blaeberry 82 N/6, Golden 82 N/7
Groomed for classic and skate skiing

These trails are great for a short workout, and they are just a quick drive from town. The trails are mostly flat, making it a good place for beginners. The golf course gets significantly less snow than the Dawn Mountain trails, so these routes are usually not in good shape until later in the season. Grooming is done by the Golden Nordic Ski Club.

Facilities: There is a log cabin at the parking area, with a woodstove, tables and seating. There is an outhouse around the back.

Note: Up-to-date information on the trails can be found at www.goldennordicclub.ca. There is a donation box at the parking lot for trail use (suggested amount $2).

Access: Follow signs in town for Kicking Horse Mountain Resort. After crossing the Columbia River bridge, take your first right onto Golf Course Drive. Turn right after reaching the clubhouse and park in front of the trailhead cabin.

The warming hut located at the Golden golf course trailhead. Photo Darren Farley

81. COLUMBIA VALLEY NORDIC TRAILS (BAPTISTE LAKE)
Nordic Skiing, ATR 1

Grade Most trails are easy
Distance 14 km of trails
Max elevation 1000 m

Map Radium Hot Springs 82 K/9
Groomed for classic skiing

The Columbia Valley trails are a bit of a local secret, offering views of the Rockies, the Columbia River valley, and the Purcell range across the valley. In the middle of the trail system is Baptiste Lake, which has two benches along its north end offering a nice spot to relax and have a snack. Most of the terrain is gentle, with rolling hills. The trails are set with two classic tracks but no skate lane, which is perfect for a sociable ski with friends.

Note: The trails are trackset and maintained by volunteers. There is a day-use fee of $4 per person. An annual pass costs $25 per person, a family annual pass $35. All of the trails are on private land. Dogs are welcome.

Access: From Radium drive north on Highway 95 for 9.5 km. Shortly after the turnoff for Edgewater, turn right onto Hewitt Road and follow it for 1.1 km. The trailhead is on the right.

Vincent Prenioslo skis along the shore of Baptiste Lake. Photo Darren Farley

LAKE LOUISE AREA

82. **Lake Louise Loop** Easy/Intermediate, p. 203

83. **Fairview Loop** Easy/Intermediate, p. 204

84. **Tramline Trail** Easy, p. 207

85. **Peyto Trail** Intermediate, p. 208

86. **Upper Telemark Trail**
Intermediate/Advanced, p. 209

87. **Lower Telemark Trail** Easy, p. 209

88. **Great Divide Trail** Easy, p. 210

89. **Bow River Loop** Easy, p. 211

90. **Moraine Lake Road** Easy, p. 213

91. **Paradise Valley** Intermediate, p. 214

92. **Plain of Six Glaciers** Intermediate, p. 216

93. **Pipestone Trails** Easy/Intermediate, p. 218

94. **Baker Creek** Intermediate, p. 220

95. **Baker Creek Power Line** Easy, p. 222

96. **Taylor Lake** Advanced, p. 222

Lake Louise is known worldwide as a mountaineering centre and downhill ski resort. It also offers extensive opportunities for cross-country skiing – Nordic skiing along set tracks or ski touring in a wilderness setting. The scenery is outstanding and the area gets lots of snow, so it is the perfect place for a ski holiday.

Facilities: The facilities here are spread out in three distinct centres collectively referred to as Lake Louise. These are: the Lake Louise townsite, Upper Lake Louise (near the lake) and the Lake Louise Ski Resort. All amenities that you might require can be found at these locations.

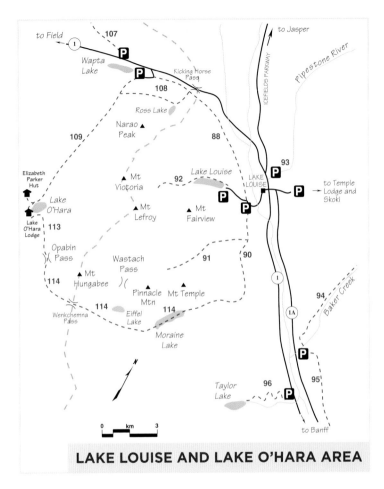

LAKE LOUISE AND LAKE O'HARA AREA

Lake Louise Townsite

There are two service stations here; several restaurants and lounges; and three hotels: the Mountaineer Lodge (403-522-3844), the Post Hotel (403-522-3989) and the Lake Louise Inn (403-522-3791). The Lake Louise Alpine Centre and Hostel (403-522-2200) offers excellent low-cost accommodation with lovely ambiance. Wilson Mountain Sports

(403-522-3636, 866-929-3636) can help with all your equipment needs. There is also a medical centre and a national park visitor information centre. In addition there is a post office, liquor store, bookstore, grocery store and a bakery and coffee shop called Laggan's. These businesses are located in or near Samson Mall.

Upper Lake Louise

On the shore of Lake Louise itself, about 3 km up the hill from the townsite, is the famous Canadian Pacific hotel called the Chateau Lake Louise. Just a short distance down the road is Deer Lodge, which is a little less grand but still very elegant. Many trails begin near here and are referred to collectively as the Upper Lake Louise Trails.

Lake Louise Ski Resort

This facility is located across the valley from the lake, about 2.5 km northeast of the townsite. Ski lifts begin from the Lodge of the Ten Peaks, and the access to Skoki Lodge begins nearby.

A little history

Lake Louise was not the original home of mountaineering in Canada – that honour rests with Rogers Pass, where there was a luxurious hotel called Glacier House. However, the focus shifted over the years, and when Glacier House closed in autumn 1925 because the rail line had been rerouted through a tunnel under the mountains, Lake Louise had already become the alpine centre for Canada.

For years prominent mountaineers from around the world met at the Chateau to plan their trips into the backcountry and climb the glittering peaks. Today Lake Louise is still a great climbing centre – the massive north face of Mount Temple, the airy ridge of Mount Victoria and the steep quartzite cliffs at the end of the lake draw adventure seekers from around the world. Lake Louise has also grown in stature as a ski destination. Skoki Lodge opened its doors in the winter of 1931 and has now grown into the downhill ski giant known as Skiing Louise.

An extensive array of Nordic ski trails has also developed all around the valley. The Chateau, which for years was only open in the summer, now does a healthy business in the winter, and the once-rustic Post Hotel has grown into the sophisticated operation we see today.

Upper Lake Louiise Trails

There are ten well-maintained and trackset trails in this network, which provide wonderful Nordic skiing opportunities for all levels of ability. They are easy to access and are located in the heart of beautiful country. Nearby are amenities such as toilets, telephones and restaurants. These trails are perfect for a family outing or for those who are new to the sport. After a day of skiing it is pleasant to visit the Chateau for a cup of hot chocolate in luxurious surroundings.

Before skiing these trails you may wish to stop by the National Park Visitor Information Centre, located in Samson Mall in the Lake Louise townsite, and pick up one of the excellent trail maps that are available. Park employees at the centre will also have current information about the state of the trails and which ones have recently been trackset and are in the best shape. You can also visit www.pc.gc.ca/banfftrails to view reports of recent and planned trail grooming.

Many of the Upper Lake Louise trails are accessed from the large parking lot on the left, just before you reach the Chateau.

82. LAKE LOUISE LOOP
Nordic Skiing, ATR 1

National Park Trail #4
Grade Easy/intermediate
Distance 4 km return
Time 1–2 hours return

Elevation gain Nil
Max elevation 1730 m
Map Lake Louise 82 N/8

This loop is actually two completely different trails. One runs across the lake and is flat and very easy. It offers a pleasant introduction to cross-country skiing in magnificent surroundings. The other part of the loop runs along the hillside, about 100 m above the lake. It rolls up and down and is much more challenging.

Facilities: There are toilets and heated washrooms at the west end of the parking lot, nearest Chateau Lake Louise. Restaurants and shops are available at the Chateau.

Hazards: Do not ski across the lake unless it is well frozen and covered with a substantial cushion of snow.

Options: This trail joins up with the Plain of Six Glaciers Trail (see page 216).

Access: A large parking lot is located on the left, just before the Chateau. Park at the west end of the lot (nearest to the Chateau).

From the parking lot, walk around to the front of the Chateau. The ski trail across the lake begins near the ice castle and skating rink directly in front of the hotel. It crosses the lake, keeping close to the right-hand (northwest) shore. The trail is flat and usually trackset but may be damaged by the footprints of walkers. Most people ski to just before the end of the lake, where you can look up to the right and see a frozen waterfall. This is called Louise Falls and is a favourite with ice climbers. Look closely and perhaps you can see some. About this point a current of water from near the shore can make the snow wet underneath, so proceed with caution.

From here it is possible to take off your skis and ascend the hiking trail about 100 m up the hillside toward Louise Falls, where you will find another trail, also #4, heading back toward the Chateau. This route can be tricky if your skis are fast. The track rolls up and down through the forest and eventually emerges from the trees just a few metres west of the Chateau, near the start of the hiking trail to Lake Agnes and the telemark ski trail

83. FAIRVIEW LOOP
Nordic Skiing, ATR 1

National Park Trail #2
Grade Easy/intermediate
Distance 7.5 km to complete the loop
Time 2 hours

Elevation gain (loss) 50 m
Max elevation 1730 m
Map Lake Louise 82 N/8

Karen Kunelius enjoys the falling snow along Fairview Trail. Photo Chic Scott

Highly recommended, this trail traverses forests and clearings, giving a nice open feeling, plenty of variety and good views. There are moderate little uphills, downhills and turns, which help to make the trail entertaining and interesting.

Facilities: There are heated toilets and washrooms at the west end of the parking lot, nearest to the Chateau.

Options: This trail forms a pleasant alternative start to the tour along Moraine Lake Road. It can also be combined with Tramline Trail to the townsite of Lake Louise.

Access: A large parking lot is located on the left, just before you reach Chateau Lake Louise. Park at the east end of the lot (farthest from the hotel), near the start of the trail.

From the east end of the parking lot the trail goes up to the right for a short distance, then turns left into the trees. It rolls up and down for several kilometres below Fairview Mountain before reaching an

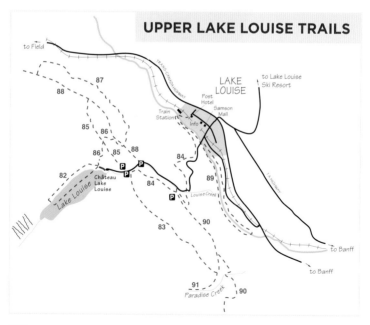

exhilarating downhill run that is enjoyable even for beginners. The trail splits in two for a short distance along here and you should stay to the right. After about 3 km the trail turns sharply to the left and descends to Moraine Lake Road. The trail splits in two again for a short distance along here and again you should stay right.

Turn left when you reach Moraine Lake Road and follow it to the junction with Tramline Trail, located at the edge of the parking area. Turn left and ski up the gradual grade of Tramline Trail back to the parking lot and your car.

84. TRAMLINE TRAIL
Nordic Skiing, ATR 1

National Park Trail #3
Grade Easy
Distance 4.4 km one way
Time 30–45 minutes downhill;
   1.5 hours uphill

Elevation gain (loss) 180 m
Max elevation 1730 m
Map Lake Louise 82 N/8

This is a fun trail and an interesting way to connect Upper Lake Louise with the townsite. It is a good idea to ski this in one direction, have a cup of tea and a rest, then return along the same trail to your starting point. The route can be a lot of fun to ski downhill but a bit of a grind to ski back up again. The trail follows the railbed of an old tramline that carried guests to the Chateau from the railway station between 1912 and 1930. Consequently it is wide and has a gentle grade. Halfway along, there is a beautiful view east over the Bow Valley.

Facilities: There are heated toilets and washrooms at the west end of the parking lot, nearest the Chateau. Services are available at both ends of the trail (Chateau Lake Louise or the Lake Louise Townsite).

Hazards: The route can be challenging when it is icy. Beware!

Options: This trail links up nicely with the Bow River Loop.

Access: A large parking lot is located on the left, just before you reach the Chateau. Park at the east end of the lot (farthest from the hotel), near the start of the trail.

From the east end of the parking lot, the trail heads gently downhill, parallel to the road. After about 1.6 km it crosses Moraine Lake Road, then descends into the forest. After a short distance it curves to the left to reach the Upper Lake Louise access road. You must take off your skis and cross the road. (Be careful!) The trail crosses Louise Creek, then descends to the Bow River, directly across from the Lake Louise Railway Station and Restaurant. From here the trail is complex and convoluted but it can be skied almost all the way. Cross the Bow River on a footbridge, then turn right and follow a trail along the river. After about 500 m the trail crosses a road to the left, then continues to the right (east), parallel to the railway tracks. Finally the route goes underneath the tracks at the railway bridge over the Pipestone River. You are now on the doorstep of the Post Hotel, and Samson Mall is just a few hundred metres to the east.

85. PEYTO TRAIL
Nordic Skiing, ATR 1

National Park Trail #5
Grade Intermediate
Distance 2.2 km one way
Time 30 minutes downhill;
    1 hour uphill

Elevation gain (loss) 45 m
Max elevation 1760 m
Map Lake Louise 82 N/8

This is an enjoyable little trail that starts at Deer Lodge and connects with the Great Divide trail and the Lower Telemark trail.

Access: The Peyto Trail starts at a small parking lot located directly behind Deer Lodge. Alternatively you can park across the Upper Lake Louise access road in the main parking lot.

To begin with, the trail rolls up and down through the woods, passing behind the Brewster barbecue building. After another short rolling stretch it briefly joins the Upper Telemark trail coming in from the left. Beyond here the Peyto trail descends gently, bypassing a steep descent to the right. The last part of the Peyto is a moderate descent to join the Great Divide trail.

86. UPPER TELEMARK TRAIL
Nordic Skiing, ATR 1

National Park Trail #7
Grade Intermediate/advanced
Distance 1.4 km one way
Time 30 minutes downhill;
   1 hour uphill

Elevation gain (loss) 65 m
Max elevation 1780 m
Map Lake Louise 82 N/8

The Upper Telemark trail is a little more difficult than the Peyto. There are sections rated green, blue and even black (the latter can be avoided, however).

Facilities: There are toilets and heated washrooms at the west end of the parking lot, nearest the Chateau.

Access: A large parking lot is located on the left, just before you reach the Chateau. Park at the west end of the lot (nearest to the hotel).

From the parking lot, walk around to the front of the Chateau, then continue along the trail to a point just beyond the hotel where the trail to Lake Agnes begins. Walk a short distance up the Lake Agnes trail to find the start of the Upper Telemark trail, which winds its way behind the Chateau. The trail soon begins to descend and makes its way down the hillside to join the Great Divide trail. There are several variations you can take, depending on the level of difficulty you are looking for. On the way back up you can avoid climbing the steep section by taking a green alternative out to the right to briefly join up with the Peyto trail.

87. LOWER TELEMARK TRAIL
Nordic Skiing, ATR 1

National Park Trail #8
Grade Easy
Distance 4.4 km one way
Time 1 hour one way

Elevation gain (loss) 110 m
Max elevation 1670 m
Map Lake Louise 82 N/8

This is a delightful trail that rolls up and down through woods and meadow.

Access: To reach this route, ski along the Great Divide trail for several kilometres or descend either the Peyto or the Telemark trail to reach the Great Divide trail.

From the Great Divide trail there are four short connectors which take you onto the Lower Telemark trail, which runs through the woods parallel to the Great Divide trail. It is possible to ski one way along Lower Telemark, then for variation return along Great Divide.

88. GREAT DIVIDE TRAIL
Nordic Skiing, ATR 1

National Park Trail #6
Grade Easy
Distance 15 km to Great Divide
   return

Time 4 hours
Elevation gain (loss) 30 m
Max elevation 1670 m
Map Lake Louise 82 N/8

This trail is actually a snow-covered paved road. It is flat and usually trackset and is an excellent place for novice skiers to practise or for expert skiers to train. The snow comes early here and the road requires only 20–30 cm to be skiable.

Facilities: There are toilets at the parking lot. At the Great Divide there are toilets, picnic tables and camp shelters.

Hazards: Commercial dogsled operators also use this trail, but the teams are controlled and well organized. They run in a separate track from the skiers.

Options: It is possible to carry on beyond the Great Divide for another 3 km to the start of the Lake O'Hara fire road (see page 261). You can leave a car here and ski just one way (11 km) or, for the really hard-core, you can ski the whole round trip (22 km). The Lower Telemark trail runs parallel to the Great Divide trail and offers a variation for your return.

Access: Follow the road that climbs from the Lake Louise townsite

Setting off along the Great Divide trail. Photo Chic Scott

up the hill toward the Chateau. After several kilometres the road makes a sharp turn to the left to begin the final climb to the Chateau. At this point proceed straight ahead and park in the plowed lot on the right.

Put on your skis and head down the road straight in front of you. You can ski as far as you like. The road is almost all flat except for a short hill just before reaching the Great Divide.

89. BOW RIVER LOOP
Nordic Skiing, ATR 1

National Park Trail #9
Grade Easy
Distance 7 km loop
Time 2 hours

Elevation gain Nil
Max elevation 1550 m
Map Lake Louise 82 N/8

This trail follows the bank of the Bow River and the views are excellent. The drawback of this trail is that it crosses several roads and this requires removing your skis. Because the trail is so near to town, there may have been a lot of pedestrian traffic, causing damage to the ski track.

Facilities: Shops, restaurants and public toilets can be found nearby at Samson Mall.

Hazards: Be careful crossing roads – take your skis off!

Options: The Tramline trail and the Bow River loop make a good combination. The Campground Loop trail (#10) makes a short, pleasant variation.

Access: Parking is available at Samson Mall, the Post Hotel and the Lake Louise Railway Station restaurant. The trail is accessible from any of these locations. The route is described starting from the Railway Station restaurant.

From the restaurant parking lot, cross the Bow River on the footbridge. Turn left and continue east along the river. After a short distance the trail drops down to the left and continues along close to the river. Soon you reach the Upper Lake Louise access road, where you must take off your skis and cross the road.

Continue through the trees for about 1 km to reach the edge of the campground. Here you cross the Campground Loop trail (#10). Continue ahead on the Bow River Loop trail (#9) through the campground. About halfway through the campground you can turn left and cross a large bridge over the Bow. You can also continue ahead on trail #9 to the far end of the campground, where you cross the west end of Campground Loop (#10).

Continue straight ahead for about 1 km on a pleasant trail beside the river to reach another footbridge, which crosses to the north side of the Bow. The route now continues west along the north bank of the river to reach the Upper Lake Louise access road. Take off your skis and cross the road.

From here it is easiest to cross the bridge to rejoin Bow River Loop (#9) on the opposite bank, then return to your car the way you came along the south bank.

It is also possible to continue straight ahead, but the way becomes complex. To begin, the ski trail continues for a short distance to reach the Railway Station road. You can take off your skis here and walk west along the road for several hundred metres (crossing a bridge over Pipestone Creek), then put your skis on again, ski down left into the forest and follow this trail back to your car. It is also possible to cross the road and work your way along a trail that crosses under the railway tracks to reach the Post Hotel or Samson Mall (see the description for Tramline Trail at page 207).

90. MORAINE LAKE ROAD
Nordic Skiing, ATR 1
to the viewpoint

National Park Trail #1
Grade Easy
Distance 16 km to viewpoint and return
Time An hour or two or all day if you like

Elevation gain 250 m to the viewpoint
Max elevation 1880 m
Map Lake Louise 82 N/8

This tour follows a paved road that is not plowed in the winter. Consequently it requires little snow to be in condition and is one of the first trails to be skiable each season. Because the route contours around the shoulder of Mount Temple, high above the valley, the views down the Bow Valley, and later into Consolation Valley and the Valley of the Ten Peaks, are excellent.

Hazards: Be sure to leave enough time and energy for the return trip.

Options: This tour links up with more advanced ones such as the traverse of Wenkchemna and Opabin passes to Lake O'Hara.

Access: A large parking lot is located on the left about halfway up the Upper Lake Louise access road from the Lake Louise townsite, at the turnoff for Moraine Lake Road.

From the end of the parking lot, ski around the road closure gate, then simply head up the road. The trail is trackset and on a weekend will be

Skiing along Moraine Lake Road. Photo Chic Scott

busy. After about 2.5 km the trail crosses Paradise Creek, then climbs for another kilometre. The way now levels out as far as the viewpoint overlooking Consolation Valley. This is a good place to stop for lunch and is as far as most people go. To continue another 3 km to Moraine Lake involves exposing yourself to avalanche risk from high on Mount Temple.

OTHER TRAILS IN THE LAKE LOUISE AREA

91. PARADISE VALLEY
Ski Touring, ATR 2

Grade Intermediate
Distance 20 km return from
   Moraine Lake Road trailhead
Time Full day for most parties

Elevation gain 410 m to meadow
   at head of valley
Max elevation 2090 m at
   meadow
Map Lake Louise 82 N/8

This is a popular tour offering interesting skiing and some of the most impressive scenery in the Canadian Rockies.

The north face of Mount Temple towers above the ski trail in Paradise Valley. Photo Chic Scott

Hazards: Do not linger in the slide paths that descend from mounts Haddo and Aberdeen.

Access: There is a large parking lot on the left side of the road about halfway up the hill between the Lake Louise townsite and the Chateau. The tour begins along Moraine Lake Road.

From the parking lot, ski around the road closure barrier and head up the snow-covered road. After about 2 km, angle right and climb up a hill through the woods. After a short distance another route (Fairview Trail) branches off to the right and curves back to the northwest. Do not follow this. Instead, carry on ahead and climb a steep bank to gain the crest of a forested ridge. Continue climbing through the trees for about 500 m until the trail intersects with the main summer trail between Lake Louise and Moraine Lake.

Turn to the right toward Lake Louise and ascend for a short distance to another trail junction. Now turn left into Paradise Valley. The trail climbs for a short distance, then makes a long descent to the valley, breaking out of the trees at Paradise Creek. This is a good spot to rest and admire the impressive north face of Mount Temple towering 1500 m above.

The trail now crosses the creek on a bridge and continues over rolling terrain along the south bank. After 500 m the route again crosses the creek to the north side and continues working its way up the valley through mature forest. After several kilometres the track makes its way left to the creek.

The trail now works its way up a steep hillside, in the space between the two arms of the creek, eventually following along the north bank of the south arm to a large meadow. There are good views of the great face of Mount Hungabee at the end of the valley, and high above to the south can be seen a solitary spire called Grand Sentinel.

92. PLAIN OF SIX GLACIERS
Ski Touring, ATR 3

Grade Intermediate
Distance 10 km return
Time 4–6 hours

Elevation gain 200 m
Max elevation 1900 m
Map Lake Louise 82 N/8

This is an outstanding tour that takes you into the heart of one of the most impressive mountain settings in North America. The skiing is not difficult and the route is not long. The last half of the tour follows a creekbed, so wait until after Christmas when there should be adequate snow.

Facilities: Toilets and heated washrooms are available at the west end of the parking lot nearest Chateau Lake Louise. A hot drink in the Chateau at the end of the day is a real treat.

Hazards: Beyond the end of the lake you should not follow the summer trail that is located high on the northwest side of the valley, as it is exposed to avalanches. The valley bottom is also crossed by several large avalanche paths and care should be taken in choosing rest stops so that you are not on one of these paths. This tour is not recommended when the avalanche hazard is high.

Mounts Lefroy and Victoria tower above skiers approaching the Plain of Six Glaciers. Photo Kathy Madill

Access: A large parking lot is located on the left, just before you reach the Chateau. Park at the west end of the lot (nearest to the hotel).

From the parking lot walk around to the front of the Chateau. Follow a ski trail that starts from the ice castle and skating rink in front of the hotel and crosses the lake, staying near to the right (northwest) shore. Be certain the lake is well frozen before you head out on it.

The trackset trail only goes as far as the end of the lake, below the prominent Louise Falls, which can be seen high up on the right. Beyond the end of the lake the trail passes beneath large cliffs on the right. Follow the creekbed for about 2 km, climbing gently, negotiating humps and slopes. Eventually you reach a large, open area surrounded by impressive mountains. It is best to stop here, eat your lunch and enjoy the view. Travel beyond this point will soon take you into terrain that requires glacier travel experience and equipment. Skiing back down the creekbed is fun, but the plod across the lake at the end of the day can be a little tedious.

93. PIPESTONE TRAILS
Nordic Skiing, ATR 1

National Park Trails 20, 21, 22, 23

Grade Mainly easy; one intermediate trail

Distance 21 km of trails

Time From a few hours to all day if you like

Elevation gain 120 m between low point and high point of entire system

Max elevation 1670 m

Map Lake Louise 82 N/8

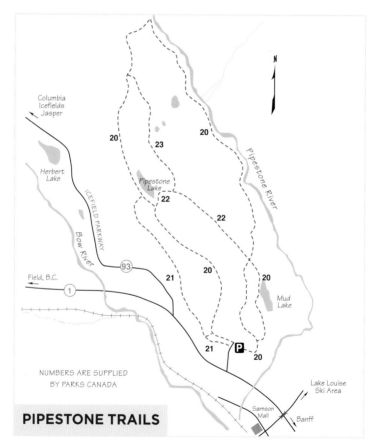

NUMBERS ARE SUPPLIED
BY PARKS CANADA

PIPESTONE TRAILS

BAKER CREEK MOUNTAIN RESORT

Baker Creek Mountain Resort is an excellent location for your cross-country ski holiday. Trackset trails can be accessed from the resort and the marvellous trail network at Lake Louise is just a few minutes away.

Location On the southwest side of the Bow Valley Parkway, 11 km east of Lake Louise.

Map Lake Louise 82 N/8

Accommodation Luxury accommodation in a wilderness setting with all the comforts of home. Suites in the main lodge or individual log chalets are available.

Dining Fine dining available in the Baker Creek Bistro

Cost $200–300/person/night

Contact Baker Creek Mountain Resort
Box 66, Lake Louise, AB TOL 1E0
403-522-3761
bakerinfo@bakercreek.com
www.bakercreek.com

Baker Creek Mountain Resort. Photo Kathy Madill

The Pipestone trails offer excellent skiing for beginner and expert alike. It is a great place to get a few hours of fresh air if you have limited time. The routes are all easy with the exception of #20, which has some steep hills and is graded intermediate. These trails are regularly trackset.

Hazards: It is easy to get turned around when you are skiing these trails, so keep a close check on your progress at each intersection.

Access: Turn north off the Trans-Canada Highway 700 m west of the Lake Louise overpass and follow the signs. The road climbs uphill for several hundred metres and then turns to the right, into a parking lot.

The Pipestone network comprises four numbered trails: #20 (Pipestone Loop) is 13.3 km; #21 (Hector), 3 km; #22 (Drummond), 2.7 km; and #23 (Merlin), 2.3 km. The trails run through a mix of forest and meadow. The open area around Pipestone Pond along the west arm of route #20 is an excellent spot for a sunny lunch break. The trails are laid out so that you will be climbing uphill almost continuously when skiing north (away from the parking lot) and then getting a thrilling downhill run on the way back. The view of the Lake Louise peaks across Mud Lake on trail #22 is excellent.

94. BAKER CREEK
Ski Touring, ATR 1

Grade Intermediate
Distance 12 km to meadow and return
Time 4–5 hours

Elevation gain 210 m
Max elevation 1700 m
Map Lake Louise 82 N/8

Facilities: There are toilets at the parking lot

Hazards: This trail is no longer maintained by Parks Canada and there may be deadfall across it.

Access: Park across the Bow Valley Parkway from Baker Creek Mountain Resort, about 14 km west of Castle Junction. The parking lot is located on the northeast side of the bridge.

Looking towards Mount Temple from the Pipestone trails. Photo Chic Scott

From the far left end of the parking lot, ski about 75 m along the creek and cross a bridge to the north side. From here ski back to the left, under the hill and away from the creek, for about 100 m. Then turn right, into a draw, and start climbing. The route rises steeply for a short distance, angling up to the left, then makes a long switchback to the right and crosses under power lines. It continues to climb at a moderate angle for several kilometres through a mature forest of lodgepole pines. Keep your eye open for viewpoints on the right, high on the hillside above Baker Creek. Eventually the trail flattens out for several more kilometres as far as a beautiful meadow under the slopes of Lipalian Mountain.

95. BAKER CREEK POWER LINE
Nordic Skiing, ATR 1

Grade Easy
Distance 7 km return
Time 2 hours

Elevation gain Nil
Max elevation 1480 m
Map Lake Louise 82 N/8

This tour offers a good view of the peaks surrounding the Bow Valley. It is an easy ski and may be trackset.

Facilities: There are toilets at the parking lot.

Access: Park across the Bow Valley Parkway from Baker Creek Mountain Resort, about 14 km west of Castle Junction. The parking lot is on the northeast side of the bridge.

From the far right-hand corner of the parking lot, head straight back into the woods. The trail may occasionally be marked with a sign as "#2." After about 100 m the route reaches a clearing, turns right and for the next few kilometres follows power lines. Eventually the power lines run up a steep hillside to the left, while the trail turns to the right into the trees. Ski through the trees to reach a campground, where you can do a circuit on the roads and then return to your car the way you came.

96. TAYLOR LAKE
Ski Touring, ATR 1

Grade Advanced
Distance 12.5 km return
Time 5-6 hours return

Elevation gain 600 m
Max elevation 2070 m
Map Lake Louise 82 N/8

Steep and tricky, this is hardly a cross-country ski trail at all, yet many people still ski it. It is to be avoided when conditions are icy.

Options: It is possible to traverse southeast to reach O'Brien Lake. Powder turns can be found to the north of Taylor Lake on a spur that comes out from Panorama Ridge.

Access: A parking lot is located on the southwest side of the Trans-Canada Highway, 8 km west of Castle Junction.

Near Taylor Lake.
Photo Gabriel Altebaeumer

The first 2 km of this trail are reasonable as they work their way up the hill through the trees. The route then steepens and is a continuous climb to the lake. Be careful on your way back down, as the trail is narrow and the corners are tight.

"... a man is rich in proportion to the number of things which he can afford to let alone."

—*Henry David Thoreau*, Walden

"*The air was still, the sun incredible, the cornices and ice towers were balanced on a slender spire of rock.... A soft mist rose to the east of the crest. I turned for a moment and was completely lost in silent appraisal of the beautifully sensuous simplicity of windblown snow.*"

—*Allen Steck*

SKOKI

97. **Hidden Lake** Easy/Intermediate, p. 230

98. **Wolverine Valley** Intermediate, p. 231

99. **Skoki via Boulder and Deception Passes**
Intermediate, p. 232

100. **Skoki Mountain Loop** Intermediate, p. 234

101. **Natural Bridge** Easy, p. 238

102. **Oyster Lake** Easy/Intermediate, p. 238

103. **Fossil Mountain Loop** Intermediate, p. 239

104. **Merlin Valley** Advanced, p. 240

105. **Packer's Pass** Intermediate, p. 241

106. **Skoki to Lake Louise via Pipestone River**
Intermediate, p. 242

Getting some turns at Skoki, p. 244

The Skoki region is one of the most popular destinations in the Rockies for cross-country skiing. There is good snow, the scenery is spectacular and there are plenty of trails. In the heart of it all is historic Skoki Lodge, a delightful place to relax for a few days and enjoy the Canadian backcountry ski experience.

Access: From the overpass along the Trans-Canada Highway, near the Lake Louise townsite, drive toward the Lake Louise Ski Resort. If you are a Skoki Lodge guest you should check in with guest services at the resort and they will give you a pass so that you can take the ski lifts over the shoulder of Whitehorn Mountain to Temple Lodge, where the trail to Skoki Lodge begins.

If you are not staying at Skoki Lodge, turn right after 1.6 km onto the Temple Lodge access road and continue for 1 km to the Fish Creek parking lot. From here you can ski 3 km up the ski-out to Temple Lodge. From Temple Lodge it is possible to ski to Skoki, enjoy a cup of tea and some delicious baked goods and return to your car before dark, but

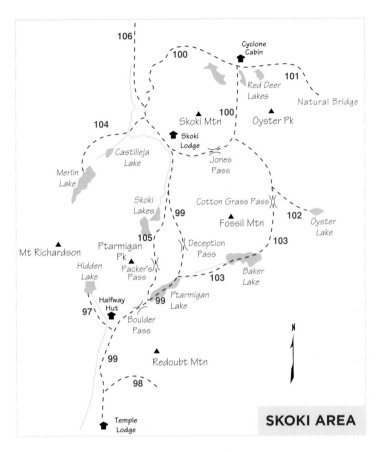

SKOKI AREA

you must be fit. It is a better idea to stay overnight at the lodge and savour its old-time ambience.

A little history

Skoki was one of the earliest ski lodges in the Canadian Rockies. Built by Earl Spencer in the autumn of 1930 for a group led by Cliff White and Cyril Paris, it welcomed its first guests the following winter. The lodge was enlarged to its present size in 1936. During its glory days of the 1930s the world came to Skoki to experience the magic of winter in the Rockies. Folks would ski all the way from the Lake Louise

225

Niall Rankin's black and white photo from 1932 captures the magic of skiing at Skoki. Photo WMCR Niall Rankin V683-Ic2B-pa139-824

railway station (near the townsite) to Skoki, sometimes overnighting at Halfway Hut. Temple Lodge was built in 1938 and the two lodges formed the core that would eventually grow into the Lake Louise Ski Resort.

There is a magical world of ski history associated with Skoki Lodge. Two of the earliest guests were Lady Jean Rankin (lady in waiting to the Queen) and her husband Niall, who stayed for a month in 1932. The first European ski guides in the region, Vic Kutschera and Herman Gadner, worked here alongside local guides like Cliff White, Peter Whyte, Cyril Paris, Ken Jones and Sam Evans. Some of the first avalanche fatalities in the region occurred near Skoki: Raymond "Kit" Paley was killed on Fossil Mountain in 1933 and Herman Gadner on Mount Richardson in 1945. Their ghosts are said to play cards at night in Halfway Hut.

SKOKI LODGE

This beautiful log lodge has been in continuous operation since 1931.

Location Beneath the west flank of Skoki Mountain, along the right bank of Skoki Creek (564100 E 5708400 N)

Maps Lake Louise 82 N/8, Hector Lake 82 N/9

Facilities There is a central lodge surrounded by several guest cabins. Not much has changed at Skoki since the 1930s, and this is a great place to step back in time and experience our romantic past. Dinner is still served by candlelight. Outdoor toilets.

Capacity 22

Hosts Leo and Katie Mitzel

Cost $160/person/night (two-night minimum)

Reservations Skoki Lodge,
Box 5, Lake Louise, AB T0L 1E0
1-888-997-5654 or 403-522-3555; fax 403-522-2095
info@skoki.com
www.skoki.com

Note The two-night minimum is for reservations well in advance. If you book within two weeks of your visit, it may be possible to book only one night if there is space available.

Skoki Lodge in 2012. Photo Chic Scott

The cozy interior of Skoki Lodge. Photo Chic Scott

Katie Mitzel prepares delicious meals at Skoki Lodge. Photo Chic Scott

The original Skoki Lodge in 1931. WMCR Lloyd Harmon V108 331A

Today Skoki Lodge is just as beautiful and romantic as ever. And it still attracts royalty: Prince William and his wife Kate stayed there in 2011. For more Skoki stories, read Kathryn Manry's *Skoki: Beyond the Passes* (Rocky Mountain Books, 2001).

97. HIDDEN LAKE
Ski Touring, ATR 2

Grade Easy/intermediate
Distance 8 km return (from Temple Lodge)
Time 4–6 km return (from Temple Lodge)

Elevation gain 250 m to Hidden Lake
Max elevation 2270 m
Map Lake Louise 82 N/8

The tour to Hidden Lake is a delightful trip in beautiful surroundings. It passes historic Ptarmigan Hut, also known as Halfway Hut. Once in Hidden Bowl there is an opportunity to make some turns on the slopes of Richardson Ridge above the lake. The view down the valley to the Lake Louise peaks is outstanding.

Facilities: Toilets and restaurants can be found at Temple Lodge.

Access: Take the Lake Louise exit from the Trans-Canada Highway and head up the hill toward the Lake Louise Ski Resort. After 1.5 km turn right and drive 1 km to the Fish Creek parking lot. From here you can ski 3 km up the ski-out to Temple Lodge. This trail crosses the road beside the Fish Creek parking lot. Be careful of skiers descending the ski-out and stay to the side of the trail. The trail is steep, so wear skins or have a good grip wax.

The trail to Hidden Lake starts about 100 m above Temple Lodge, along the northeast edge of the ski run. It heads northeast, through the trees along the east flank of the valley, and is usually well packed by the many guests on their way to Skoki Lodge. After about 2 km the trail breaks out into the open and Halfway Hut can be seen about 100 m off to the left, on the other side of Corral Creek.

From Halfway Hut ski northwest, directly up Hidden Creek. After about 500 m the terrain begins to open up and Hidden Lake is another 500 m. Moderate-angled slopes can be found off to the left on Richardson Ridge, where you can make a few turns.

The return trip is a fun downhill run and you can make it all the way back to your car at Fish Creek with only the occasional uphill section.

98. WOLVERINE VALLEY
Ski Touring, ATR 2

Grade Intermediate
Distance 6 km return from
   Temple Lodge
Time 4–6 hours

Elevation gain 500 m
Max elevation 2500 m
Map Lake Louise 82 N/8

This tour is an excellent way to get away from the noise of the ski resort and into some beautiful alpine scenery. This has been a popular tour since 1938, when Temple Lodge was first built. It was originally referred to as Purple Bowl, but most folks now call it Wolverine Valley.

Facilities: Toilets and restaurants are available at Temple Lodge.

Hazards: The slopes above the southwest side of the valley on

Wolverine Ridge are attractive and offer good skiing but there is serious avalanche potential. Use caution.

Access: The trail begins near Temple Lodge. See the Hidden Lake tour on page 222 for details on how to reach the lodge.

The route begins along the northeast edge of the ski run, about 100 m uphill from Temple Lodge. This is actually the trail that goes to Skoki Lodge. Follow the trail for several hundred metres, then angle up to the right on a man-made cut through the trees. The trail angles up and curves to the right, turning southeast in Wolverine Valley. It runs high above a stream and after about 1 km breaks out of the trees into the open. Continue along, gradually gaining elevation towards the high alpine terrain at the end of the valley. It is possible to ski several kilometres to reach a high pass (564000 E 5698700 N) from where you can look down into Baker Creek far below. This is a glorious spot on a sunny day and there are gentle slopes up here to make turns on.

99. SKOKI VIA BOULDER AND DECEPTION PASSES
Ski Touring, ATR 1

Grade Intermediate
Distance 11 km one way from Temple Lodge
Time 4–5 hours one way

Elevation gain 540 m
Max elevation 2510 m
Maps Lake Louise 82 N/8, Hector Lake 82 N/9

The tour to Skoki is a classic that locals repeat over and over as the years pass by. The scenery is outstanding, the trail is interesting but not too difficult, and Skoki Lodge is a marvellous place, rich in history. You can get a hot drink here before skiing back to your car. Better still, why not stay several nights and discover the roots of our skiing heritage.

Facilities: There are toilets and restaurants at Temple Lodge. Halfway Hut is located several kilometres up the trail from Temple Lodge but is a bare-bones structure with no stove. It can provide shelter on a windy day but is not intended for overnight use.

Hazards: This tour takes you through avalanche country. Although there is little danger if you stay on the correct trail, you must be careful not to stray onto surrounding terrain, which may not be safe. This tour is real backcountry skiing and you should be prepared to deal with emergencies. Crossing Ptarmigan Lake on the return journey can be difficult if the wind is blowing in your face.

Options: There are a number of excellent ski trails in the vicinity of Skoki Lodge. A pleasant alternative on the return trip is to ski through Jones Pass, around Fossil Mountain, through Cottongrass Pass and across Baker Lake to regain the trail at Ptarmigan Lake. If you are really ambitious it is possible to descend Skoki Creek to Little Pipestone Creek and then down to the Pipestone River, which can be followed back to Lake Louise (see page 242).

Access: Take the Lake Louise exit from the Trans-Canada Highway and proceed up the road towards the Lake Louise Ski Resort. After 1.6 km turn right, onto the Temple Lodge access road. Follow this road for 1 km to the Fish Creek parking lot, which is on the right.

Ski up the ski-out to Temple Lodge. This trail passes close by the Fish Creek parking lot, just a few metres uphill. The terrain is steep here, so use skins or have a good grip wax. After 3 km you reach Temple Lodge, where the trail to Skoki can be found on the far (northeast) side of a ski run, about 100 m uphill from Temple Lodge.

The Skoki trail heads into the woods, rolling up and down. After a short distance there may be a branch heading down to the left. Do not take this but continue straight ahead, crossing some open areas for about 2 km, gradually gaining elevation. The trail is normally well packed and easy to follow. Eventually the route breaks out of the woods into a large, open meadow with a beautiful view all around. Over on the left, on a small hill above the creek, you will see Halfway Hut.

Continue up the valley, staying generally to the left side, and at the end climb a moderately steep hill to Boulder Pass. Here you will come out into the open and into the wind. Descend a short distance and ski across Ptarmigan Lake, following stakes in the snow, to the base of Deception Pass.

Halfway Hut, along the trail to Skoki, is said to be the home of several ghosts. Photo Chic Scott

The climb to the pass gains about 180 vertical metres and becomes steep near the top. Use skins if you have them or put on extra grip wax.

From Deception Pass it is a fun run down to Skoki Lodge. From the pass the trail (well marked with stakes) continues north over open terrain across the slopes of Fossil Mountain, then angles left down into the trees. The track through the trees to the lodge is packed down by snowmobiles and is usually easy to follow. The lodge is located on the right bank of Skoki Creek, beneath the slopes of Skoki Mountain.

100. SKOKI MOUNTAIN LOOP
Ski Touring, ATR 2

Grade Intermediate
Distance 9 km loop
Time 4–5 hours

Elevation gain 80 m
Max elevation 2200 m
Map Hector Lake 82 N/9

This is an interesting trail that can be started after a leisurely breakfast

Leo Grillmair on the trail to Skoki Lodge, with the Valley of the Ten Peaks and Mount Temple in the background. Photo Chic Scott

Hans Gmoser climbs towards Deception Pass on the return journey from Skoki Lodge to Lake Louise. Photo Chic Scott

and will bring you back to the lodge in time for afternoon tea. The route can be skied in either direction, the prime consideration being the steep hill rounding the northwest side of Skoki Mountain. It is challenging and it is a personal choice whether you want to struggle up it or struggle down it. Many people take off their skis and walk.

Facilities: The Cyclone warden cabin can be visited on this trip but it will be locked.

Options: This trail can be combined with a trip to the Natural Bridge (see page 238).

Access: The trail begins and ends at Skoki Lodge.

From the lodge ski south, up the valley, toward Deception Pass. Within a few hundred metres the route leaves the main trail and angles to the left, climbing through the trees to Jones Pass. Descend the other side, staying to the left and being sure not to linger on the large avalanche paths. Continue down the draw for about 1 km, then through the forest to reach the large, open meadow at Red Deer Lakes. The Cyclone warden cabin is across the far side of the meadow, up against the forest (566600 E 5710700 N). This is a good place to relax and enjoy a cup of tea and a sandwich.

To complete the Skoki Mountain Loop, ski west for several kilometres across the meadows from the Cyclone warden cabin. The trail eventually enters the forest on the south side of the valley. This spot can be hard to locate but often there is a piece of flagging hanging from a tree.

From here the trail makes its way through trees and glades on the north side of Skoki Mountain, eventually descending very steeply to reach the main trail in the Skoki Creek Valley. This descent can be tricky, particularly if the snow is crusty or icy and many people take off their skis and walk. The last part of the tour ascends the trail up the Skoki Creek Valley to the lodge and is usually well packed.

Lunch break on the porch of the Cyclone warden cabin. Photo Chic Scott

Hans Gmoser skis across the meadows near
Red Deer Lakes. Photo Chic Scott

101. NATURAL BRIDGE
Ski Touring, ATR 1

Grade Easy
Distance 16 km return
Time 5–6 hours
Elevation gain 80 m

Max elevation 2200 m
Maps Hector Lake 82 N/9, Barrier
Mountain 82 O/12

This route is an extension of the trail around Skoki Mountain and makes for a full-day tour. The destination is a rock bridge at the end of a small valley behind Oyster Peak.

Facilities: The Cyclone warden station can be visited on this trip but it will be locked.

Hazards: A map and some proficiency in using it will be very helpful on this tour. In the vicinity of Red Deer Lakes, where several valleys meet, it can be difficult to decide which one to follow.

Access: The trail begins and ends at Skoki Lodge.

Follow the Skoki Mountain Loop as far as the Cyclone warden cabin. From here continue east down the Red Deer River for several kilometres, then work your way to the right, through the woods and over to the drainage behind Oyster Mountain. An alternative is to follow the summer trail from the Cyclone cabin along the hillside on the left-hand side of the valley to a trail junction. Turn right on a branch trail that goes up a small valley to the Natural Bridge. This trail can be hard to follow at first, but toward the end just follow a creekbed to the Natural Bridge. To return to Skoki Lodge, ski back to the Cyclone cabin, then continue either direction along the Skoki Mountain Loop.

102. OYSTER LAKE
Ski Touring, ATR 3

Grade Easy/intermediate
Distance 12 km return
Time 4–5 hours

Elevation gain 150 m
Max elevation 2290 m
Map Hector Lake 82 N/9

This is a very pleasant tour which leads you through open terrain to a scenic destination. There is even a fun ski run back down the creekbed from the lake to Cottongrass Pass.

Hazards: There is avalanche potential on this tour and you should be prepared for emergencies. When you round the corner of Fossil Mountain, do not try to take the high line. Instead, take the low trail through the trees, as it is much safer.

Options: This tour can be combined with the Fossil Mountain Loop.

Access: The trail begins and ends at Skoki Lodge.

From the lodge ski south, up the valley toward Deception Pass. Within a few hundred metres the route leaves the main trail and angles to the left, climbing through trees to Jones Pass. Descend the other side, staying to the left, and do not linger on the large avalanche paths. Ski down the draw, keeping your eye out for flagging and a sign marking a trail to the right. This trail works its way up and to the right, through trees and out into the open again. Ski across the meadow to Cottongrass Pass below the drainage coming down from Oyster Lake. From here you can either ski up the drainage or ascend the sparsely treed shoulder on the right. Near the top, climb the drainage, up an open slope to the right, then cut sharply to the left and ski over a little notch to the lake.

103. FOSSIL MOUNTAIN LOOP
Ski Touring, ATR 2

Grade Intermediate
Distance 11 km loop
Time 5–6 hours
Elevation gain 300 m

Max elevation 2470 m
Maps Lake Louise 82 N/8, Hector Lake 82 N/9

This is one of the most challenging tours from Skoki Lodge and will take most of a day to complete. Some experience with route finding and map reading will be an asset. There will probably also be some trail-breaking across the open areas because the track will drift over in the wind. This tour can be skied in either direction.

Hazards: There is some avalanche potential on this tour and you should be prepared for emergencies.

Options: This tour can be combined with a trip to Oyster Lake. It can also be used as an alternative return route from Skoki to Temple Lodge.

Access: The trail begins and ends at Skoki Lodge.

Follow the Oyster Lake tour (see page 238) as far as Cottongrass Pass. From here work your way around to the right through open trees to reach Baker Lake at its northeast corner. Ski across the lake, then climb the headwall at the west end to the flats above, being sure to stay away from the steep slopes on the right. Ascend the slopes above to Deception Pass (565200 E 5705500 N).

From the pass, the trail (well marked with stakes) continues north across the slopes of Fossil Mountain, following open terrain, then angles left down into the trees. The track through the trees to the lodge is packed down by snowmobiles and is usually easy to follow.

104. MERLIN VALLEY
Ski Touring, ATR 1

Grade Advanced
Distance 6 km return
Time 3–4 hours

Elevation gain 210 m
Max elevation 2230 m
Map Hector Lake 82 N/9

This is a challenging trail which takes you into a beautiful high valley. You can find excellent terrain for making turns in the upper Merlin Valley. The climb from the meadows to Lake Merlin is steep and difficult and requires some route finding.

Hazards: This trail is demanding and only experienced skiers will be able to handle the descent back down from Lake Merlin. If you plan on skiing the slopes above Lake Merlin, be aware that you are in potential avalanche terrain and should be properly equipped and prepared to deal with emergencies.

Access: The trail begins and ends at Skoki Lodge.

Ski down the trail north of Skoki Lodge to the large meadows. Turn left and cross the meadows in a southwest direction for several hundred metres, then climb up on the right bank at a very large and tall tree. Continue across an avalanche path and work your way into the trees. After several hundred metres the trail begins to climb to the right up an open area with sparse trees. The angle is very steep but eventually eases and the trail cuts left into the trees, where it continues to climb but at a more moderate rate. There are numerous blazes along here, which makes the trail relatively easy to follow. It climbs up to the base of some cliffs, then traverses left across very steep terrain (in the trees) just below them. After a few hundred metres the terrain flattens out. If you are only going to the lake, you can reach it easily now by a short descent down to the left. If your destination is Merlin Ridge, continue climbing and angling up to the right.

An alternative ascent route crosses the meadows to the farthest southwest end, then climbs an open slope on the right (this is a rock slide in the summer). From the top, traverse left to Castilleja Lake. Climb the treed slope above the lake, working your way up by traversing back and forth through the trees. Traverse left (southwest) to Lake Merlin when you are high enough.

The real problem with both these routes is the steep descent back to the valley afterward. Neither one is easy.

105. PACKER'S PASS
Ski Touring, ATR 3

Grade Intermediate
Distance 11 km from Skoki to
   Temple Lodge
Time 3–4 hours

Elevation gain 300 m
Max elevation 2470 m
Maps Lake Louise 82 N/8,
   Hector Lake 82 N/9

This tour offers a slightly more direct route from Skoki Lodge back to Temple Lodge. It takes the pass between Packer's Peak and Ptarmigan Peak (564300 E 5705000 N). It is a more difficult tour than via Deception Pass and is subject to more avalanche risk.

Facilities: There are toilets and restaurants at Temple Lodge. Halfway Hut is located several kilometres up the trail from Temple Lodge but is a bare-bones structure with no stove. It can provide shelter on a windy day but is not intended for overnight use.

Hazards: This tour is subject to significant avalanche hazard and should be undertaken only by experienced backcountry skiers.

Access: The route begins at Skoki Lodge.

From the lodge, ski south, up the trail toward Deception Pass. In less than a kilometre turn right, up the creek that drains Skoki Lakes. Direct access to the lakes is blocked by cliffs, so one must climb the small drainage to the left below Packer's Peak, then cut back to the right above the cliffs. Rather than descend along the bench down to Skoki Lakes, angle up and over the shoulder of Packer's Peak, then make a rising traverse high on the west slope of Packer's Peak up to Packer's Pass. Descend easily down the other side along a ramp to the southwest, to reach Ptarmigan Lake. Here you rejoin the regular trail from Skoki to Temple Lodge.

106. SKOKI TO LAKE LOUISE VIA PIPESTONE RIVER
Ski Touring, ATR 1

Grade Intermediate
Distance 24 km one way
Time Full day
Elevation loss 600 m

Max elevation 2160 m at Skoki Lodge
Maps Lake Louise 82 N/8, Hector Lake 82 N/9

This tour offers an alternative way to ski from Skoki Lodge to Lake Louise, but it is a long way and trail-breaking will most likely be required. It is a full-day tour for most of us and in deep snow it might be even more than that. Still, the Pipestone Valley is wide and beautiful and the peace and solitude are wonderful.

Hazards: If the snow is deep and you expect you will be breaking trail, give yourself plenty of time.

Access: The tour begins at Skoki Lodge and ends at the parking lot for the Pipestone trails (page 218), where you should have a second car waiting.

From Skoki Lodge follow the trail heading north, down Skoki Creek. After about 1 km, at the meadows, ski through the campground and carry on straight ahead (do not take the trail that climbs up to the right over to Red Deer Lakes). Carry on down Skoki Creek on a good trail, staying on the right bank a short distance above the creek. The route descends steeply for another kilometre and then flattens out. Continue along the valley bottom through the trees on the right side of the creek. After one more kilometre the valley begins to open up as you reach Little Pipestone Creek, and it is best here to simply follow the creekbed.

Cross some large, open meadows with huge avalanche paths above on the right and then climb up onto the right bank of the creek, where you will find a very clear and well-defined trail through the trees. Follow

Faye Atkinson studies the map in Pipestone Valley. Photo Chic Scott

this track easily for about 2 km until it starts to descend. The trail drops steeply for a short distance, then levels out and you leave the trees and enter an open meadow.

From here the route is tricky to follow, although there are a large number of blazes on the trees. Doing your best to follow the blazes, head west through the trees to the junction with the Pipestone River. You could also head for Little Pipestone Creek and follow it down to the junction with the Pipestone River. Along this section of the tour it might be advisable to pull your compass out and follow it.

From the junction of Little Pipestone Creek and the Pipestone River, head down the river across beautiful open meadows for about 5 km. Eventually the trees close in and the meadow narrows but it is still best to follow the river for another 7 km. About 6 km before reaching the highway, look for the Pipestone trails up on the right bank of the Pipestone River – they can be easy to miss. Ski down the Pipestone trails back to your waiting car at the parking lot.

GETTING SOME TURNS AT SKOKI
Ski Touring, ATR 2

There are several areas at Skoki where you can get a few turns. Be careful, though, as these areas pose some avalanche risk.

Packer's Pass: The northwest flank of Packer's Peak, above Zigadenus Lake, offers excellent skiing on a slope of about 300 vertical metres. See the tour to Packer's Pass at page 241.

Merlin Ridge: The slopes above Lake Merlin offer excellent opportunities for making turns on moderate terrain. The descent is about 360 vertical metres from top to bottom. This area can be tricky to reach due to the steep climb from the valley to the lake. See the tour to Merlin Valley on page 240.

Wolverine Slopes: These slopes are found low down on the west flank of Fossil Mountain, just above the trail from Skoki Lodge to Deception Pass. They are short but offer some entertaining skiing.

Skoki Valley: Good terrain for making turns can be found in several locations near the lodge:

Cliffy White, the grandson of ski pioneer Cliff White, carves telemark turns near Packer's Pass. Photo Brad White

- Just above the lodge on the slopes of Skoki Mountain there are opportunities for tree skiing. Years ago, runs were actually cleared and groomed here.
- There is some open-glade skiing across from Skoki Lodge, in the trees at the base of The Wall of Jericho.

A little history

Cliff White, a great ski pioneer of the Canadian Rockies, was one of the first to see the ski potential of this region. He was a founding member of the Banff Ski Club in 1917, and in 1928 he was one of the leading organizers in building the first ski cabin on Mount Norquay. In 1930, with Cyril Paris and others, he established Skoki Lodge. For many years during the late 1930s and 1940s he managed Temple Lodge and introduced many skiers to our Canadian mountains. Cliff's son, Clifford J. White, said of him, "He was ahead of his time, a primary force in bringing skiing as a successful business to the Canadian Rockies." As historian Ted Hart put it: "There were lots of people in the 1930s who enjoyed skiing, but he actually made it his life's work." All of us today benefit from Cliff's pioneering vision.

A little history

Skoki Lodge has been the home of many colourful characters over the years. Sir Norman Watson, a British baronet, became the major shareholder in the Ski Club of the Canadian Rockies and had dreams of turning the Skoki and Temple areas into a little Austria, complete with cows in the meadows.

Peter and Catharine Whyte ran Skoki Lodge during the winters of 1932 and '33. Two of the finest artists in the Canadian Rockies, the pair created the Whyte Museum of the Canadian Rockies in Banff. For her exceptional generosity and leadership, Catharine Whyte received the Order of Canada in 1978.

One of the most wonderful individuals to have been associated with Skoki Lodge was Lizzie Rummel, who ran the lodge from 1943 to 1949. Her personality, generosity and love of the mountains was eventually rewarded with the Order of Canada in 1980.

Cliff White was a ski pioneer who saw the future potential of skiing in the Rocky Mountains. Photo WMCR V683-Ic2b-pa139-112

Ken Jones near Skoki. Photo Chic Scott

Ken Jones first came to Skoki Lodge in 1936 to work on the addition and the second storey on the building. It was Ken who brought the 60-foot ridge pole to Skoki from Red Deer Lakes. For many years during the 1930s, '40s and '50s he worked as a packer and guide at Skoki Lodge. Ken loved to tell stories, and for decades he entertained guests at Skoki with his tales of pioneer days in the Canadian Rockies.

YOHO NATIONAL PARK

107. **Sherbrooke Lake** Intermediate/Advanced, p. 258

108. **Ross Lake Circuit** Intermediate, p. 258

109. **Lake O'Hara Road** Easy, p. 259

110. **Lake O'Hara Circuit** Easy, p. 262

111. **McArthur Pass** Intermediate, p. 263

112. **Morning Glory Lakes** Intermediate, p. 264

113. **Opabin Plateau** Intermediate/Advanced, p. 265

114. **Opabin/Wenkchemna Circuit** Advanced, p. 266

115. **Yoho Valley Road** Easy, p. 269

116. **Little Yoho Valley** Intermediate/Advanced, p. 271

117. **Kiwetinok Pass** Easy, p. 273

118. **Field to Emerald Lake** Intermediate, p. 274

119. **Emerald Lake Trails** Easy, p. 276

120. **Kicking Horse Trail** Easy, p. 277

121. **Amiskwi Fire Road to Amiskwi Pass** Easy, p. 280

122. **Ottertail Valley Fire Road** Easy, p. 281

123. **Ice River Fire Road** Easy, p. 282

124. **Wapta Falls** Intermediate, p. 282

Yoho National Park offers some of the finest cross-country skiing in the Rocky Mountains and sees lots of activity. There are two Alpine Club of Canada (ACC) huts, a backcountry lodge and a frontcountry lodge in the park, all of which provide a wonderful overnight experience. The park gets lots of snow and offers spectacular scenery. It also has a long tradition of ski activity. In fact the ACC ran its first ski camp at Lake O'Hara in 1936, and held one in the Little Yoho Valley almost every year during the 1940s. These two areas are now amongst the most popular in the Rockies.

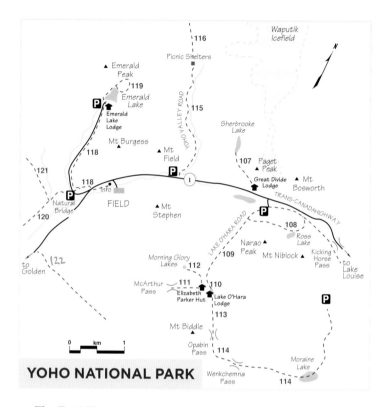

YOHO NATIONAL PARK

The Field/Emerald Lake region has a number of fine ski trails too, trackset by the Kicking Horse Ski Club (www.KHSC.ca).

Access: The Trans-Canada Highway (Highway 1) traverses Yoho Park as it makes its way from Lake Louise to Golden. The road is kept in good driving condition during the winter, as it is the main highway across Canada. The only town in the park is Field, located along the Trans-Canada Highway, 26 km west of Lake Louise.

Facilities: There is a service station along the highway at the turnoff to Field, and the town offers a large number of guest houses, a small hotel, liquor store, post office, grocery store and two restaurants. Emerald Lake Lodge features luxurious accommodation, with ski trails starting right from the front door. It is reached via a road which exits the Trans-Canada 3 km west of town. Ten km east of Field is the Great Divide Lodge/Wapta Lodge, with a gas station, hotel, restaurant and lounge.

Information: Due to budget cuts, the Parks Canada Information Centre located along the Trans-Canada Highway at the entrance to Field is closed in the winter. However, the Friends of Yoho National Park are attempting to keep the facility open several hours each day on weekends. Toilets at the Information Centre are open year round.

LAKE O'HARA LODGE

This luxurious lodge was built by the Canadian Pacific Railway in the winter of 1925/26 and offers a truly comfortable winter experience.

Location On the west shore of Lake O'Hara
(546200 E 5689700 N)

Maps Lake Louise 82 N/8;
GeoBC Yukness Mountain 082N039

Elevation 2010 m

Facilities During the winter, only the central lodge is open, offering guest rooms, lounge, dining room, indoor plumbing and central heating

Capacity 16 in winter

Hosts Bruce and Alison Millar

Season Mid-June to September and mid-January to mid-April

Cost About $350/person/night (two-night minimum); includes all meals and guiding service

Reservations Lake O'Hara Lodge,
Box 55, Lake Louise, AB T0L 1E0
250-343-6418 (summer and winter as specified above)
403-678-4110 (off-season)
www.lakeohara.com

Guide Bernard Faure on the porch of Lake O'Hara Lodge. Photo Chic Scott

Dinner time at Lake O'Hara Lodge. Photo Chic Scott

ELIZABETH PARKER HUT

This beautiful, historic log building is surrounded by some of the most spectacular peaks in the world.

Location In a meadow about 500 m west of Lake O'Hara (545600 E 5689500 N)

Elevation 2040 m

Maps Lake Louise 82 N/8;
GeoBC Yukness Mountain 082N039

Facilities Fully equipped with foamies, cooking and eating utensils, propane cookstoves and lanterns and a wood heating stove

Capacity 20 in winter

Water During the winter, flowing water can be found in the creek about 100 m east of the hut

Reservations The Alpine Club of Canada, 403-678-3200

Note This hut is locked when no custodian is present; a combination number is required.

Arriving back at Elizabeth Parker Hut after a day of skiing. Photo Chic Scott

EMERALD LAKE LODGE

Emerald Lake Lodge is a frontcountry lodge and you can drive right to the door. Ski trails begin directly in front of the lodge. This is a perfect destination for those new to the sport of cross-country skiing.

Location On the shores of Emerald Lake, about 6 km northwest of the town of Field, BC. From Field drive west on the Trans-Canada for 3 km, then turn north and follow the paved access road for another 8 km to the lodge.

Elevation 1300 m

Map Golden 82 N/7

Facilities Emerald Lake Lodge is fully equipped with indoor plumbing, hot and cold running water, deluxe dining etc.

Reservations Emerald Lake Lodge
Box 10, Field, BC V0A 1G0
403-410-7417
1-800-663-6336 (toll free Canada and usa)
info@crmr.com
www.crmr.com/emerald

Emerald Lake Lodge. Photo Orange Girl Photography

Lake O'Hara is world famous for its summer hiking trails. It is also a great destination for cross-country skiing and ski touring. The region is so beautiful that many people simply come here to look and enjoy the grandeur of the mountains. Lake O'Hara Lodge is a luxurious place to spend a few nights in the backcountry, and for those on a more limited budget Elizabeth Parker Hut is very popular in winter.

The Little Yoho Valley also offers great backcountry skiing. In fact this valley has been the scene of ACC ski camps for seven decades. Much of the skiing is in high alpine terrain but there are also some Nordic tours lower down. The presence of Stanley Mitchell Hut makes this the perfect destination for a ski adventure. It is always a treat at the end of a hard tour to return to a hut and warm yourself around the fire.

STANLEY MITCHELL HUT

This delightful log hut sits on the edge of a meadow in a high alpine valley. Out the front window is a spectacular view of the President Range.

Location At the edge of the trees, about 100 m back from the right bank of the creek, near the head of the Little Yoho Valley (530200 E 5708400 N)

Elevation 2050 m

Maps Blaeberry River 82 N/10;
GeoBC Trolltinder Mountain 082N058
Summits and Icefields Map

Facilities Fully equipped with foamies, cooking and eating utensils, propane cookstoves and lanterns and a wood heating stove.

Capacity 22 in winter

Water From the creek directly south of the hut (you must dig down in the snow to reach the creek)

Reservations The Alpine Club of Canada, 403-678-3200

Note This hut is locked when no custodian is present; a combination number is required.

Stanley Mitchell Hut, a winter paradise. Photo Tomasz Gehrke

107. SHERBROOKE LAKE
Ski Touring, ATR 1

Grade Intermediate/advanced
Distance 6 km return
Time 3 hours return
Elevation gain 180 m

Max elevation 1800 m
Maps Lake Louise 82 N/8;
GeoBC Sherbrooke Lake
082N049

This is a steep and challenging trail, and if it is icy or rutted it can be even more difficult. Sherbrooke Lake is a beautiful destination, though, and the trail is popular.

Facilities: Great Divide Lodge/Wapta Lodge is located next to the trailhead and features toilets, telephones and a restaurant.

Hazards: The trail is marked incorrectly on older topographical maps.

Access: Park at the Great Divide Lodge/Wapta Lodge, which is located on the north side of the Trans-Canada Highway near the summit of Kicking Horse Pass, 12 km east of Field or 15 km west of Lake Louise.

The trail begins just a few metres west of the hotel and climbs up and left through the trees. Most of the tour ascends at a moderately steep angle. After about 1 km the trail levels out and you come to a junction sign. Continue straight ahead. After 2 km the trail rounds the shoulder of Paget Peak, breaks out of the trees and continues easily through the open area along the creek to the lake.

108. ROSS LAKE CIRCUIT
Ski touring, ATR 1

Grade Intermediate
Distance 9 km loop
Time 3 hours
Elevation gain 200 m

Max elevation 1830 m
Maps Lake Louise 82 N/8;
GeoBC Sherbrooke Lake
082N049

This is an interesting tour that takes you into an impressive mountain cirque. There are very nice views over Kicking Horse Pass from this tour, but the experience can be marred somewhat by the noise of the Canadian Pacific Railway and the Trans-Canada Highway.

Facilities: There are toilets at the Lake O'Hara fire road parking lot.

Access: Turn south off the Trans-Canada Highway near the summit of Kicking Horse Pass, about 12 km west of Lake Louise. Drive a short distance, cross the railway tracks, turn right and then drive down the hill for several hundred metres to the parking lot for the Lake O'Hara fire road.

Mike Galbraith on the Ross Lake trail. Photo Chic Scott

Walk back up the entrance road for a short distance, turn right, put on your skis and head along the snow-covered Highway 1A. After about 2 km you will see a trail sign on the right for Ross Lake. Turn right and climb gradually up a trail through the forest for about 1.5 km to reach Ross Lake, surrounded by great mountain walls. At the lake turn right (west) along another trail and continue for about 3 km to reach the Lake O'Hara fire road. Turn right again and ski down the fire road back to your car in the parking lot.

If you ski this trail clockwise as described here, there are several steep hills descending to the Lake O'Hara fire road. If you ski the route anticlockwise, you must climb these steep little hills, but later you get a very pleasant downhill run to the lake and then another good descent from the lake to Highway 1A. Either way, you must gain about 200 vertical metres in elevation.

Skiing up the Lake O'Hara fire road. Photo Chic Scott

109. LAKE O'HARA ROAD
Ski Touring, ATR 1

Grade Easy

Distance About 11 km one way

Time 3–4 hours to Lake O'Hara; only 2–3 hours back to parking

Elevation gain 430 m

Max elevation 2030 m

Maps Lake Louise 82 N/8; GeoBC Yukness Mountain 082N039, Sherbrooke Lake 082N049

This is a very popular tour and many folks stay overnight at Lake O'Hara Lodge or Elizabeth Parker Hut. The trail requires little snow to be skiable, as it follows a road. And the snow comes early in the season here, so this is one of the first trails to be in shape. Often this tour can be skied by mid-November. The route is very easy to follow and usually the trail is well packed.

Facilities: There are toilets at the parking lot.

Options: At Lake O'Hara there are several pleasant tours you can do. Occasionally, fit and adventurous skiers continue over Opabin Pass and Wenkchemna Pass to Lake Louise, or over Opabin and then down Tokumm Creek to the Kootenay Highway, or over McArthur Pass and out the Ottertail fire road. You must be a strong and experienced skier for these tours.

Access: Turn south off the Trans-Canada Highway near the summit of Kicking Horse Pass, about 12 km west of Lake Louise. Drive a short distance, cross the railway tracks, turn right and drive down the hill for several hundred metres to the parking lot for the Lake O'Hara fire road.

The route to Lake O'Hara follows the snow-covered summer road, which leaves the parking lot from its southeast corner. To begin, the road climbs at a steady angle for about 2 km. Then, for the next 5 km, the road is level and you are surrounded by wonderful scenery. Before crossing the creek the route begins to climb again and gains elevation until just before the lake.

The first buildings you see as you reach the lake are the warden's cabin on the left and the summer kiosk called Le Relais on the right.

Richard Guy skiing to Lake O'Hara at age 91. Photo Chic Scott

Louise Guy skiing to Lake O'Hara at age 89. Photo Chic Scott

Walk quietly in any direction and taste the freedom of the mountaineer. Camp out among the grass and gentians of glacier meadows, in craggy garden nooks full of Nature's darlings. Climb the mountains and get their good tidings. Nature's peace will flow into you as sunshine flows into trees. The winds will blow their own freshness into you, and the storms their energy, while cares will drop off like autumn leaves. As age comes on, one source of enjoyment after another is closed, but Nature's sources never fail. Like a generous host, she offers here brimming cups in endless variety, served in a grand hall, the sky its ceiling, the mountains its walls, decorated with glorious paintings and enlivened with bands of music ever playing.

— *John Muir*, Our National Parks *(1901)*

Lake O'Hara Lodge is just a few hundred metres beyond, on the shore of the lake.

To reach Elizabeth Parker Hut you must follow a trail which turns off to the right at Le Relais. At first the trail climbs steeply through the forest. Then it crosses a crest and descends a short distance to the left, where it breaks out of the trees at the edge of the creek. Turn sharply to the right and ski along the edge of the creek for several hundred metres to a large meadow where you will see Elizabeth Parker Hut in front of you.

The return trip to the parking lot can be quick and lots of fun, particularly if the trail is well packed and there are good tracks.

110. LAKE O'HARA CIRCUIT
Ski Touring, ATR 1

Grade Easy
Distance 2 km loop
Time 1 or 2 hours
Elevation gain Nil

Max elevation 2030 m
Maps Lake Louise 82 N/8;
GeoBC Yukness Mountain
082N039

Access: This trail begins and ends at Lake O'Hara Lodge. From the lodge, ski along the shoreline trail on the south side of the lake. As the trail rounds the east end of the lake, beneath cliffs, it goes out onto the lake and returns to the lodge by crossing the lake. Do not attempt to follow the shoreline trail on the north side, as it is up on a small cliff above the lake. Also, keep your distance from the north shore while you cross, for there are big avalanche slopes above. Be sure the lake is well frozen, and be careful of getting your feet wet, as the water can percolate up through the ice and snow.

111. McARTHUR PASS
Ski Touring, ATR 2

Grade Intermediate
Distance 4 km return from
    Elizabeth Parker Hut
Time 3–4 hours
Elevation gain 150 m

Max elevation 2210 m
Maps Lake Louise 82 N/8;
    GeoBC Yukness Mountain
    082N039

This is a delightful tour that gets you up high where you have superb views of Mount Victoria across the valley. There is a pleasant run back down the draw to the hut.

Options: There is opportunity to make some turns on the slopes of Odaray Mountain above the pass.

Hazards: People often ski on the open slopes above Schaffer Lake. While this area does offer good ski potential, it is very dangerous and has been the scene of several fatal avalanches in the past.

Tami Knight leads her friends across Schaffer Lake. Photo Chic Scott

Access: This trail begins and ends at Elizabeth Parker Hut. From the back door of the hut, ski straight ahead, just to the right of the trees. After about 150 m you will find an open draw which leads up the hill. Ski up this draw, gaining about 150 metres in elevation, to reach the meadow beside Schaffer Lake. If it is early season it may be best to follow the summer trail through the trees above the draw on the left.

To reach McArthur Pass, cross the meadow, aiming for the lowest point in the pass. Follow the drainage towards the pass for several hundred metres until the way is barred by a cliff band. Make several short switchbacks through the trees on the left of the drainage to get above the cliff, then follow open terrain to the pass.

Good ski terrain can be found to the north on the lower slopes of Odaray Mountain . This is a great spot to sit in the sun and eat your lunch.

112. MORNING GLORY LAKES
Ski Touring, ATR 1

Grade Intermediate
Distance 7 km return
Time Easy day
Elevation loss 40 m

Max elevation 2050 m
Maps Lake Louise 82 N/8;
GeoBC Yukness Mountain
082N039

This is an enjoyable ski tour that takes you into a deep cirque beneath the impressive northeast face of Odaray Mountain. There is a long climb back up at the end of the day.

Hazards: Do not attempt this trail when conditions are icy or crusty.

Access: This trail begins and ends at Elizabeth Parker Hut. Ski north from the hut across the meadows and then continue up a sparsely treed draw for a short distance to reach a crest. Just before the ground begins to drop away to the north, turn left and locate a trail through the woods. This trail runs level for about 500 m, then descends moderately steeply for about 1 km to Morning Glory Lakes. Note that you will need skins or a good grip wax to climb back up the hill again.

113. OPABIN PLATEAU
Ski Touring, ATR 2

Grade Intermediate/advanced
Distance 7 km return
Time Full day
Elevation gain 300 m

Max elevation 2320 m
Maps Lake Louise 82 N/8;
GeoBC Yukness Mountain
082N039

This is a delightful tour that takes you to a high alpine plateau with superb views of some of the great peaks of the Rockies.

Options: You can carve a few turns at the toe of Opabin Glacier. It is also possible to continue over the Opabin/Wenkchemna Circuit or the Opabin/Tokumm Creek trail

Hazards: Coming down from Opabin Plateau to Lake O'Hara can be tricky if the snow is icy or crusty.

Access: This tour begins and ends at Lake O'Hara Lodge.

Skiing across Opabin Plateau towards Opabin Pass.
Mounts Hungabee and Biddle tower above. Photo Chic Scott

From the lodge, ski along the shoreline trail on the south side of the lake to find the east Opabin trail, which climbs steeply through the trees just east of the creek to reach Opabin Plateau. This is a steep grade and climbing skins are recommended. Once you reach the plateau, follow the creek draw out onto the plateau. It is possible to wander at will out here and find some nice hills on which to make a few turns.

To return to Lake O'Hara, follow your trail down the draw to the top of the steep hillside above the lake and then follow the creekbed down. Partway down, an open scree slope to the left of the creekbed offers a good opportunity for some turns. Use caution on this descent, as there is some avalanche hazard.

114. OPABIN/WENKCHEMNA CIRCUIT Ski Touring, ATR 3

Grade Advanced

Distance 24 km one way (Lake O'Hara to Lake Louise)

Time Some parties do this tour in one long, hard day. You could overnight at Elizabeth Parker Hut, but this would mean carrying a sleeping bag.

Elevation gain 430 m from parking to Lake O'Hara; 570 m from Lake O'Hara to Opabin Pass; 340 m from Eagle Eyrie to Wenkchemna Pass

Elevation loss 330 m from Opabin Pass to Eagle Eyrie; 730 m from Wenkchemna Pass to Moraine Lake

Max elevation 2600 m at both Opabin Pass and Wenkchemna Pass

Maps Lake Louise 82 N/8; GeoBC Yukness Mountain 082N039

This is one of the best tours of its type in the Canadian Rockies. It is long and challenging and takes you through superb high mountain terrain. It is a serious trip and there is some very real avalanche terrain to negotiate. Use caution!

Options: It is possible to cross Wastach Pass to reach Paradise Valley, then exit down the Paradise Valley trail. This makes for a longer and harder day.

It is also possible to continue down Tokumm Creek (Prospector's

Valley) to reach the Kootenay Highway 93 at Marble Canyon (see page 176).

Facilities: There are camp shelters with wood stoves at the Moraine Lake campground.

Hazards: The slopes below all three passes – Opabin, Wenkchemna and Wastach – have significant avalanche risk. Take all safety precautions. This trip is not recommended unless the avalanche hazard is low. There are small glaciers on both sides of Opabin Pass and there are some crevasses. It is advisable to carry a rope just in case.

Access: Begin this tour by skiing up the Lake O'Hara fire road (see page 261).

From Lake O'Hara Lodge follow the Opabin Plateau trail (see page 266). Cross Opabin Plateau heading southeast toward Opabin Pass (548600 E 5686600 N). The terrain is open, and when visibility is good the way is not hard to find. The route ascends a small glacier with some large crevasses, so use caution and put on a rope. The final climb to the pass is steep and may require some step kicking.

The descent from Opabin Pass is steep for a short distance, then becomes a very pleasant ski run for about 300 vertical metres down to Eagle Eyrie. The climb from here up to Wenkchemna Pass is a risky slope. The angle is moderately steep and the ground surface under the snow is smooth scree. Use caution! The last part of the climb to the pass is often windblown and bare and you may be climbing over loose rocks.

The descent from Wenkchemna Pass to Moraine Lake is pleasant and follows an easy line over moraine and open meadow. Stay well south of Eiffel Lake and marvel at the walls of the Ten Peaks high above. Ski along the margin of forest and moraine until you reach the drainage which flows down to Moraine Lake. Descend this drainage and then ski across the lake to reach Moraine Lake Lodge on the opposite side. Continue to Lake Louise along Moraine Lake Road (see page 213).

115. YOHO VALLEY ROAD
Ski Touring, ATR 3

Grade Easy
Distance 26 km return if you go all the way to Takakkaw Falls
Time Full day if to Takakkaw Falls
Elevation gain 150 m

Max elevation 1480 m
Maps Lake Louise 82 N/8; GeoBC Wapta Mountain 082N048; Summits and Icefields Map

This is a straightforward and easy ski up a snow-covered road. You can ski just a few kilometres or all the way to Takakkaw Falls, where you will get a great view of the frozen waterfall in its winter splendour. You might even see some ice climbers on it.

Facilities: There are toilets at the parking lot. There is a campground at Takakkaw Falls which has toilets and an enclosed camp shelter.

Hazards: The avalanche paths off Wapta Mountain reach the road and should be crossed quickly. This trail should be avoided in periods of high avalanche hazard.

Options: It is possible to ski beyond Takakkaw Falls to Stanley Mitchell Hut in the Little Yoho Valley.

Access: The large parking lot at the trailhead is reached by taking the turnoff for the Yoho Valley, 4 km east of Field. If you are coming from Lake Louise, turn right just after you descend the big hill from Kicking Horse Pass and after crossing the bridge over the Kicking Horse River.

This ski tour follows a road which begins at the east end of the parking lot and is simple to follow. After a short distance there is a turnoff to the left to the campground, but continue straight ahead up the hill. After about 1 km the road crosses a bridge and continues climbing. After about 5 km the route ascends several switchbacks, then levels out again. Just beyond the switchbacks the road is threatened by giant avalanche paths high on Wapta Mountain. In fact the road is often piled high with avalanche debris. Proceed as quickly as possible across this area without stopping.

When the road reaches Takakkaw Falls you can continue straight

Descending the Yoho Valley road. Photo Chic Scott

ahead for several hundred metres along a trail to reach the campground, where there is a camp shelter and toilets, and a pile of firewood buried somewhere under the snow.

116. LITTLE YOHO VALLEY Ski Touring, ATR 3

Grade Intermediate/advanced

Distance 10 km one way from Takakkaw Falls to Stanley Mitchell Hut (Note that the trip from the highway to the hut and back to your car is about 46 km!)

Time From the highway the ACC hut can be reached in one very long day, depending on conditions and the strength of the party. Some, however, will find that two days are necessary. The return journey, from the hut back to the highway, can be done by most skiers in one day.

Elevation gain 150 m from the highway to Takakkaw Falls; 575 m from Takakkaw Falls to Stanley Mitchell Hut.

Max elevation 2060 m

Maps Lake Louise 82 N/8, Hector Lake 82 N/9, Blaeberry River 82 N/10 GeoBC Wapta Mountain 082N048, Trolltinder Mountain 082N058, Summits and Icefields Map

The tour to the Little Yoho Valley and an overnight stay at beautiful Stanley Mitchell Hut is one of the great ski experiences of the Canadian Rockies. The cabin is the postcard image of what a mountain hut should look like, and the area abounds in great skiing. However, it is a very long and arduous ski tour, particularly if you have a heavy pack.

Facilities: There are toilets at the parking lot. There is a camp shelter at Takakkaw Falls that is completely enclosed and can be used by parties who cannot make it to Stanley Mitchell Hut in one day. There are toilets nearby and a pile of firewood buried under the snow. Usually there is an axe in the shelter.

Hazards: Cross the Wapta slide paths quickly and without stopping. Allow plenty of time for this tour and if necessary spend a night at the Takakkaw Falls shelter. It is better to spend a moderately comfortable night here rather than push on late in the day and find yourself in the dark frantically trying to find the hut. It has happened many times before.

On your return trip, ski carefully on the steep descents of Laughing Falls Hill and Hollingsworth Hill, particularly if conditions are icy or crusty.

Access: The large parking lot at the trailhead is reached by taking the turnoff for the Yoho Valley, 4 km east of Field. If you are coming from Lake Louise, turn right just after you descend the big hill from Kicking Horse Pass and after crossing the bridge over the Kicking Horse River.

Folks begin this trail by skiing up Yoho Valley Road (see page 269) to the campground.

The trail to the Little Yoho Valley and Stanley Mitchell Hut leaves from the far (north) end of the campground, crosses a large open area that in summer is a stream outwash, then enters the woods on the opposite side. The route is easy to see at first, as it follows a wide, straight cut through the forest. After several kilometres it climbs a long, uniform slope (Hollingsworth Hill), then continues through the woods beyond, eventually descending to the Yoho River, which it follows to the Little Yoho River, crossing it near Laughing Falls. The trail can be hard to follow in this area if it has snowed recently.

After 4.5 km (from the campground) the trail turns left just after crossing the Little Yoho River and begins to climb out of the Yoho Valley to reach the Little Yoho Valley. The turnoff is sometimes hard to find, particularly if the trail signs are buried deep under the snow. Nowadays there is enough traffic in this area that the trail should be easier to follow. The route now switchbacks through mature forest up the west wall of the valley and can again be hard to follow at times.

After gaining about 240 vertical metres, the incline begins to ease and the trail angles out left towards the Little Yoho River. It continues along the north bank, above the river, into the valley. After a while the steep hillside the trail is traversing levels off and the route meanders through forest and open glades to the hut. Stay on the north bank throughout. Following the trail can be tricky, as it crosses meadows and re-enters the forest on the opposite side at points that are hard to find. The hut is located on the edge of a meadow, on the north side of the Little Yoho River (530200 E 5708400 N) about 5 km from the Laughing Falls turnoff

The return journey to the highway can be an exciting challenge for less experienced skiers. This is particularly true in the springtime, when the trail can be icy. The descent of the steep hillside above Laughing Falls is not a laughing matter if you are unsure on your skis. Be careful and take your time. The same is true for Hollingsworth Hill, which is steep and long. For your return journey be sure to get going early in the morning and allow plenty of time to reach the highway in one day.

117. KIWETINOK PASS
Ski Touring, ATR 2

Grade Easy
Distance 7 km return
Time 3-4 hours
Elevation gain 400 m
Max elevation 2450 m

Maps Blaeberry River 82 N/10;
GeoBC Trolltinder Mountain
082N058; Summits and
Icefields Map

This is a superb tour in beautiful mountain surroundings and is highly recommended.

Access: The route begins and ends at Stanley Mitchell Hut.

From the hut ski across the creek and follow it upstream for about 150 m. Turn left and follow a shallow draw in the trees for about 100 m up into a small bowl. Climb up and to the right, out of the bowl and over a crest to reach a large open area that is the drainage of the President Glacier. Cross this in a southwest direction to reach a draw along the left margin of the trees. Continue ascending, staying on the left edge of the trees in open terrain. Near the edge of treeline there is a moderately steep slope to climb. Remain on the left side of the creekbed and ascend the slope at its lowest and least steep point. High on the left

Ken Jones leads Alan Brunelle and Louise Guy back to Stanley Mitchell Hut after a tour to Kiwetinok Pass. Photo Chic Scott

are prominent cliffs. Above the steep hill, traverse out to the right and into the creekbed, then continue climbing over open terrain to reach Kiwetinok Lake and, a short distance beyond, Kiwetinok Pass. You can ski through the pass to the brow of a hill overlooking the Amiskwi Valley and sit here in the sun while you eat your lunch.

118. FIELD TO EMERALD LAKE
Nordic Skiing, ATR 1

Grade Intermediate
Distance 10 km one way
Time 3–4 hours one way
Elevation gain 200 m
Max elevation 1300 m

Maps Golden 82 N/7; GeoBC Wapta Mountain 082N048, Mount Duchesnay 082N038

This is an excellent trail with a stunning view of Mount Stephen along the way. It is regularly trackset.

Facilities: There are toilets and telephones at the Yoho Park Visitor Information Centre in Field and at Emerald Lake Lodge.

Options: This trail can be skied one way if you leave a second car at the end, or it can be skied return if you have only one car.

Access: Park at the Yoho Park Visitor Information Centre on the south side of the Trans-Canada Highway, near the entrance to the town of Field. If you are only skiing one way, leave your second car at Emerald Lake.

From the Information Centre ski west along the flats between the highway and the river. After 1 km cross the highway to the right. Take your skis off and use caution! On the other side a wide trail climbs at a moderate angle through the trees for about 1 km, then levels off and rounds the shoulder of the mountain to the right. Descend gradually for about 500 m to a trail junction.

If you take the left-hand branch you descend steadily for about 1 km to the Emerald Lake access road at the parking lot for the Natural Bridge. If you take the right-hand branch it is about 8 km to Emerald Lake.

Sharon and Al Cole approach Field after skiing
to Emerald Lake. Photo Chic Scott

To begin with, the trail is a wide road, but after about 2 km it narrows and meanders up and down through the woods. There are several steep, narrow hills to deal with. Eventually the route comes out at the parking lot at Emerald Lake.

119. EMERALD LAKE TRAILS
Nordic Skiing, ATR 1

Grade Easy

Distance About 7 km to end of lake and around extension loop

Time 2 hours for complete route

Elevation gain Nil

Max elevation 1300 m

Maps Golden 82 N/7; GeoBC Wapta Mountain 082N048

This is a lovely tour in a beautiful setting. The skiing is easy and the trail is regularly trackset. The valley is oriented southwest and gets sunshine most of the day.

Facilities: There are toilets at the parking lot, and Emerald Lake Lodge is nearby with all the amenities. Emerald Sports and Gifts (250-343-6000) is located beside the bridge, near the start of the trail. Here you can rent skis, get information and enjoy a cup of hot apple cider.

Hazards: You should not linger on the large avalanche path on the northwest side of the lake.

Access: Turn north off the Trans-Canada Highway 3 km west of Field and follow the road to the end, where there is a large parking lot at Emerald Lake.

The trail starts at the north end of the parking lot, passes the toilets, then continues into the woods. In about 100 m the route crosses a large avalanche path (do not linger) and ascends a few metres up left into the trees. Another trail, for snowshoers only, drops down to the right and travels near the lakeshore. (Note that this start to the trail exposes you to avalanche risk and should be avoided if there is any likelihood of avalanche.) Continue through the woods on an interesting, rolling trail to the end of the lake, where the trail comes out of the woods and

David Jones skis at Emerald Lake below Mount Burgess. Photo Chic Scott

descends out to the right onto alluvial flats. From here you can turn left at a junction and ski another 3 km around a loop, which brings you back to the same spot. Return to the parking lot the way you came. The trail along the other side of the lake (the south side) is now designated for snowshoe enthusiasts.

If the avalanche hazard is high you should avoid the avalanche path on the north side of the lake entirely and begin your tour by crossing the lake from Emerald Lake Lodge (beware of wet spots on the lake).

120. KICKING HORSE TRAIL
Nordic Skiing, ATR 1

Grade Easy
Distance 13 km return
Time 4–5 hours return
Elevation gain 60 m
Max elevation 1220 m

Maps Golden 82 N/7;
GeoBC Mount Duchesnay
082N038, Wapta Mountain
082N048

Kathy Madill skis beside the Kicking Horse River. Photo Chic Scott

This is a very nice half-day tour. Most of the trail runs through the forest but there are a few open views along the way. The route is regularly trackset.

Access: Turn north off the Trans-Canada Highway onto the Emerald Lake access road, 3 km west of Field. Continue 1.5 km and park in the Natural Bridge parking lot.

The trail starts from the right (north) side of the parking lot. Ski gently downhill on a wide road for about 2.5 km and cross a small bridge over the Emerald River. In another 100 m cross a larger bridge over the Amiskwi River. Continue another 100 m through a picnic area to a trail junction. Turn left and for about 50 m the trail narrows but then opens up. Ski about 2 km along a road through the forest to a large open area where there is a terrific view of the surrounding peaks. On the left is the Kicking Horse River.

After you've skied another kilometre on a wide road, the trail narrows and continues another kilometre to a trail junction. The branch to the right heads up the Otterhead River (ski touring/trail-breaking). If you turn left you can ski about 500 m to a bridge over the Otterhead River. The trackset trail ends a few hundred metres beyond the bridge.

121. AMISKWI FIRE ROAD TO AMISKWI PASS
Ski Touring, ATR 2

Grade Easy
Distance 76 km return
Time From several hours to several days
Elevation gain 800 m
Max elevation 1960 m
Maps Golden 82 N/7,
Blaeberry River 82 N/10;
GeoBC Mount Duchesnay
082N038, Mount Horsey
082N047, Wapta Mountain
082N048, Mount Keays
082N057

This trail offers a long tour in a wilderness setting. You will likely be all by yourself to enjoy the exercise and fresh air.

Facilities: Amiskwi Lodge (**522700** E **5718900** N) is located near Amiskwi Pass.

Access: Turn north off the Trans-Canada Highway onto the Emerald Lake access road, 3 km west of Field. Continue 1.5 km and park in the Natural Bridge parking lot.

The trail starts from the right (north) side of the parking lot. Ski gently downhill on a wide road for about 2.5 km, then cross a small bridge over the Emerald River. In 100 m cross a larger bridge over the Amiskwi River. Continue another 100 m through a picnic area to a trail junction. Turn right, take a deep breath and start skiing. It is about 35 km to Amiskwi Pass.

122. OTTERTAIL VALLEY FIRE ROAD Ski Touring, ATR 2

Grade Easy

Distance 28 km return to McArthur Creek

Time Full day to McArthur Creek and back, but you can just ski as far as you like before turning back

Elevation gain 300 m

Max elevation 1500 m

Maps Golden 82 N/7, Lake Louise 82 N/8; GeoBC Mount Ennis 082N028, Mount Oke 082N029, Mount Duchesnay 082N038

This is an easy and enjoyable tour that is not often skied. It is a pleasant way to get some fresh air and solitude.

Options: Occasionally skiers will cross McArthur Pass from Lake O'Hara, then descend McArthur Creek to the Ottertail Fire Road, then continue skiing out to the highway. This is a good adventure for those looking for something a little different.

Access: There is a plowed parking area on the southeast side of the Trans-Canada Highway, 8 km west of Field.

This tour follows a fire road, so the trail is wide and the grade is gentle. The road does most of its climbing over the first 3 km and then levels off. Ski as far as you like and turn back when you have had enough. If you have the time and energy to make it all the way to the McArthur Creek warden cabin you will be treated to a spectacular view of the towers of Mount Goodsir to the south.

123. ICE RIVER FIRE ROAD
Ski Touring, ATR 1

Grade Easy
Distance 32 km return if all the way to park boundary at Ice River
Time As long or short as you wish
Elevation gain 150 m

Max elevation 1300 m
Maps Mount Goodsir 82 N/1, McMurdo 82 N/2; GeoBC Aquila Mountain 082N018, Mount Ennis 082N028

This is a long and easy ski along a fire road. It offers an opportunity for a solitary jaunt along a quiet trail.

Access: Park your car at the Hoodoo Creek campground on the southeast side of the Trans-Canada Highway, 22 km west of Field.

From the parking lot, ski along the road for about 500 m. Just before the entrance to the campground, turn right and ski down a side road for about 500 m. The fire road starts here. Ski around the gate and head up the road. Put your mind in neutral, breathe deeply and listen to your skis as they swish through the snow.

124. WAPTA FALLS
Ski Touring, ATR 1

Grade Intermediate
Distance 9 km return
Time 3–4 hours return
Elevation gain 80 m

Max elevation 1120 m
Maps McMurdo 82 N/2; GeoBC Mount Hunter 082N027

This is a pleasant half-day ski tour. Although it is only graded intermediate, the trail is narrow toward the end and requires caution and skill. There is a limited view of the falls from the top of the hill. To see them properly one should really descend the hill, which can be tricky. Walking down is a good idea.

Hazards: Take care at the viewpoint above the falls. It is slippery and the bottom is a long way down. Walk down the hill if you are unstable on your skis.

Access: There is a small parking lot on the south side of the Trans-Canada Highway, 25 km west of Field. The parking lot is about 2 km west of the Leanchoil bridge over the Kicking Horse River – keep a sharp eye out, as it comes into view very quickly.

From the parking lot, ski around the closure barrier and head down the road. The first 1.5 km is along a road and is wide and easy. At the end of this section the trail continues along a cutline for another 1.5 km, following the left side of the slash. Eventually the slash peters out and the trail enters the woods.

For the next kilometre the trail is narrow and climbs at a moderate angle. This takes you to a viewpoint above the Kicking Horse River, overlooking Wapta Falls. Unfortunately, it is not easy to see the falls from here and you must continue along the trail for another 500 m to get a good look. The trail is steep, particularly at the start, and you should walk down if you are unsteady on your skis. The trail initially angles out to the right, then lower down traverses back to the left.

At the bottom of the hill you can ski a few metres along the river to the base of the falls. They are large and impressive from this vantage point.

"Nature is not a place to visit; it is home."

—*Gary Snyder*

THE ICEFIELDS PARKWAY

125. **Mosquito Creek to Molar Meadows**
Intermediate, p. 286

126. **Dolomite Peak Circuit** Advanced, p. 288

127. **Lake Katherine/Lake Helen Circuit** Advanced, p. 290

128. **Crowfoot Pass** Intermediate, p. 291

129. **Bow Hut** Advanced, p. 293

130. **Bow Summit** Easy/Intermediate, p. 296

131. **Glacier Lake** Intermediate, p. 298

132. **Nigel Pass** Intermediate, p. 299

133. **Wilcox Pass** Intermediate/Advanced, p. 301

134. **Sunwapta Falls/Athabasca River**
Intermediate, p. 302

135. **Poboktan Creek** Easy, p. 304

136. **Maligne Pass** Advanced, p. 305

137. **Fryatt Creek** Advanced, p. 308

The Icefields Parkway, between Lake Louise and Jasper, is one of the most scenic drives in the world, and terrific cross-country ski touring can be found along it. In the winter this is a remote stretch of road and there are no service stations for 230 km. The pavement is not salted but it is sanded and often snow covered. It is maintained between 7:30 am and 3:00 pm only. Snow tires (look for the snowflake symbol) are mandatory on the Parkway until April 1. Sometimes the road is closed due to avalanche danger or heavy snowfall, so be sure to check road conditions at Alberta 511 (www.alberta511.ca or dial 511) before setting out. Be certain you are prepared to deal with cold weather and snow – your car

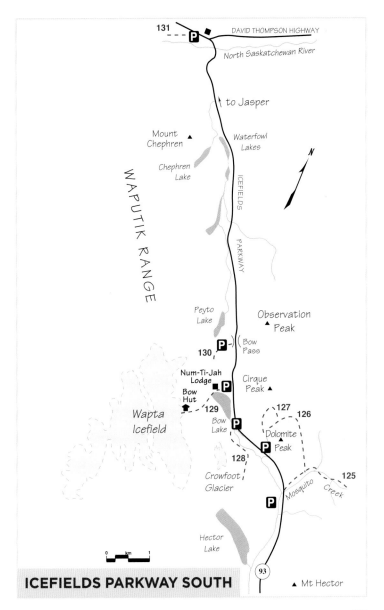

131 DAVID THOMPSON HIGHWAY

North Saskatchewan River

to Jasper

Mount Chephren ▲

Waterfowl Lakes

N

Chephren Lake

ICEFIELDS

WAPUTIK RANGE

PARKWAY

Peyto Lake

Observation Peak ▲

130 Bow Pass

Num-Ti-Jah Lodge

Cirque Peak ▲

Bow Hut

129

Bow Lake

127

126

Wapta Icefield

Dolomite Peak ▲

128

125

Crowfoot Glacier

Mosquito Creek

Hector Lake

93

▲ Mt Hector

ICEFIELDS PARKWAY SOUTH

0 ___ km ___ 1

battery should be strong and you should carry jumper cables, a shovel, extra food and survival gear.

For emergencies there is a warden station near Saskatchewan River Crossing, about 2 km south of the junction of the Icefields Parkway with the David Thompson Highway (Highway 11), where a pay telephone can be found. There is also a pay telephone at the warden station at Poboktan Creek, about 30 km north of the Columbia Icefield. These warden stations are now closed in winter. There are hostels at Mosquito Creek, Rampart Creek, Hilda Creek, Beauty Creek and Athabasca Falls, all of which, except Hilda Creek, have telephones. Num-Ti-Jah Lodge, at Bow Lake, is closed during the winter. Note that there is no cell phone reception along the Icefields Parkway. For further information on the Parkway in winter and an up-to-date list of payphones, ask for the winter Icefields Parkway brochure at Jasper, Banff or Lake Louise visitor centres, or download a copy from the Jasper National Park website, www.parkscanada.gc.ca/Jasper.

Accommodation: You can have a very comfortable and inexpensive night in any of the hostels at Mosquito Creek, Rampart Creek, Hilda Creek, Beauty Creek and Athabasca Falls. All of these are open in winter. Winter camping is allowed at the Wapiti campground, at the Jasper end of the Icefields Parkway, and bivvying is allowed at the Wilcox Pass trailhead.

125. MOSQUITO CREEK TO MOLAR MEADOWS
Ski Touring, ATR 2

Grade Intermediate
Distance 18 km return
Time Full day
Elevation gain 450 m

Max elevation 2270 m at the meadows
Map Hector Lake 82 N/9

This is a very popular tour that gets you up high into alpine meadows. It is an easy trail at first, but towards the end it climbs at a steady angle

Karen Kunelius enjoys a quiet moment along Mosquito Creek. Photo Chic Scott

through the trees up to Molar Meadows. On a sunny day this is a beautiful place to make a few turns.

Options: For strong, well-prepared skiers it is possible to continue beyond Molar Meadows, over North Molar Pass and down to Fish Lakes. You can then descend to the Pipestone River and follow it back to Lake Louise. This tour would take several days and involve winter camping.

Access: Parking is available in the Mosquito Creek Hostel lot on the west side of the Icefields Parkway, 24 km north of the junction with the Trans-Canada Highway. The parking lot is located just before the highway crosses Mosquito Creek.

From the hostel parking lot walk across the road and cross the bridge. Put your skis on and locate the trail, which starts very near to the bridge. At first the trail climbs steeply through the trees, then continues at a more moderate angle. The route then levels off and rambles through the forest, descending to the creek after about 2.5 km.

The trail follows along the valley floor for another 1.5 km, then begins to curve right. Cross two small creeks and continue through the woods for about a kilometre, eventually crossing Mosquito Creek to the right (west) side of the valley. From here the trail climbs steeply, so make sure you have good grip wax or skins. Gain about 150 vertical metres, then drop down left into the creekbed again. Cross the creek and climb steeply for another 120 vertical metres up to Molar Meadows. The trail is hard to follow on this last climb but it is possible to switchback through the trees where necessary.

126. DOLOMITE PEAK CIRCUIT
Ski Touring, ATR 3

Grade Advanced
Distance 19 km loop
Time Full day

Elevation gain 650 m
Max elevation 2500 m
Map Hector Lake 82 N/9

The Dolomite Peak Circuit is one of the finest ski tours in the Canadian Rockies. The first part, up Helen Creek, is straightforward, and the final run down Mosquito Creek is an exhilarating way to end the day. But the middle section of the tour, crossing alpine snowfields high above treeline, can present difficult route finding.

Hazards: Route finding on this tour can be a problem in poor visibility and it could be very easy to get lost in a whiteout. There is significant avalanche potential, so caution is advised. Much of the route is out in the open and above treeline, so warm clothing is required.

Access: Because this tour does not return to the same point on the highway as it departed from, two cars are required. It is customary to begin the tour at the Helen Creek trailhead, just north of the Helen Creek Bridge, 29 km north on the Icefields Parkway. Leave a second car at the Mosquito Creek hostel parking lot, along the highway about 5 km south of this point.

The trail climbs steeply above the Helen Creek trailhead for about 100 vertical metres, to the crest of a ridge. The angle eases here and the route

The Dolomite Traverse takes you high above treeline and is a perennial favourite. Photo Tim Johnson

continues northwest, along the crest of the ridge, for a short distance, then descends to the right to the creek. Cross the creek on a bridge and continue along the opposite bank. The trail along here crosses large avalanche paths with thick forests in between. After about 1.5 km it starts to climb, then crosses the creek again and works its way up through the trees to an elevation of about 2150 m, where the trees begin to thin out.

From here there is no clearly defined trail and you work your way up and right over steep rolls, then over a rocky shoulder to gain a broad pass at about 2400 m. Be careful of avalanche hazard here. A gentle descent now takes you to Lake Katherine.

Cross the lake and continue through Dolomite Pass. A huge boulder on the right makes a good windbreak for a lunch stop. From the pass descend about 70 vertical metres down the drainage to the northeast until it is possible to begin turning right (southeast) towards an unnamed pass (544100 E 5726700 N) which can now be seen about 2 km distant. It is not advised to cut this corner along a high line, because you will encounter steep and potentially dangerous avalanche slopes. The climb from the valley to the unnamed pass gains about 150 vertical metres and is straightforward.

From the pass, carefully descend the slope to the southeast, then follow the drainage down to a large open area. Carry on descending the drainage until you reach a point where the right bank is threatened by slopes above. During periods of elevated avalanche hazard it would be advisable to continue for a short distance down the sparsely treed slopes on the left bank, away from the danger. At an elevation of about 2150 m, cross the creek on a large bench to gain the right-hand bank. Continue descending and traversing in a southerly direction (trending to the right). Some glades can be found through the trees, where you can get a few turns. Do not descend directly down the creekbed, as its steep banks pose a serious avalanche threat.

At the bottom, just before reaching Mosquito Creek, you will reach the trail. Turn right and follow it back to the Icefields Parkway (see page 286).

127. LAKE KATHERINE/ LAKE HELEN CIRCUIT
Ski Touring, ATR 2

Grade Advanced
Distance 8 km return
Time 4–6 hours

Elevation gain 650 m
Max elevation 2470 m
Map Hector Lake 82 N/9

This is an excellent tour that takes you high above treeline into alpine terrain. The trip requires good weather and good visibility.

Hazards: You will be in the high alpine far from shelter, so you should be well clothed and prepared for emergencies. You will also be in potential avalanche terrain, so take the appropriate precautions.

Access: There is a small parking lot on the northeast side of the Icefields Parkway, just across the bridge over Helen Creek, 29 km north of the junction with the Trans-Canada Highway.

Follow the Dolomite Peak Circuit tour (see page 288) as far as Lake Katherine. From here ascend open slopes to the west for about 1 km to gain the pass (540500 E 5726800 N) located immediately south of Cirque Peak. Cross the pass and descend the southwest slopes to Lake Helen. At the top the slopes are steep and you should proceed with caution. Stay to the right on the descent, as there are small cliffs below on the left. Descend to Lake Helen and cross it, heading south towards the valley. From the south end of the lake, contour around to the left at about the same level, then ski through a notch and into a draw. You can descend this draw or traverse a little farther to your left to reach your up-track. It is also possible to descend directly down Helen Creek from Lake Helen, but the creek can be awkward at the point where it reaches treeline, and there is considerable avalanche danger.

128. CROWFOOT PASS
Ski Touring, ATR 2

Grade Intermediate
Distance 10 km return
Time Full day

Elevation gain 430 m
Max elevation 2350 m
Map Hector Lake 82 N/9

The tour to Crowfoot Pass is one of the finest in the Rockies. There are excellent views down the Bow Valley to Mount Temple and Pilot Mountain and farther south to the tower of Mount Assiniboine. Save this one for later in the season when there is lots of snow and the sun lingers in the pass.

Hazards: There is avalanche hazard on this tour and the Creek Route has claimed a life in the past.

Options: People have crossed this pass and descended to Hector Lake, but this is not recommended, as the descent is very steep.

Access: The best place to park is at the Crowfoot Glacier viewpoint on the west side of the Icefields Parkway, about 32 km north from the junction with the Trans-Canada Highway. This viewpoint is 3 km south of the turnoff for Num-Ti-Jah Lodge. Many people park farther south along the highway, but this is not a good idea, particularly if snowplows are active.

From the parking lot, head straight over the snowbank and down a short, steep hill to the trees below. This hill is about 20 vertical metres high and may require several kick turns. Once in the trees, ski out into the valley bottom to reach the flats at the end of Bow Lake. Turn left and ski down the open flats, then round a corner into another open area. From here there are two routes to the pass.

The Ramp Route

After skiing about 1 km from the main body of Bow Lake, turn right, up a small but clearly defined creekbed. This soon curves left and goes through a large boulder field, then across an open area. It then curves right and soon you head left through the trees. Within about 100 m you enter a draw and you begin to climb (539600 E 5722000 N). If there is lots of snow you can continue ascending the draw. If not you can traverse left onto a crest and wind your way upwards. After about 200 vertical metres of ascent the angle lays back and the trees begin to thin out. From here the tour continues along the ramp, gradually gaining elevation. Eventually the angle again lays back and you continue for several kilometres across to the pass. On the last 2 km there are several small, steep hills and rolls that must be treated with caution.

The Creek Route

If you choose to ascend the Creek Route, continue skiing down the Bow River flats until they pinch out and the river begins. Ski up onto the right bank and proceed through the trees. Travel is excellent along here, and after about 1 km through the open forest you reach the drainage (541200 E 5722000 N) coming down from Crowfoot Pass. At this point the drainage is a small canyon which is easily entered. Put your skins on and begin skiing up the creek. Travel is easy and the angle is not too steep. The creek gains about 100 vertical metres and approaches a cliff looming above through the trees. At this point the creek begins to curve to the left. Continue up the creek for some distance more. It is usually distinct and easy to follow. At one point the way levels out for a short distance but soon begins to climb again through open trees. Eventually you break completely out of the trees and can continue straight ahead up the drainage to the pass, where there is a nice outcrop of quartzite rock to sit on.

129. BOW HUT
Ski Touring, ATR 3

Grade Advanced
Distance 8 km one way to Bow Hut
Time 4–6 hours
Elevation gain 390 m

Max elevation 2330 m
Maps Hector Lake 82 N/9, Blaeberry River 82 N/10; Summits and Icefields Map

This is a serious ski tour that takes you up high to the edge of the Wapta Icefields. Its destination, Bow Hut, is the largest and most luxurious of the huts on the Wapta Icefield. There is no glacier travel on this route, but beyond Bow Hut all travel is on glaciers. The trail is usually broken and easy to follow, but if there has been a heavy snowfall and you are unfamiliar with the route, this tour can be more challenging.

Facilities: There are toilets at the parking lot. Note that Num-Ti-Jah Lodge is no longer open during the winter.

Hazards: This tour takes you into high alpine terrain. You should have warm clothes, avalanche safety equipment and survival gear and be prepared for any emergency. There is avalanche hazard on this route in several places: along the narrow canyon; while climbing the hillside above the canyon; and on the final steep hill before Bow Hut. Use caution! Be particularly aware that the large cirque below St. Nicholas Peak is threatened by avalanches from the ice cliffs high above. Move through this exposed area quickly.

Access: There is a large parking lot along the access road to Num-Ti-Jah Lodge, just west of the Icefields Parkway about 34 km north of the intersection with the Trans-Canada Highway or 6 km south of Bow Pass.

From the parking lot ski or walk a short distance down the road toward Num-Ti-Jah Lodge and then angle left out to Bow Lake. Cross the lake (be certain it is well frozen and snow covered) to the gravel flats on

Skiing up the second canyon on the way to Bow Hut.
It is best not to linger here. Photo Chic Scott

BOW HUT

A thoroughly modern hut and the flagship of the Wapta Fleet, set amid spectacular surroundings.

Location Northeast of St. Nicholas Peak on a rocky ridge overlooking the drainage leading down to Bow Lake
(535400 E 5720500 N)

Elevation 2350 m

Maps Hector Lake 82 N/9;
Summits and Icefields Map

Facilities Two buildings (a cooking room and sleeping quarters) separated by a vestibule; foamies, cooking and eating utensils, propane cookstoves and lanterns and a woodstove for heating

Capacity 30

Water Snowmelt in winter, dug from the snowbank at the west end of the hut. In spring and summer water can be had from a small creek to the west of the hut.

Reservations The Alpine Club of Canada, 403-678-3200

Note The cooking room is locked when a custodian is not present; a combination number is required.

Bow Hut. Photo Chic Scott

the far side. Continue up the stream for about 500 m until you can see that the way ahead is blocked by a narrow canyon. At this point angle left and follow a trail through the trees, climbing gradually up a small drainage. Soon the trail bumps up against a steep mountainside beneath a large avalanche path. Do not linger here, but climb quickly up a short, steep hill to the right. After reaching the crest, traverse around the corner, then descend into the main drainage again. You have now circumvented the first canyon.

Follow the creek, heading almost due south up the second canyon. The walls above you are steep and draped with snow – you should not linger here. In the late spring this creek may be open in places and have some tricky sections. After about 1 km the way ahead narrows and becomes steep and difficult as the route ascends to the left, up onto the east bank. Continue now through open forest, climbing gradually, until the trees end and the route breaks out into a large mountain cirque.

Cross the cirque in a southerly direction, climbing gradually, and contour around to the base of the steep hillside on the right. It is critical that you pick the safest point to climb this hillside, as there is avalanche potential here. The best route ascends a shallow groove at the left end of the hillside, making several traverses and kick turns, eventually breaking out to the right over the edge of the groove onto lower-angled slopes above. Continue ascending these slopes, gaining about 100 vertical metres, to reach Bow Hut (535400 E 5720500 N).

130. BOW SUMMIT
Ski Touring, ATR 2

Grade Easy/intermediate
Distance 1 km to base of ski slope
Time A few hours or all day
Elevation gain 100 m for most popular slope; about 330 m for parking lot to highest area skied to

Max elevation 2250 m on bench above most popular slope
Maps Hector Lake 82 N/9, Blaeberry River 82 N/10; Summits and Icefields Map

Mike Galbraith enjoys the magnificent view from Bow Summit. Photo Chic Scott

Bow Summit has long been a popular destination for ski touring and making turns. On a sunny day this is a magical spot: there is lots of snow, the slopes are only a short distance from the car and the views are excellent. Note that this area is closed to skiers early in the season until there is sufficient snow to prevent damage to the fragile alpine vegetation.

Hazards: Bow Summit has been the scene of several avalanche fatalities in the past. Although the slopes are not large, they should be treated cautiously.

Access: Turn west off the Icefields Parkway at Bow Pass, 40 km north of the junction with the Trans-Canada Highway. Drive a short distance up the road towards the Peyto Lake viewpoint, then turn right into a large, plowed parking lot.

From the parking lot ski up the unplowed road for 300–400 m, then angle out left to the base of a prominent hill. This hill is the main attraction at Bow Summit, and although it's not large, it can give many hours of enjoyable skiing.

There is also a bowl higher up where turns can be made. To get there, ski along the bench which runs along the top of the hill (this is actually an old road). The trail crosses a creek drainage after about 1 km and just beyond turns upward into a wild alpine cirque. Some of the slopes here are skiable but offer avalanche potential.

The Bow Summit area is good for ski touring as well as making turns. It is possible to just wander through the forest at the base of the hill, breaking trail and enjoying the beauty and freedom of ski touring.

131. GLACIER LAKE
Ski Touring, ATR 1

Grade Intermediate
Distance 14 km return
Time Moderate day
Elevation gain 50 m following river; 250 m following trail

Max elevation 1420 m following river; 1670 m following trail
Map Mistaya Lake 82 N/15

Although this can be a wonderful ski tour in a wilderness setting, the valley is low in elevation and receives little snowfall. Consequently the river flats are often blown bare, and when spring comes, what little snow there is disappears quickly.

Access: There is a parking lot on the southwest side of the Icefields Parkway, about 1 km north of the turnoff for the David Thompson Highway (Highway 11).

The trail starts from the southwest corner of the parking lot, heads south for a short distance, then turns west and continues for about 1 km to a bridge over the North Saskatchewan River. Cross the bridge and continue west until the trail descends to the flats of the Howse River. From here follow the river flats for 5 km. At about 512400 E 5752100 N, turn north up the creek which drains Glacier Lake. If the creek is open and it is not possible to ski up the canyon, climb up onto the right bank to find the trail and follow it to Glacier Lake.

Instead of following the river flats, it is also possible to follow a summer trail which works its way into the forest and climbs 250 vertical metres over a hill before descending steeply to the lake.

132. NIGEL PASS
Ski Touring, ATR 2

Grade Intermediate
Distance 16 km return
Time 4-6 hours return

Elevation gain 280 m
Max elevation 2120 m
Map Columbia Icefield 83 C/3

This is a very pleasant tour through spectacular mountain terrain. It is varied and interesting but not too difficult and gets a lot of sun.

Hazards: Approach the pass with caution, as cornices can overhang the cliffs above the Brazeau River.

Access: There is a parking lot, signed Nigel Creek, on the northeast side of the Icefields Parkway, about 12 km south of the Columbia Icefield Centre.

From the parking lot ski straight ahead up the old road. After about 1.5 km, where a large avalanche path descends from the left, turn rightward into the trees for a short distance to the Camp Parker warden cabin. At the cabin turn left on the summer trail to Nigel pass. The trail angles down through open timber to Nigel Creek. Follow the creekbed for another kilometre until the sides begin to pinch in. It is possible to continue up the creek if there is lots of snow, but it is better to climb up onto the right bank and gain a bench about 50 m higher where there is a trail in the woods. Follow the trail along this bench for 1 km until the terrain starts to open up and the canyon disappears. Continue easily, just above the creek, for another kilometre until it is necessary to climb up onto the right bank again to bypass a rocky canyon. Soon the trail descends to the creek and the way ahead is clear. Follow the drainage straight ahead, climbing gradually through meadows and clumps of trees, up to Nigel Pass. If you stay to the left and ski to the lowest point in the pass, you will end up looking down a very steep cliff into the headwaters of the Brazeau River.

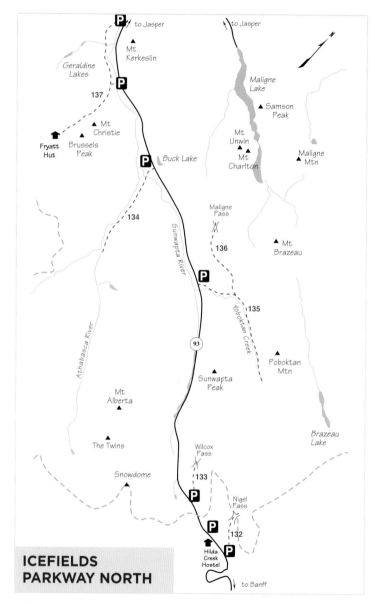

ICEFIELDS
PARKWAY NORTH

133. WILCOX PASS
Ski Touring, ATR 2

Grade Intermediate/advanced
Distance 8 km return
Time 4-6 hours return

Elevation gain 360 m
Max elevation 2360 m
Map Columbia Icefield 83 C/3

This is an exciting tour that gets you up high very quickly. There is an outstanding view of the Columbia Icefield to the west.

Hazard: The steep initial section of this tour may be tricky to descend.

Access: Park in the plowed turnoff into the Wilcox campground on the northeast side of the Icefields Parkway, 2.5 km south of the Columbia Icefield Centre.

The trail climbs up the hillside almost immediately above the parking area and it is advisable to put skins on your skis for the initial part of the tour. The trail angles up left into the trees, then climbs through the

Dean Lister and Shawn McDonald at Wilcox Pass, with mounts Athabasca and Andromeda in the distance. Photo Chic Scott

Shawn McDonald carves some turns on the way back from Wilcox Pass. Photo Chic Scott

forest at a steep but reasonable angle. After a short distance the trail enters a gully and it becomes necessary to make several switchbacks. After gaining about 75 m in elevation, ski out left to the brow of a hill. Ascend the crest, then traverse left on a gentle bench which climbs gradually through the trees. After a short distance you can climb directly up to the right through some trees for about 75 vertical metres onto a higher bench. Follow this higher bench easily to the northwest across large, open slopes for about 3 km to reach the pass.

134. SUNWAPTA FALLS/ ATHABASCA RIVER
Ski Touring, ATR 1

Grade Intermediate
Distance 12 km return to junction with Athabasca River
Time 4–5 hours return

Elevation loss 100 m
Max elevation 1390 m
Maps Athabasca Falls 83 C/12, Fortress Lake 83 C/5

Dave Agnew breaks trail along the Athabasca Valley. Photo Chic Scott

This is a pleasant and popular trail and there are great views of the surrounding peaks from the Athabasca River. The trail actually descends on the way out and climbs as you return to your car.

Options: You can continue along the Athabasca River flats for another 8 km to the junction of the Athabasca and Chaba Rivers.

Access: Turn west off the Icefields Parkway onto the Sunwapta Falls access road, 55 km south of Jasper. The road is no longer plowed in winter, so park here in the little cleared space next to the Parkway.

From the Icefields Parkway ski about 500 m along the Sunwapta Falls access road to the trailhead kiosk in the snow-covered parking lot. The trail descends steeply and crosses a bridge over the chasm of Sunwapta Falls. Climb a few feet on the other side of the bridge, then continue through the woods. The trail descends gradually for about 2.5 km, then flattens out for another 2 km. The final kilometre is a moderately steep descent to the Athabasca River.

135. POBOKTAN CREEK
Ski Touring, ATR 1

Grade Easy

Distance 26 km return

Time Full day

Elevation gain 400 m

Max elevation 1940 m

Map Sunwapta Peak 83 C/6

The tour up Poboktan Creek is a pleasant valley trip but is closed until later in the season (March 1) to protect the caribou population. Please check with Jasper National Park at 780-852-6176, http://is.gd/WtT5fU, for the current status.

Facilities: There are toilets at the parking area.

Hazards: Do not attempt to ski along the bed of Poboktan Creek, as there is a narrow canyon about 4 km below the Waterfall warden cabin which is impassable.

Access: There is a large parking lot on the east side of the Icefields Parkway, on the south side of Poboktan Creek, about 70 km south of Jasper (across the creek from the Sunwapta warden station).

From the parking lot walk across the road bridge into the warden station's yard. The trail starts behind the office building, beside the creek, in the southeast corner of the yard. Ski for about 500 m along the north side of the creek. The trail begins to climb steeply and soon gains 100 vertical metres. It now continues high on the north slope, working its way into the valley. After about 3 km the route drops down to the creek again and follows it for a short distance. Then it once again climbs up onto the north bank and for several kilometres works its way through the trees, until it reaches Poligne Creek. At this point a trail branches north to Maligne Pass (see page 305).

Cross Poligne Creek and follow the Poboktan Creek trail as it winds its way through the woods for about 1 km until it reaches another creek. The trail crosses this creek and continues up the valley, climbing steadily. After several kilometres of traversing along the northeast side of the valley, the trail descends to Poboktan Creek. Follow the creekbed for about 1 km to a major fork. The way up the left fork looks clear but is actually a dead end. Follow the right fork for a very short distance, then climb the open slope up onto the left bank. In the angle between the two forks you will find the trail again (and the Waterfall campground as well). Follow the trail through the trees for about 1 km until it descends to the open meadow along Poboktan Creek. Ski across the meadow to the far end (1.5 km), where the Waterfall warden cabin is located at the edge of the trees on the northeast side of the meadow.

136. MALIGNE PASS
Ski Touring, ATR 2

Grade Advanced
Distance 28 km return
Time Long day

Elevation gain 700 m
Max elevation 2240 m
Map Sunwapta Peak 83 C/6

This area is closed until later in the season (March 1) to protect the caribou population. Check the Jasper National Park website, http://is.gd/WtT5fU, for current status.

This tour should only be undertaken by experienced skiers who can handle very tricky skiing on narrow trails. The way up the narrow valley of Poligne Creek is very difficult and the route does not get any easier until near Maligne Pass. The descent back to Poboktan Creek is an exciting ride, to say the least. However, Maligne Pass is very beautiful and well worth the trip.

Access: There is a large parking lot on the east side of the Icefields Parkway, on the south side of Poboktan Creek, about 70 km south of Jasper (across the creek from the Poboktan Creek warden station).

From the parking lot follow the Poboktan Creek trail for 7 km to its junction with Poligne Creek (see page 304). From the junction ski north up the hill for several hundred metres, then cross a bridge to the east bank of Poligne Creek. The route climbs very steeply now and skins are recommended. The trail does one very long switchback to the right, then swings to the left and heads into the valley at a more reasonable angle.

Looking out over Maligne Pass. Photo Tony Hoare

The track continues along horizontally for some way, then descends to the creek.

Cross a bridge and continue along the trail as it climbs into the trees on the west bank. The route descends to the creek again after about 1 km. Cross the creek on a bridge at the edge of a large avalanche path. Follow along through the trees, climbing steadily, high above the east bank of the creek. After another kilometre the trail again descends to the creek. Cross a bridge to the west bank. You are now in the V-angle formed by the junction of two creeks.

Continue following a trail through the trees to reach the most westerly of the two creeks, the one that descends from Maligne Pass. Follow this creek, staying on the east bank, for about 500 m, until you cross it on a small bridge. You are now on the west bank of the most westerly creek. Continue angling up the treed hillside above and soon the trail peters out. Traverse rightward into the creekbed itself and follow it for a short distance until you come out into the open at a giant avalanche path. Cross the avalanche path and ski up a draw to the right to regain safer ground in the trees. Now work your way through the trees towards the pass, staying well back from the avalanche slope on the right. After a while the trees thin out, then disappear. Continue climbing at a moderate angle for several kilometres to the pass. The last 4 km, beyond the avalanche path, is very beautiful and the pass itself is outstanding.

137. FRYATT CREEK
Ski Touring, ATR 2

Grade Advanced
Distance 15 km one way from
    Athabasca River crossing;
    22 km one way from Geraldine
    fire road parking lot

Time Full day to hut
Elevation gain 780 m
Max elevation 1980 m
Map Athabasca Falls 83 C/12

This is an adventurous ski tour with a cozy cabin as your reward. The headwall at the end of the tour, up to the cabin, can be a killer. Try to leave plenty of time to deal with this obstacle in the daylight.

Facilities: Fryatt Hut is located just above the headwall. Note that it is incorrectly marked on some maps – the correct grid reference is 440200 E 5817600 N.

Hazards: Crossing the frozen Athabasca River is a very dangerous undertaking and should only be attempted when you are sure the ice is solid and will support your weight.

Access: There are two options for starting.

1. Safe start: Turn west off the Icefields Parkway at about 31 km south of Jasper and drive 1 km along Highway 93A to a plowed parking area at the Geraldine fire road. Ski up the fire road for about 2 km to the junction with the Fryatt trail. Turn left again and follow the trail along the valley bottom for about 10 km to where it crosses Fryatt Creek.

2. Alternative start: If the river is well frozen it is possible to cross on skis and thus cut about 7 km off the tour. USE CAUTION AND DO NOT ATTEMPT TO SKI ACROSS THE RIVER UNLESS YOU ARE SURE IT WILL SUPPORT YOUR WEIGHT. If you choose to attempt this shortcut, park on the west side of the Icefields Parkway at a plowed parking lot about 41 km south of Jasper. Once across the river, climb up onto the bank and ski into the woods to find the trail. Then turn left and ski about 4 km to reach Fryatt Creek.

Cross Fryatt Creek and climb steeply through the forest along the south side of the valley for about 4 km. The creek is reached again and the way becomes easier. Follow the drainage up the valley, cross the lake, then continue up the drainage to the headwall.

The summer trail is hard to follow up the steep headwall and it is best to take off your skis and climb the hill on foot. Ascend the hill on a diagonal from right to left, staying to the right of the waterfall. There may be several yellow trail markers in the trees to guide you. This climb in deep snow can be a real challenge.

The cabin is located just above the northwest side of the creek, not far beyond the rim of the headwall.

SYDNEY VALLANCE (FRYATT) HUT

This is a very pleasant hut in a beautiful location. It has been completely refurbished in recent years.

Location Above the headwall at the end of Fryatt Creek (440200 E 5817600 N)

Elevation 2000 m

Map Athabasca Falls 83 C/12

Facilities Wood heating stove; propane lighting and cooking; all pots, pans, dishes and utensils; foamies

Capacity 12

Water From the creek a few metres east of the hut or from snowmelt

Reservations The Alpine Club of Canada, 403-678-3200

Note The hut is locked and a combination number is required.

Sydney Vallance (Fryatt) Hut. Photo Josée LaRochelle

JASPER

138. **Athabasca Falls Loop** Easy, p. 313

139. **Geraldine Fire Road** Advanced, p. 314

140. **Leach Lake Trail** Easy, p. 314

141. **Whirlpool Trail** Easy, p. 315

142. **Whirlpool Campground Loop** Easy, p. 316

143. **Wabasso Campground Trails** Easy, p. 316

144. **Mount Edith Cavell Road** Easy, p. 317

145. **Whistler's Campground Loop** Easy, p. 318

146. **Pyramid Lake Resort Trail** Easy, p. 318

147. **Palisade Lookout** Advanced, p. 320

148. **Decoigne Trails** Easy, p. 321

149. **Summit Lakes/Jacques Lake**
     Easy/Intermediate, p. 322

150. **Moose Lake Loop** Easy/Intermediate, p. 323

151. **Upper Moose Lake Loop** Intermediate, p. 325

152. **Evelyn Creek Loop** Intermediate/Advanced, p. 325

153. **Bald Hills Lookout** Intermediate, p. 326

154. **Little Shovel Pass** Intermediate/Advanced, p. 327

155. **Shangri La** Intermediate, p. 329

Tours at Shangri La, p. 331

Jasper National Park is the largest of the mountain parks, covering 11,228 square kilometres, and offers extensive opportunities for cross-country skiing in a wilderness setting. The town of Jasper is quiet in winter but still has everything you may require. The Athabasca Valley is low in elevation, and consequently Jasper area trails can often suffer from lack of snow. The trails near Maligne Lake, however, have a much deeper snowpack.

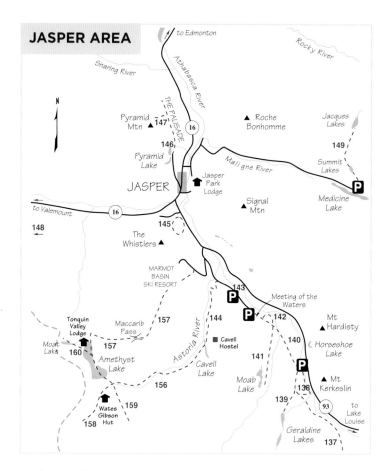

JASPER AREA

to Edmonton
Rocky River
Snaring River
Athabasca River
THE PALISADE
Pyramid Mtn ▲ 147
16
Roche Bonhomme ▲
Jacques Lakes
149
N
146
Pyramid Lake
Maligne River
Summit Lakes
JASPER
Jasper Park Lodge
P
to Valemount
16
Signal Mtn ▲
Medicine Lake
148
145
The Whistlers ▲
MARMOT BASIN SKI RESORT
P 143
Meeting of the Waters
P 142
Mt Hardisty ▲
Tonquin Valley Lodge
Maccarib Pass
157
144
Astoria River
Cavell Hostel
140
Horseshoe Lake
Moat Lake
157
160
Amethyst Lake
141
Mt Kerkeslin ▲
P
138
Cavell Lake
Moab Lake
156
139
93
to Lake Louise
Wates Gibson Hut
159
158
Geraldine Lakes
137

Access: Jasper is most easily reached by a 360 km drive from Edmonton via Highway 16. One can also reach Jasper after a 230 km drive along the Icefields Parkway from Lake Louise. Mount Robson Provincial Park is located 88 km west of Jasper along Highway 16. Many of the ski trails in this chapter are found along the Maligne Lake road, which branches off from Highway 16 some 4 km east of Jasper.

Facilities: The town of Jasper has a population of about 5,000 and offers all the amenities you might need. There are gas stations, grocery stores, restaurants, hotels, a liquor store and a post office. The best bargains in accommodation are the Jasper Hostel, 7 km from town along the road to the Sky Tram, or Maligne Canyon Hostel, 11 km east of Jasper on the road to Maligne Canyon (phone 778-328-2220 or 1-866-762-4122 for reservations at both these hostels). The Wapiti campground, 3 km south of town along the Icefields Parkway, is open in winter. For your equipment needs try Gravity Gear (780-852-3155, www.gravitygearjasper.com) or Totem Ski Shop (780-852-3078, totemskishop.com).

Information: The Jasper Park Visitor Information Centre (780-852-6176) is located across from the VIA Rail station in the centre of town. The Parks visitor safety office can be reached at 780-852-6155. Before setting out on any of these trails it is recommended that you visit the information centre or the Parks webpage at http://is.gd/SUzEyx to get the latest update on the state of the trails. Winter recreation around Jasper is evolving very fast and park officials are doing their best to accommodate changing interests.

138. ATHABASCA FALLS LOOP
Nordic Skiing, ATR 1

Grade Easy

Distance 7 km loop

Time 2 hours

Elevation gain 40 m

Max elevation 1220 m

Map Athabasca Falls 83 C/12

This is a very pleasant trail over varied terrain.

Facilities: There is a toilet at the parking lot.

Access: Drive south from Jasper for 31 km along the Icefields Parkway, then turn right and follow Highway 93A about 1 km to the Geraldine fire road parking lot.

Ski up the fire road for about 2 km, gradually gaining elevation through the forest, to the Fryatt Creek trailhead. Turn left and follow the trail for about 1 km until it veers left along a marsh. Follow the trail east for 1 km to the Athabasca River, then turn left again and ski along the shore back to the road. Turn left and walk along Highway 93A for about 500 m to your car.

Note: The section along the river is frequently used by snowshoers as well. The loop is not trackset.

139. GERALDINE FIRE ROAD
Nordic Skiing, ATR 1

Grade Advanced
Distance 6 km one way
Time 3–4 hours

Elevation gain 500 m
Max elevation 1700 m
Map Athabasca Falls 83 C/12

This is a steep trail, groomed for both classic and skate. You will be sweating on the way up. Bundle up for the windy ride back down.

Facilities: There is a toilet at the parking lot.

Access: Drive south from Jasper for 31 km along the Icefields Parkway, then turn right and follow Highway 93A for about 1 km to the Geraldine fire road parking lot.

The trail follows the Geraldine fire road. After skiing 2 km you reach a trail junction where you should stay right.

140. LEACH LAKE TRAIL
Nordic Skiing, ATR 1

Grade Easy
Distance 9 km one way
Time 3 hours one way
Elevation gain 60 m

Max elevation 1240 m
Map Athabasca Falls 83 C/12
Regularly groomed for both
   skate and classic

This is a gentle trail that follows snow-covered Highway 93A. There are good views of the valley and the surrounding peaks.

Options: This trail can be extended by skiing Whirlpool Trail and/or Whirlpool Campground Trail.

Facilities: There is a toilet at the parking lot.

Access: Drive south from Jasper for 31 km along the Icefields

Parkway, then turn right and follow Highway 93A about 1 km to the Geraldine fire road parking lot.

Known also as Sunnyside Trail, this ski excursion begins from the Geraldine fire road parking lot and follows snow-covered Highway 93A to Leach Lake and beyond to Whirlpool Trail.

141. WHIRLPOOL TRAIL
Nordic Skiing, ATR 1

Grade Easy
Distance 18 km return
Time 5–6 hours return
Elevation gain 110 m

Max elevation 1230 m
Map Athabasca Falls 83 C/12
Regularly groomed for both
   skate and classic

This is a long, easy ski tour, much of it following a road through the forest. Some portions of the route run parallel to the Whirlpool River, offering expansive views.

Facilities: There is a toilet at the parking lot.

Access: Drive south of Jasper for 6.5 km along the Icefields Parkway, turn right onto Highway 93A and continue for about 13 km to the Meeting of the Waters picnic site. This is as far south as the road is plowed.

From the parking lot, ski south along the snow-covered road. After 2 km, turn right onto the Whirlpool River fire road and follow it for another 6.5 km to what is the summer parking lot and trailhead. If you continue about 500 m beyond this point, you will see the trail for Moab Lake leaving the road to the right (large sign). The lake is just a short distance down the hill.

George Rodway skis along the Whirlpool River fire road. Photo Chic Scott

142. WHIRLPOOL CAMPGROUND LOOP Nordic Skiing, ATR 1

Grade Easy
Distance 4.5 km return
Time 1–2 hours
Elevation gain Nil

Max elevation 1130 m
Map Athabasca Falls 83 C/12
Trackset when conditions allow

This is a short and pleasant ski tour with some nice views.

Facilities: There are toilets at the parking lot.

Access: Drive south of Jasper for 6.5 km along the Icefields Parkway, turn right onto Highway 93A, and continue for about 13 km to the Meeting of the Waters picnic site. This is as far south as the road is plowed.

From the parking lot ski 2.2 km south along the snow-covered road, as far as the Whirlpool River bridge. Turn left and circle back through the campsite to return to the parking lot.

143. WABASSO CAMPGROUND TRAILS Nordic Skiing, ATR 1

Grade Easy
Distance 6.5 km of trails
Time A few hours or all day
Elevation gain Nil

Max elevation 1130 m
Map Athabasca Falls 83 C/12
Trackset for classic and skate except one loop for classic only

These trails offer a variety of options for all cross-country ski enthusiasts.

Facilities: There are toilets and a telephone at the parking lot.

Access: Drive south of Jasper for 6.5 km along the Icefields Parkway, turn right onto Highway 93A and continue for about 9.5 km to the Wabasso campground (on the left).

The Wabasso trails start directly in front of the parking area. There are four short loops. The 3.6 km outer one, which parallels the Athabasca River part of the way, is a fabulous tour offering outstanding views of the surrounding peaks. This outer loop is trackset for classic only.

Kathy Madill skis beside the Athabasca River on the Wabasso Outer Loop. Photo Chic Scott

144. MOUNT EDITH CAVELL ROAD Ski Touring, ATR 1

Grade Easy
Distance 11 km one way to hostel
Time 4–5 hours to hostel;
   2–3 hours return to parking

Elevation gain 500 m
Max elevation 1740 m
Maps Jasper 83 D/16,
   Amethyst Lakes 83 D/9

This tour follows a road that is not plowed in the winter. It is a steady uphill plod. In an effort to protect the endangered woodlands caribou the route is closed until February 15.

Options: This tour is the start for the trip into Tonquin Valley and Amethyst Lakes.

Access: From Jasper drive south on the Icefields Parkway for 7 km to Highway 93A. Turn right and follow 93A for 5 km, past the turnoff to Marmot Basin ski resort, to a large parking lot at the Mount Edith Cavell road, located on the left, just across a bridge over the Astoria River.

The Mount Edith Cavell road begins directly across the highway from the parking lot. It climbs for several kilometres in long switchbacks, then rounds a shoulder into the drainage of the Astoria River. For the rest of the way the road climbs at a gentler angle and is very easy to follow.

The hostel is located on the left. After getting settled in and enjoying a hot drink, it is nice to round off the day with a short trip up the remainder of the road to Cavell Lake and admire the impressive north face of Mount Edith Cavell.

145. WHISTLERS CAMPGROUND LOOP Nordic Skiing, ATR 1

Grade Easy
Distance 4.5 km loop
Time A few hours or all day

Elevation gain Nil
Max elevation 1060 m
Map Jasper 83 D/16

The trackset trails of Whistlers Campground provide excellent skiing for people of all ages and abilities. Take a break for a wiener roast and a campfire at Marmot Meadows.

Facilities: There are tables and firepits for picnics and a toilet at the parking area.

Access: Drive south from Jasper along the Icefields Parkway and after 2 km turn right at Whistlers Road. Immediately turn left onto the campground road and follow it for about 500 m to a parking lot.

From the parking lot, ski a short distance along the access road to join a road that forms a loop around the campground and offers enjoyable, easy skiing.

146. PYRAMID LAKE RESORT TRAIL Nordic Skiing, ATR 1

Grade Easy
Distance 1 km loop
Time 30 minutes for complete loop

Elevation gain Nil
Max elevation 1180 m
Map Jasper 83 D/16

When conditions allow, a short loop is trackset on Pyramid Lake in front of the Pyramid Lake Resort.

Facilities: There is a restaurant at Pyramid Lake Resort as well as toilets and telephones.

Hazards: Before you venture onto the ice be sure that it is well frozen and snow-covered. Beware of water seeping up through the ice and snow. Although you will not go through the ice, your skis will get wet and eventually ice up completely.

Access: Drive about 6 km up the Pyramid Lake road from the edge of Jasper. There is a public parking lot on the right about 50 m before the resort.

From the parking lot, cross the road and walk to the edge of the lake. You can ski around the lake in either direction. There are stunning views of Pyramid Mountain to the northwest and Mount Edith Cavell to the south down the valley.

Kathy Madill skis on the perfectly trackset trail on Pyramid Lake below Pyramid Mountain. Photo Chic Scott

147. PALISADE LOOKOUT
Nordic Skiing, ATR 1

Grade Advanced
Distance 11 km to Palisade
Lookout
Time 6–8 hours return

Elevation gain 840 m
Max elevation 2020 m
Map Jasper 83 D/16
Trackset for first 7 km only

This ski tour follows a fire road and gives you great views if you reach the top.

Access: Park at the end of the Pyramid Lake road, 7 km from Jasper.

This tour follows a road through forest all the way to the lookout. The grade is moderately steep much of the way. After 7.5 km the road forks and you should follow the right-hand branch. The view from the top is worth the effort.

Kathy Madill skis up the Palisade Lookout trail. Photo Chic Scott

148. DECOIGNE TRAILS
Nordic Skiing, ATR 1

Grade Easy
Distance About 15 km of trails
Time A few hours or all day
Elevation gain Nil

Max elevation 1120 m
Map Jasper 83 D/16
Trackset for both classic and
  skate

This network of cross-country trails is new as of 2014. The routes follow old highways and railways, so they offer level and easy skiing (beware of a couple of very short but steep hills).

Access: Drive west of Jasper along Highway 16 for 20 km. About 100 m before the west park gate, turn right down a small road and follow it for about 1 km to a parking area.

Facilities: There is a warming hut to the south of the parking area, just to the left of a couple of residences. It is a converted garage, but on cold days it can be a good place to wax your skis or eat lunch.

Kathy Madill skis along the trackset Decoigne Trails. Photo Chic Scott

The cross-country trails start just west of the parking lot and run pretty well straight west up the valley. Another set of trails can be found by skiing north from the parking lot for a few metres through the trees then turning right (east) and continuing for several kilometres back along the valley toward Jasper.

149. SUMMIT LAKES/JACQUES LAKE Ski Touring, ATR 1

Grade Easy to First Summit Lake; intermediate to Jacques Lake

Distance 10 km round-trip to First Summit Lake; 24 km round-trip to Jacques Lake

Time Half-day to First Summit Lake and back; full day to Jacques Lake and back

Elevation gain 80 m to Summit Lakes

Max elevation 1530 m at Summit Lakes; 1490 m at Jacques Lake

Map Medicine Lake 83 C/13

This is an excellent novice trail as far as Summit Lakes. The scenic trail follows the valley along Beaver Creek between the Colin Range and the Queen Elizabeth Range. To carry on to Jacques Lake is more challenging and it may be necessary to break trail along this narrow path.

Facilities: There is a toilet at the trailhead.

Hazards: Do not linger in the obvious avalanche path which crosses the valley just before Summit Lakes.

Access: Drive 27 km along the Maligne Lake road to the Beaver Creek picnic area, which is on the left at the southeast end of Medicine Lake.

For the first 2 km, as far as Beaver Lake, the trail is a wide, gentle road. The route then continues along the west shore of Beaver Lake, offering superb views of the immense, slabby wall of the Queen Elizabeth Range. Beyond the lake the trail crosses briefly to the east side of the valley, then returns to the west side. Shortly after crossing an avalanche path, the wide trail ends at First Summit Lake. To carry on to Jacques Lake, follow the right-hand (northeast) shore of both lakes before finding the summer trail again. Follow this trail through dense forest to Jacques Lake.

MALIGNE LAKE TRAILS

At Maligne Lake the snow is excellent, the scenery beautiful, and there is a variety of trails to chose from. The touring into alpine terrain, high above treeline, is also superb, with scope for making turns.

The area west of the lake is closed until March 1 for caribou conservation. The lake itself and the eastern side of the valley are open year-round. Check the Jasper National Park webpage, www.parkscanada.gc.ca/jasper.

To reach Maligne Lake, drive 4 km east of Jasper on Highway 16, turn right onto the Maligne Lake road and follow it for another 45 km to the lake. Before March 1, park in the lot in front of the Maligne Lake Tours building (closed in winter). After March 1 you can also cross the bridge over the Maligne River and park in the lot on the west side of Maligne Lake. Many of the trails begin along the Bald Hills fire road, which starts where the access road turns left into the parking lot. None of these trails will be trackset but some may be skier-packed. Unfortunately these trails may also be damaged by snowshoers. The Maligne Lake trails vary from short and easy to long and advanced.

Note: As mentioned earlier, the Maligne Lake area is the wintering ground for woodland caribou, so dogs are not permitted on these trails.

150. MOOSE LAKE LOOP
Nordic Skiing, ATR 1

Grade Easy/intermediate
Distance 4.5 km loop
Time 1 hour

Elevation gain 60 m
Max elevation 1740 m
Map Athabasca Falls 83 C/12

Open from March 1 onwards. This would be an easy trail if it were not for the hill down to the lake. Moose Lake is a lovely spot for a rest and a cup of tea.

Facilities: Toilets at the trailhead.
Hazards: Be sure the lake is well frozen and snow-covered.
Options: This trail can be linked with Upper Moose Lake Loop.

Access: The trail begins from the parking lot located on the west side of the lake. Start along the Bald Hills fire road, which begins just opposite the entrance to the parking lot. In about 100 m turn left at the Maligne Pass trail sign. There is some very nice, rolling skiing along here to the junction with Upper Moose Lake Loop. Turn left again and ski a fast downhill to Moose Lake. From here the trail continues more easily to the shore of Maligne Lake. Turn left once more and ski past the warden station to the parking lot.

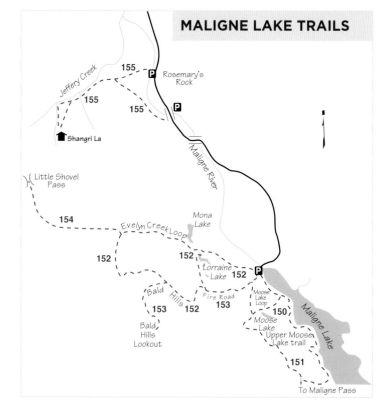

151. UPPER MOOSE LAKE LOOP
Nordic Skiing, ATR 1

Grade Intermediate
Distance 7.5 km loop
Time 2 hours

Elevation gain 90 m
Max elevation 1780 m
Map Athabasca Falls 83 C/12

Open March 1 onwards, this is a fun trail, always interesting, and the views along the lakeshore are beautiful. It should be skied in the anti-clockwise direction.

Hazards: Be sure the lake is well frozen and snow-covered.

Access: The trail begins from the parking lot located on the west side of the lake.

The first part of this trail is as described for Moose Lake Loop, but at the junction continue ahead up the steep hill. After this it is a winding and narrow trail to the Maligne Pass trail junction. From here the fun begins. Turn left and descend a draw, curving easily back and forth to the lake. Turn left again and follow the trail along the lakeshore, winding in and out at every indentation and rounding immense boulders, to eventually join up with the last part of Moose Lake Loop.

152. EVELYN CREEK LOOP
Nordic Skiing, ATR 1

Grade Intermediate/advanced
Distance 12 km loop
Time 3 hours

Elevation gain 280 m
Max elevation 1960 m
Map Athabasca Falls 83 C/12

Open from March 1 onwards, this is a longer trail with a challenging downhill section. It is best skied in a clockwise direction to get the thrill of the long downhill run (about 140 m elevation loss).

Facilities: Toilets at the trailhead.

Access: The trail begins from the parking lot located on the west side of the lake.

Head up the Bald Hills fire road, which starts just opposite the entrance to the parking lot. After about 3.5 km, and at the end of a long, straight, level section, leave the fire road to the right and continue straight ahead on the narrow Evelyn Creek trail. Make a long traverse across the hillside. Then, just past the Evelyn Pass hiking trail turnoff, turn right and descend to Evelyn Creek. At this point you will see on your left the bridge over Evelyn Creek. This is a long and exciting downhill run and it keeps the snow well. Turn right again and continue along a very pleasant rolling section passing Mona Lake. Continue along a narrow, twisting trail, mostly downhill, to emerge on the access road just north of the parking lot entrance.

153. BALD HILLS LOOKOUT
Ski Touring, ATR 2

Grade Intermediate
Distance 1500 m return
Time Moderate day
Elevation gain 480 m
Max elevation 2170 m
Map Athabasca Falls 83 C/12

Open from March 1 onwards, this trail takes you high above treeline where the terrain and the scenery are beautiful. It is worth spending a few hours up here exploring the area.

Facilities: Toilets at the trailhead.

Hazards: You should be prepared on this tour for the cold and the wind. If you wander off into the meadows, be careful of avalanche terrain.

Options: If you have time, it is pleasant to explore across the meadows to the south.

Access: The trail begins from the parking lot located on the west side of the lake.

This trail follows the Bald Hills fire road to the site of the old fire lookout. The fire road starts directly opposite the entrance to the parking lot. After the Evelyn Creek Loop turnoff (3.5 km) the fire road steepens considerably and climbs to the open ridge at treeline. The trail continues

Kathy Madill admires the view over Maligne Lake from Bald Hills Lookout. Photo Chic Scott

along the ridge in a southerly direction, over meadows and rises, to reach the lookout site, which is on the left (east) side of the ridge. All along here are wonderful views to the right of Mount Tekarra and the ridges of the Skyline Trail. However, when you reach the lookout site you are treated to the celebrated view of Maligne Lake and surrounding peaks.

154. LITTLE SHOVEL PASS
Ski Touring, ATR 2

Grade Intermediate/advanced
Distance 20 km to the pass and back
Time Full day

Elevation gain 650 m
Max elevation 2320 m
Map Athabasca Falls 83 C/12

Open March 1 onwards, this is one of the finest ski tours in the Jasper area. It gets you up high into the alpine where there are some outstanding views and some turns can be made.

Facilities: Toilets at the trailhead.

Hazards: This tour takes you above treeline, so be prepared to deal with avalanche terrain, extreme weather and limited visibility.

Options: From Little Shovel Pass you can ski north into Snow Bowl and down to Shangri La Cabin. This is one of the finest spots for ski touring in the Rockies and is highly recommended (see p. 332).

Access: The trail begins from the parking lot located on the west side of the lake.

From the entrance to the parking lot, walk about 25 m back along the access road to the Skyline trailhead. This is the exit from the Lorraine Lake and Evelyn Creek loops. The trail is excellent as it climbs and descends at a moderate angle through the trees for about 5 km to the Evelyn Creek bridge. Keep a sharp eye out for skiers coming down the trail.

From the bridge it is best to follow the drainage to the pass. Head up Evelyn Creek for several hundred metres, then angle up the right-hand fork (452400 E 5842900 N) that comes down from Little Shovel pass. This branch is not very distinct to begin and it may be hard to find. It might be best to ski up Evelyn Creek for about 200 m and then angle up and right through a clearing in the trees. The going is easy but the creek is hard to follow. After several hundred metres the creek becomes more distinct and easier to follow. Follow this branch of the creek for about 1.5 km until the creekbed flattens out and you cross an open meadow near the end of the valley. At this point (450200 E 5842200 N) angle up to the right into a very small drainage coming down from the pass. This creek is also not very distinct to begin with and is hard to find. Follow the drainage to the pass (448400 E 5843200 N).

The summer trail that switchbacks up the hillside above the valley is not recommended, as it traverses several open slopes higher up.

155. SHANGRI LA
Ski Touring, ATR 1

Grade Intermediate
Distance 8 km one way
Time This tour takes all day and should really be combined with an overnight stay at the cabin.

Elevation gain 420 m
Max elevation 2000 m
Maps Medicine Lake 83 C/13, Athabasca Falls 83 C/12

Open March 1 onwards, Shangri La is a beautiful log cabin located high in the mountains near Jasper. It is an outstanding destination for skiers of all abilities. Stay a few nights and enjoy the peace and quiet of the Canadian Rockies.

The bowl above the hut is 7 km across, rimmed with many small peaks, and offers excellent skiing. Days can be filled touring in the meadows, admiring the scenery or carving turns. The descents are not long, generally 200 to 300 vertical metres, but are more than adequate for a good day of skiing.

Access: From Jasper drive east of town along Highway 16 for about 4 km to the Maligne Lake turnoff and then drive up this road for about 37 km.

There are two ways to begin the tour:

1: If the Maligne River is well frozen you can cross it at Rosemary's Rock and ascend directly toward the valley of Jeffery Creek. Park your car in a plowed lot on the right at the point where the road leaves the Maligne River (453300 E 5847900 N) and cuts inland (the large rocks in the river are obvious). Cross the river, using extreme caution, and ascend the far bank. Then head northwest through the trees, following a trail with many blazes. The route initially seems to be going in the wrong direction but after several kilometres it turns west and heads up the hillside, climbing steadily.

2: If the river is open, drive another 1 km along the road and park in a plowed lot on the left, just before a bridge over the Maligne River. Cross the bridge on foot, then ski along the left bank of the river. Soon

Approaching Snow Bowl. Photo Chic Scott

the trail begins to climb and works its way up the hillside (many blazes on the trees).

Eventually the two approaches join, then ascend steeply, cross a wooded shoulder, and descend to Jeffery Creek (450800 E 5847800 N).

Follow the creekbed for about 2 km until it opens into a large meadow. Continue to follow the creek for several more kilometres, then turn left up a subsidiary stream which enters from the left (447700 E 5845900 N) and follow it for 1 km to the cabin. The cabin itself is tucked away above the left bank of the stream and can be easy to miss. Usually you spot the waterhole dug in the snow and footsteps leading steeply up the bank.

Many people take a shortcut for the last kilometre to reach the cabin. Rather than follow the small stream up to the cabin, they turn up to the left, at about 448200 E 5846100 N, and ascend directly over a wooded shoulder.

Crossing Snow Bowl near Shangri La Cabin. Photo Tony Hoare

TOURS AT SHANGRI LA
Ski Touring, ATR 2-3

From March 1 onwards, there are a variety of tours that can be done in Snow Bowl above Shangri La. All of them begin by skiing up the draw to the southwest, which you can see from the front door of the cabin. Very quickly this draw breaks out of the trees into open meadows. Do not attempt to follow the streambed itself, which continues past the cabin in a southerly direction. The walls of this streambed are very steep and pose a real avalanche threat.

Once out in the meadows you can tour for hours and find many excellent slopes for turns. Here are some suggestions:

1. There is an excellent hill for making turns on the east flank of what is called Aberhart's Nose. This is the hill directly in front of you as you enter the meadow beyond the draw. Good ski descents can be had from this ridge (446900 E 5843900 N).

2. If you feel adventurous, you can ski and scramble along the

SHANGRI LA CABIN

This delightful log cabin was built in 1936 by legendary outfitter and guide Curly Phillips and Doug Jeffery. It is steeped in the history and magic of a bygone era. The cabin is owned by the Maligne Lake Ski Club.

Location Near the head of Jeffery Creek, just below treeline, at 447800 E 5845000 N

Elevation 2000 m

Map Medicine Lake 83 C/13

Facilities This is a very comfortable cabin with wood and propane heating, propane cookstove, cooking and eating utensils and bunks with foam pads. Bring your own sleeping bag.

Capacity 6

Water From the creek down the hill in front of the cabin

Cost $200/night (club members) and $300/night (non-members)

Reservations can be made online at www.malignelakeskiclub.ca.

Open March and April

Colin Jones standing in front of Shangri La Cabin. Photo Chic Scott

ridge above Aberhart's Nose to reach the summit of Mount Aberhart (446300 E 5842900 N), which gives a panoramic view of the area.

3. If you want a pleasant Nordic tour you can ski northwest to Big Shovel Pass (443900 E 5848000 N).

4. At the end of the day, pleasant skiing can be had in the last rays of the sun on the west slopes of Sunset Peak (448400 E 5843700 N).

> *"Recreational development is a job not of building roads into lovely country, but of building receptivity into the still unlovely human mind."*
>
> —*Aldo Leopold,* Sand County Almanac

> *"Superfluous wealth can buy superfluities only. Money is not required to buy one necessary of the soul."*
>
> —*Henry David Thoreau,* Walden

> *"Something hidden. Go and find it. Go and look behind the ranges – Something lost behind the Ranges. Lost and waiting for you. Go!"*
>
> —*Rudyard Kipling,* The Explorer

TONQUIN VALLEY

156. **Tonquin Valley via Astoria River**
Intermediate, p.334

157. **Tonquin Valley via Maccarib Pass**
Intermediate, p. 341

158. **Fraser Pass** Intermediate, p. 344

159. **Eremite Valley** Easy/Intermediate, p. 345

160. **Moat Lake** Easy, p. 346

The Tonquin Valley offers excellent ski touring and has long been the scene of Alpine Club of Canada ski camps. The scenery is outstanding, the snow is deep and there is a variety of terrain to explore. If you visit this area, stay for a few days or even a week, exploring the valley and getting to know the region. Wates-Gibson Hut and Tonquin Valley Backcountry Lodge offer comfortable accommodation for winter visitors.

The Tonquin Valley is closed until February 15 to aid in caribou conservation. Check the Jasper National Park website for the current status.

156. TONQUIN VALLEY VIA ASTORIA RIVER
Ski Touring, ATR 2

Grade Intermediate

Distance 14 km from Mount Edith Cavell Hostel to Wates-Gibson Hut; 19 km to Tonquin Valley Backcountry Lodge

Time Full day, particularly if your packs are heavy

Elevation gain 150 m to Wates-Gibson Hut; 240 m to Amethyst Lakes

Max elevation 1890 m

Map Amethyst Lakes 83 D/9

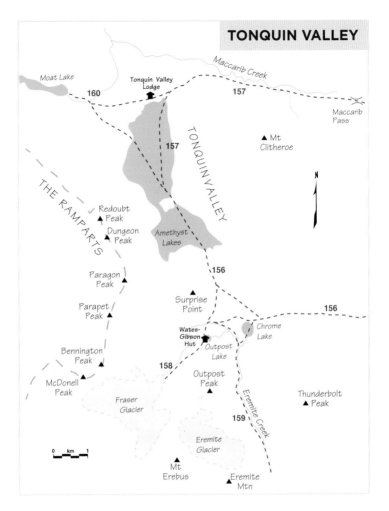

Open from February 15, this is a classic tour that takes you into the heart of one of the most beautiful regions in the world. It is worth spending a few days here, exploring the area. The trail is closed until mid-February to reduce the stress on the endangered woodland caribou that inhabit the region.

WATES-GIBSON HUT

This is a beautiful log cabin set in the middle of a ski paradise.
Location At the northwest corner of Outpost Lake
(415100 E 5835500 N); see photo map on page 337
Elevation 1890 m
Map Amethyst Lakes 83 D/9
Facilities: Foamies, cooking and eating utensils, propane cooking and lighting and a wood stove for heat
Capacity 24 in winter
Water From Outpost Lake
Reservations The Alpine Club of Canada, 403-678-3200
Open February 15 on
Note The hut is locked when a custodian is not present; a combination number is required.

Wates-Gibson Hut. Photo Chic Scott

Looking down on Outpost Lake, showing the location
of Wates-Gibson Hut. Photo Vance Hanna

Hazards: Many parties arrive late in the day and have trouble locating Wates-Gibson Hut. Plan your schedule so you arrive in daylight and have time to hunt around if need be. Refer to the photomap above for the hut location.

Options: It is common for parties to ski to the Tonquin Valley via the Astoria River and then return to the road via Maccarib Pass and Portal Creek.

Access: This trail begins at the Mount Edith Cavell Hostel (see page 317).

From the hostel ski up the road for about 75 m, then turn down a trail to the right. This trail crosses a bridge over Cavell Creek and after a few metres passes some outfitter shacks and corrals. The trail proper starts here. For the first 5 km it stays high above the Astoria River, on the northwest flank of Mount Edith Cavell. The trail traverses horizontally at first, then

TONQUIN VALLEY BACKCOUNTRY LODGE

This is a delightful and comfortable lodge located in one of the most beautiful places on earth.

Location At the northwest end of Amethyst Lakes in the Tonquin Valley (412900 E 5841500 N)

Elevation 1890 m

Map Amethyst Lakes 83 D/9

Facilities A central dining lodge surrounded by several cabins, with wood heating and outdoor plumbing

Capacity 14

Hosts Sara and Kable Kongsrud

Cost $135 per person (two-night minimum)

Reservations Tonquin Valley Backcountry Lodge, Box 550, Jasper, AB T0E 1E0
780-852-3909
horsetrip@gmail.com
www.tonquinvalley.com

Open February 15 on

Dinnertime at Tonquin Valley Backcountry Lodge. Photo Chic Scott

The view of the Ramparts above Amethyst Lakes from the front door of Tonquin Valley Backcountry Lodge. Photo Chic Scott

actually climbs for a short distance. Eventually it works its way down the hillside, reaching the Astoria River shortly after crossing Verdant Creek.

If you are skiing directly to the Tonquin Valley from Highway 93A, follow the Edith Cavell Road until a snowmobile track leaves the road to the right after approximately 6 km. You can follow this track, which descends to the river and runs along it, all the way to Amethyst Lakes. (See Exiting Down the Astoria River on page 340.)

The trail crosses to the right (north) bank of the Astoria, and for most of the next 8 km, as far as Chrome Lake, it continues along the north bank. Sometimes the trail follows the riverbed itself, but usually it is up on the north side of the river. Travel along the Astoria River and up to Amethyst Lakes is usually easy due to the snowmobile traffic that services the lodge.

Just before you reach Chrome Lake, a branch of the trail begins to climb up to the right, following the drainage which descends from Amethyst Lakes. On the map the drainage divides into two streams – follow the left (west) branch up to the lake. Here you will be treated to one of the most beautiful views in the world, the Ramparts above Amethyst Lakes.

Tonquin Valley Backcountry Lodge is located at the northwest corner of Amethyst Lakes (**412900** E **5841500** N).

To reach Wates-Gibson Hut on Outpost Lake you should continue along the Astoria River to Chrome Lake. The trail will become more difficult to follow, because the snowmobile traffic has turned off. As well, the Astoria River is not as clearly defined along here. From Chrome Lake to Outpost Lake the route finding is tricky. Starting from the outlet of Chrome Lake there are two ways you can go:

1. You can ski across the lake, angling left (south) to the inflow stream. Climb up a few metres to the right (west), through a notch and into the meadows above. Now turn right (northwest) and ski up the meadows for several hundred metres to the north end. This route has simply followed the drainage.

2. Alternatively you can take a shortcut from Chrome Lake to the meadows just beyond. From the outlet of Chrome Lake angle up to the right (west) and follow clearings through the trees for about 500 m to the meadow previously mentioned.

From the meadow the trail ascends Penstock Creek, gaining about 50 vertical metres before it flattens out into another meadow below Surprise Point. On your right (north) you will see a huge pile of jumbled rocks. Ski southwest along the left side of the meadow for about 300 m. The trail then curves around a corner to the left (south) and you will see on the hillside to the left, about 50 m in front of you, a V-shaped open slope. Ascend this hillside for about 75 vertical metres, climbing back and forth through the trees, then pop over the crest to reach the shore of Outpost Lake. The cabin is nestled in the trees a few metres above the northwest corner of the lake (see photo on page 337).

Exiting down the Astoria River

To ski back to the road and your car, it is possible to take a shortcut on your way down the Astoria River. The snowmobile trail does not climb up the hill to the hostel from the bridge but continues down the

Dean Lister and Shawn McDonald exit the Tonquin Valley down the Astoria River. Photo Chic Scott

Astoria River. Eventually the snowmobile track does climb about 75 vertical metres to the right through the trees to reach the Edith Cavell road at 428900 E 5842900 N. This is also a good route to follow on the way in if you want to do the distance in a day.

157. TONQUIN VALLEY VIA MACCARIB PASS
Ski Touring, ATR 2

Grade Intermediate

Distance 12 km to Maccarib Pass; 19 km to Tonquin Valley Backcountry Lodge; 28 km to Wates-Gibson Hut

Time It takes a full day to reach Tonquin Valley Backcountry Lodge. To ski to Wates-Gibson Hut on Outpost Lake in one push is a long, hard day indeed.

Elevation gain 300 m to the junction of Portal and Circus Creeks; 740 m to Maccarib Pass

Max elevation 2200 m at Maccarib Pass

Maps Jasper 83 D/16, Amethyst Lakes 83 D/9

Opens February 15

The ski tour to the junction of Portal and Circus creeks is pleasant enough, but the really nice terrain starts at this point and for the next 8 km, to Maccarib Pass, it is beautiful touring country. Start early and give yourself lots of time to reach your destination.

Access: Drive south from Jasper along the Icefields Parkway (Highway 93) for 7 km and turn right onto Highway 93A. Follow this highway for another 2.5 km, then turn right again onto the road to Marmot Basin ski resort. Drive up this road for about 6 km to Portal Creek. There is a parking lot on the left (west) side of the road just before it crosses Portal Creek.

From the parking lot, walk along the road and cross the bridge to the north side of Portal Creek. Put your skis on and go past some corrals and log buildings and head up the trail. The trail is straightforward to follow and provides easy going. It runs through the trees just above the right bank of the creek. In heavy snow years or later in the season it is easy to follow the creekbed itself. After about 4 km the trail drops down to the bed of Portal Creek just beyond its junction with Circus Creek. The point where you break out of the trees is a nice spot to stop for a drink and a bite to eat.

Beyond here the travel becomes much more pleasant and the skiing is lovely. For 5 km follow the creek up the valley through open, rolling terrain. Just before the end of the valley, start climbing up to the right towards Maccarib Pass. It is an easy and simple climb. The route follows open, subalpine terrain and the slopes are of a lower angle. Be sure not to turn up to the right too soon. The pass you are looking for is tucked up close to the north side of Mount Maccarib (if you turn upward too early there is another pass that looks inviting). The last part of the climb to and then through the pass is easy, but in whiteout conditions route finding can be tricky.

From the pass descend a low-angle drainage for several kilometres. The route then flattens out and you continue several kilometres across a meadow. At the point where the valley begins to close in and the creekbed starts to narrow and drop steeply, cut out left through the trees (there is a bridge across the creek at this point and a campground out on the right). It is possible now to follow a trail left and down to Amethyst Lakes or you can just ski down and left through open trees to the lake. Tonquin Valley Backcountry Lodge is located at the north-west corner of the lake (**412900** E **5841500** N).

To continue to Wates-Gibson Hut on Outpost Lake, ski south along the north arm of Amethyst Lakes. Cut across a narrow spit of land that sticks out into the lake and then continue south to the far shore. From this point the going gets tricky and there are two choices:

1. You can descend the snowmobile trail to the Astoria River and then ascend to Outpost Lake via Chrome Lake (see page 339).

2. You can attempt to cut around the corner through the trees to reach the upper valley of Penstock Creek. To do this you should maintain your elevation and not get sucked down small drainages. This 2 km stretch can prove very difficult and the author has never had much luck at getting it right. From the end of the lake follow the right-hand drainage which exits the lake on the west flank, near Surprise Point. Ski for about 1 km until this drainage begins to drop more steeply toward the valley. At this point begin angling around through the forest to the right. It is not necessary to climb up much, and a traverse line theoretical-ly should bring you into the upper reaches of Penstock Creek. There is no trail through here and you will be forced to bush-whack. You should aim to reach upper Penstock Creek in the open meadow below Surprise Point. Above you to the north, on Surprise Point, you will see a slope strewn with large boulders.

Once you reach upper Penstock Creek, ski southwest along the left side of the meadow for about 300 m. The trail then curves around a corner to the left (south) and you will see on the hillside to the left, about 50 m in front of you, a V-shaped open slope. Ascend this hillside for about 75 vertical metres, climbing back and forth through the trees, then pop over the crest to reach the shores of Outpost Lake. The cab-in is nestled in the trees a few metres above the northwest corner of the lake (see photomap on page 337).

Dean Lister and Shawn McDonald at Maccarib Pass. Photo Chic Scott

158. FRASER PASS
Ski Touring, ATR 2

Grade Intermediate
Distance 2 km one way
Time 2-3 hours one way
Elevation gain 500 m

Max elevation 2430 m
Map Amethyst Lakes 83 D/9
Opens February 15

This is an interesting tour that takes you high into alpine terrain. There is a terrific view from the pass. Some turns can be made up here as well.

Access: This tour begins at the Wates-Gibson Hut on Outpost Lake.

From the hut work your way through the trees, up the hillside to the west. After about 50 vertical metres the terrain lays back and you can continue west through sparse trees and over rolling hills into the open drainage of Penstock Creek. Be certain not to cut the corner on your left too tight, as there is a steep open slope here that could be dangerous. From here follow the drainage, which is open and straightforward.

Dean Lister and Shawn McDonald at Fraser Pass. Photo Chic Scott

The Fraser Glacier has now pulled back and it is possible to ski to Fraser Pass (**413**600 E **5833**700 N) without crossing any glacier ice. Stay well back from any steep slopes or hanging glaciers on your way up the valley.

159. EREMITE VALLEY
Ski Touring, ATR 2

Grade Easy/intermediate
Distance 5 km one way to toe of glacier
Time 2–3 hours one way
Elevation gain 400 m

Max elevation 2200 m at glacier toe
Map Amethyst Lakes 83 D/9
Open February 15 onwards

This is a beautiful day trip from the Wates-Gibson Hut. You can explore and make a few turns high in the valley.

Hazards: Do not linger beneath the avalanche slopes of Outpost Peak.

Options: If you are equipped and prepared for glacier travel you can ski to the pass between Alcove Mountain and Angle Peak. The descent from this pass is excellent.

Access: This tour begins at Wates-Gibson Hut, on the shore of Outpost Lake.

From the hut, ski north down the hill through the trees to the open meadow below Surprise Point. Continue down Penstock Creek, losing about 75 vertical metres, to reach the meadow just above Chrome Lake. Continue south along the meadows bordering Eremite Creek. Generally the route follows the creekbed up the valley, eventually breaking out into open alpine terrain after about 2.5 km, at Arrowhead Lake. The slopes on your right on Outpost Peak contain some giant avalanche paths, so you should travel quickly across any area that is threatened.

You can continue beyond Arrowhead Lake into the basin. You can also ski to an unnamed pass on the east side of the valley, which overlooks one of the side creeks of the Whirlpool River. If you are prepared for glacier travel, you can ski without difficulty up to the pass between Alcove Mountain and Angle Peak. The descent back down the glacier offers excellent skiing.

160. MOAT LAKE
Ski Touring, ATR 1

Grade Easy
Distance 8 km return
Time 2–3 hours return
Elevation gain Nil

Max elevation 1890 m
Map Amethyst Lakes 83 D/9
Open February 15 onwards

This is a beautiful and easy ski tour, one of the best in the area. The great wall of peaks to the south is spectacular.

Access: This tour begins at the Tonquin Valley Backcountry Lodge.

From Tonquin Valley Backcountry Lodge, ski west across level terrain, then gently down to Moat Lake. Cross the lake to the west end to reach

Moat Pass/Tonquin Pass. If you ascend a few metres onto the brow of a hill you will have an outstanding view of the north face of Mount Geikie towering 1300 m above you.

The north face of Mount Geikie towers above Moat Lake. Photo Chic Scott

MOUNT ROBSON PROVINCIAL PARK

161. **Berg Lake via Kinney Lake** Advanced, p. 348

Mount Robson is the highest mountain in the Canadian Rockies and one of the most spectacular peaks in the world. From the Robson River it towers almost 3000 metres above the valley. From the north it is even more majestic and awe-inspiring. A visit to Mount Robson Provincial Park is a must for those who love the Canadian Rocky Mountains.

During the winter there is little in the way of facilities at Mount Robson Provincial Park. The park information centre is not open nor is the nearby service station and restaurant. The nearest town is Valemount, about 35 km west along Highway 5.

161. BERG LAKE VIA KINNEY LAKE Ski Touring, ATR 2–3

Grade Advanced

Distance 17 km one way to Hargreaves Shelter

Time One or two days, depending on depth of snow, strength of your party and weight of your packs

Elevation gain 780 m to Hargreaves Shelter

Max elevation 1640 m

Map Mount Robson 83 E/3; GeoBC Swiftcurrent Creek 083E004, Mount Kain 083E005, Whitehorn Mountain 083E014, Lynx Mountain 083E015

A ski tour to Berg Lake on the north side of Mount Robson is the classic tour in the park. It is a long way and is truly a wilderness adventure. If you have good visibility, however, it is well worth the effort.

Facilities: There is a camp shelter along the northeast shore of Kinney Lake and another at the Whitehorn campground, located on the east side of the Robson River just after the suspension bridge near the start of the Valley of a Thousand Falls. There is a shelter at Berg Lake, along the north shore towards the northeast end of the lake. This shelter is completely enclosed and has a wood-burning heating stove.

Hazards: The climb at the north end of the Valley of a Thousand Falls, alongside White Falls and Emperor Falls, is steep and potentially dangerous.

Access: Drive west of Jasper along Highway 16 for 88 km to Mount Robson Provincial Park. Turn right and drive up a short access road to the trailhead.

Ski up the trail on the left (west) side of the Robson River for about 4 km. The trail is wide and easy to follow. Cross the bridge over the Robson River just before Kinney Lake (the river is usually open at this point). From here there are two options:

1. Turn left just across the bridge and follow a trail through the forest to Kinney Lake. Ski across the lake. This can be problematic as there is a warm current in the middle of the lake and you may get your skis wet (I did).

2. You can also follow a trail around Kinney Lake on the northeast side. The trail climbs about 50 vertical metres near the start and then descends. After about 1.5 km you reach Kinney Lake Shelter, located just above the northeast shore of the lake.

From here ski across open flats. When the valley begins to narrow, ascend the trail up the hillside on the left, crossing large avalanche paths. After about 100 vertical metres the trail enters the forest. Ascend through the forest for another 100 vertical metres, then descend and cross a suspension bridge over the Robson River. Here you will find Whitehorn Camp Shelter, where it is possible to overnight. There is a stove and also may be an axe and a saw. Hopefully there will be a pile of firewood nearby under the snow.

Ski about 1 km along the trail on the east side of the river, then cross another bridge. The trail now climbs steeply, making switchbacks up the hillside. There is exposure to avalanche along here, so caution is

HARGREAVES SHELTER

This is a rustic log building that can provide shelter on cold winter nights. The view out the front door is spectacular.

Location Along the north shore of Berg Lake, not far from the northeast end of the lake

Maps Mount Robson 83 E/3;
GeoBC Lynx Mountain 083E015

Facilities Heating stove, benches and tables. There should be an axe and saw in the shelter and hopefully a pile of wood nearby under the snow.

Water Snowmelt

Contact Mount Robson Provincial Park,
www.env.gov.bc.ca/bcparks/explore/parkpgs/mt_robson

Tony Hoare in front of Hargreaves Shelter. Photo Chic Scott

Mount Robson seen from Hargreaves Shelter. Photo Chic Scott

advised. Follow the trail steeply up to the right. A line of cliffs blocks the way. Angle out to the right and ease around a corner. The angle now lays back. Work your way up lower-angled ground through the trees to another cliff band. At the base of these cliffs, traverse out to the right. Ease around the corner at the far right end onto lower-angled slopes, then head out left. The trail can now be followed all the way to Robson Flats below Berg Lake. Cross the flats, staying left to avoid open water, then cross the lake to Hargreaves Shelter, which is located near the end of the lake.

"Let those who wish have their respectability – I wanted freedom...."

—*Richard Halliburton,* The Royal Road to Romance

MULTI-DAY
SKI ADVENTURES

162. **Jasper to Banff Ski Traverse** Advanced p. 354
163. **Southern Rockies Hut-to-Hut** Traverse, p. 365

One of the nice things about ski touring is that you can enjoy the sport at any level that suits you. You can ski for an hour or two along an easy trail, tour for 10 or 15 km into the backcountry or, if you are really adventurous, try one of these multi-day expeditions, which require a very high level of experience and skill.

The two multi-day ski adventures included here are just a sample of what you can do if you have the energy and motivation. In the Rocky Mountains you can point your skis up almost any valley and go where your spirit takes you. In this world of overcrowded ski resorts and contrived adventure it is nice to roam freely through the snow-covered hills. I hope that the information provided in this book will inspire others to leave the noise and crowds behind and discover something that is still whispered on the wind out there on the wilderness trail.

The Jasper to Banff Ski Traverse was first done in 1930 by Joe Weiss and four companions: Vern and Doug Jeffery, A.L. "Pete" Withers and Frank Burstrom. It took them 15 days, and for much of the distance they followed the valleys where the Icefields Parkway is now located. Two winters later Weiss repeated his monumental tour, this time with Cliff White and Russell Bennett. The tour from Jasper to Banff as described in this book, along the east side of the Icefields Parkway, was first done in 1976 by Don Gardner and Larry Mason. Three years later, in 1979, it was repeated by Bob Saunders and Mel Hines. Both these trips took 14 days.

The Southern Rockies Hut to Hut Traverse was first skied in 1994 by Chic Scott, Art Longair, Doug Bell and John and Louise Davidson. It is an outstanding tour and can be done in a variety of ways using a mixture of huts and some camping – whatever suits your budget.

The team that skied from Jasper to Banff in 1930 make their way along Patricia Street in Jasper. In front, Frank Burstrom, followed by Pete Withers, Joe Weiss and the Jeffery brothers, Vern and Doug. Photo Jasper/Yellowhead Museum and Archives 001_17_0

Doug Bell, Art Longair, Chic Scott, John Davidson and Louise Davidson skied the Southern Rockies Hut to Hut Traverse in 1994. Photo Art Longair

Before heading out on one of these trips it is a good idea to have a chat with Parks Canada visitor safety staff and let them know your plans. They will have good advice to offer and they always like to know of folks undertaking major ski expeditions in their park.

162. JASPER TO BANFF SKI TRAVERSE Ski Touring, ATR 3

Grade Advanced
Distance About 350 km
Time 14–21 days
Elevation gain About 7500 m
Max elevation 2500 m
Maps Medicine Lake 83 C/13,
Athabasca Falls 83 C/12,
Southesk Lake 83 C/11,
Sunwapta Peak 83 C/6,
Columbia Icefield 83 C/3,
Job Creek 83 C/7,
Cline River 83 C/2,
Siffleur River 82 N/16,
Hector Lake 82 N/9,
Lake Louise 82 N/8,
Castle Mountain 82 O/5,
Banff 82 O/4;
Jasper National Park MCR 221;
Banff, Kootenay and Yoho
National Parks MCR 220

The Jasper National Park section of this traverse is open from March 1 onwards.

This is a very challenging ski adventure and is rarely done. Plan this expedition well, train all winter, then give it everything. March is the best time of year, when the days are longer, the temperature is more moderate and the snow is deep. It is possible to escape from this tour at a number of points along the way (Poboktan Creek, Nigel Creek, David Thompson Highway, Pipestone Creek and Skoki). Additional food can be picked up when you cross the David Thompson Highway (Highway 11) about halfway along the tour, and food caches can be placed in advance from the Icefields Parkway.

The Poboktan Creek section of this tour is now closed early in the winter to protect endangered woodlands caribou. Please check with Jasper Park Information 780-852-6176, http://is.gd/WtT5fU, for the current status of this area.

Reference: The Skyline Trail, the Eight Pass route and the Six Pass

Route are all described in detail in *Summits and Icefields, vol. 1: Alpine Ski Tours in the Canadian Rockies* (RMB, 2011, 2013).

Access: The Jasper to Banff Ski Traverse begins by climbing the Signal Mountain fire road not far from Jasper. A small parking lot is located at the trailhead about 5 km along the Maligne Lake Road from its junction with Highway 16.

The Signal Mountain Fire Road is a steady uphill grind for 880 vertical metres. At an elevation of about 2000 m, where the road curves to the right near treeline, cut off left at a trail sign, 434100 E 5858600 N. The track angles up to the left through the trees and works its way out into the open. Contour across open, windblown slopes, maintaining elevation into a small drainage, 435800 E 5857600 N.

Ascend a little and contour around into a second drainage. The angling descent into the drainage is steep in places and good route finding is required. There is some avalanche hazard here. In this drainage there is a designated campsite on the east side of the creek, in the edge of the trees, at about 437900 E 5855700 N.

Ascend the drainage to the south past two lakes. Do not take the summer trail over Amber Mountain, but follow the drainage above the second lake to a pass northeast of Amber Mountain, 439300 E 5852100 N. From here it is best to descend southeast for about 100 vertical metres, cross the bowl, then ascend to the right to reach the ridge crest at 439400 E 5850900 N.

Contour southeast across windblown slopes for about 2 km to reach "The Notch," 440700 E 5850000 N. From here there is a steep descent of about 200 vertical metres. Take off your skis, traverse out east from "The Notch" to avoid a large cornice, then kick steps straight down the slope. Use extreme caution here: this slope is steep (at least 35 degrees) and could avalanche.

Put your skis on again and descend the bowl. Contour above Curator Lake on the north side, then continue contouring southeast into a large bowl which is ascended to Big Shovel Pass 443900 E 5848000 N.

Descend easily from Big Shovel Pass and cross "Snow Bowl" in a southeasterly direction. Round the northeast ridge of Mount Aberhart, then turn right at about 447500 E 5844000 N and ascend the valley to the south of Mount Aberhart, 446300 E 5842900 N. The travel is open and straightforward, but a good line following the least steep slopes should be taken to reach Connector Pass, 446600 E 5842500 N. It will be necessary to remove your skis and kick steps up a windblown slope to reach the pass. (The ascent to the small pass to the southeast, 447100 E 5842100 N, is not recommended. It is very steep and would present serious avalanche hazard.)

From Connector Pass descend about 150 vertical metres to the south-west, then contour around to the southeast on benches. A 4 km traverse takes you out into the broad flats of Hardisty Pass, 448700 E 5839400 N, the first pass on the old Eight Pass Route. Ski southeast through the pass, descend to Evelyn Creek (some tree bashing), then turn right (south) and ascend the creek.

The ascent to Evelyn Pass, 452800 E 5835000 N, is about 250 vertical metres and is a little difficult to begin. Start up a prominent drainage, but because it soon becomes a terrain trap, you should climb up onto the left shoulder and ascend through open trees. Higher up, you can traverse to the right to gain the drainage again, which is followed to the pass. Descend the other side to Trapper Creek, staying out to the right. Ski past two small lakes, cut close around the mountain at 453400 E 5832700 N, then descend to the valley bottom. At this point the traverse joins the Six Pass Route.

Cross the head of Trapper Creek, heading south, and ascend open, windswept slopes to a pass at 455400 E 5830900 N. From the summit of the pass it is best to descend in a southeast direction into the next valley (Little Creek), enjoying the skiing rather than trying to contour and maintain your elevation.

A gentle climb to the southeast will take you to another pass, 456500 E 5829600 N. The descent from this pass offers good skiing. Stay to the right on open slopes rather than follow the drainage. Lower down, on the right, you can find glades through the trees.

From this valley (Big Creek), climb straight up the other side, staying in a wedge of trees to avoid steep slopes on either side. The wedge of trees leads up to a bench from which a gentle slope continues to another pass, 459100 E 5826500 N. To get the best ski descent, climb a short distance south, up the ridge above the pass, then descend south-southeast down an open shoulder into the valley below (Short Creek).

Climb open slopes in a southeasterly direction to another pass, 461200 E 5824000 N. The descent on the far side, down southeast slopes, following the fall line into the valley (Twin Creek), offers some excellent skiing.

Continue southeast for about 7 km, gradually ascending Twin Creek Flats to what is called Elusive Pass, 467100 E 5818800 N. The ascent is straightforward but the southeast side of the pass is overhung by a large cornice and a direct descent is not possible. To solve this problem, scramble up the ridge crest to the northeast, gaining about 75 vertical metres. You may have to climb all the way to the top of the small peak, then traverse out to the right onto windblown shale slopes that can be descended to easier-angled snow slopes below. The route continues southeast into Maligne Pass, which is broad and gentle. From here descend the Maligne Pass trail (see page 305) to Poboktan Creek.

Turn left and ski east and southeast along the left bank of Poboktan Creek for about 14 km (see page 304). At about 485900 E 5805100 N begin ascending to the southeast. It is likely best to try to locate the summer trail through the forest on the left side of the creek rather than bushwhack.

Once you are out of the trees the route ascends over open terrain to Jonas Shoulder. It may be best to follow a small drainage and cross the shoulder at 487000 E 5802300 N. On the other side of Jonas Shoulder descend to the south and angle across open slopes to gain the drainage that leads to Jonas Pass.

For the next 10 km the travel through Jonas Pass is open and excellent, although the descent down Four Point Creek to the Brazeau River can be difficult. The author chose to descend the creekbed, which proved problematic but might be much better in a bigger snow year. There is a trail marked on the map but its effectiveness is unknown.

To reach Cline Pass, ski about a kilometre northeast down the Brazeau River to the point where the stream from the Kline Pass drainage reaches the Brazeau (496300 E 5793600 N). Here there is a campsite for horse packing groups in the summer. There is also a good trail (not marked on the map) that leads up through the forest, above the creek on the northeast bank. It might be quite difficult to locate this trail, however. After a couple of kilometres you emerge from the trees onto open ground which is followed to Cline Pass (**4996**900 E **5788000** N – marked incorrectly on some topo maps).

Descend into upper Cataract Creek, staying high on the northeast slopes of the valley for easier travelling. Eventually you will have to descend into the valley bottom. Travel can be both good and bad. Occasionally a trail can be found through the forest along the northeast side of the creek that can help your progress. Eventually it is best to follow the creekbed. As the route nears the Cline River the creekbed narrows and begins to drop steeply. Here it is best to ski up onto the north bank, where an old trail with much deadfall can be found through the forest. Once the trail reaches the valley bottom it is best to move out to the right and follow the open creekbed to the confluence with the Cline.

Initially, travel along the Cline River is good, on open flats. After several kilometres a trail can be found up on the right bank which works quite well for a time. Then the trail becomes difficult to locate as it leaves the forest to follow the riverbank, then re-enters the forest at unknown points. Eventually you get onto the trail on the right bank and follow it for 10–15 km to the David Thompson Highway. This is a difficult trail because it meanders back and forth and up and down through very complex terrain. There is a good chance there will not be much snow and you may be walking on a dangerous, icy trail. The topo map also shows a trail along the left bank of the Cline River. Perhaps it makes for better travelling.

From here it is necessary to make your way about 15 km west along the highway to the parking lot for the Siffleur Falls Trail.

Walk along a well-maintained trail for about 500 m, then cross a modern suspension bridge over the North Saskatchewan River. Continue walking along a boardwalk for another 500 m until the trail reaches a steep hillside. The Siffleur Falls trail leads left, but you should turn right along the base of the hillside on another trail. Follow this for a little over a kilometre until it turns left and ascends into the forest. This is the start of the trail up the Siffleur River.

To begin, the trail is excellent. It is straight (likely an old seismic line) and there is not a lot of deadfall. However, the deadfall gradually increases until the trail becomes impassable after about 15 km. A forest fire has created so much deadfall and new growth that the only recourse is to descend out left to the river flats. Travel is actually very good along the flats for many kilometres. At about 540400 E 5741100 N, turn up left through the forest on a well-maintained trail towards Pipestone Pass. After a few kilometres the valley opens up and travel becomes easier. Pipestone Pass is open and beautiful. It is best to take the north option around a small peak that is in the centre of the pass. On the southeast side of the pass some caution will be necessary if snow stability is not good.

Travel is good down the Pipestone River, following the riverbed most of the time. At the confluence of Little Pipestone Creek, turn southeast and ascend a good trail in the trees above the creek on the left bank. Often folks from Skoki have skied this trail, so you might have a packed trail. To get to Skoki Lodge you can follow the direct trail that ascends high above Skoki Creek or you can climb up the trail towards Red Deer Lakes. Then either choose a cutoff that takes you from the flats near the first lake around the north side of Skoki Mountain to reach Skoki Lodge or ski around the east and south sides of Skoki Mountain to Skoki Lodge (see pages 227, 234).

From Skoki, ski via Jones Pass and Cottongrass Pass to reach the headwaters of Baker Creek. The descent of Baker Creek will be difficult and it may be best to stay high above the creek on the left. Descend to the creekbed about 1.5 km above the junction with Wildflower Creek.

The ascent of Wildflower Creek will be steep and difficult. Ski on either side of the creek or in the creekbed as the terrain dictates. From the top of Wildflower Creek there is a short descent to the flats below Pulsatilla Pass. Ski across the flats beneath some huge avalanche slopes.

The ascent to Pulsatilla is steep and you should very seriously assess the avalanche hazard. From the top of the pass there is a descent route about 500 m to the left that offers enjoyable skiing through glades and open forest to the Johnston Creek drainage. Descend Johnston Creek following the summer trail (see page 170). About 4 km below the pass the trail crosses to the right side and stays high above a canyon for 1–2 km. You may spot some blazes along here. Once below the canyon, cross to the left side of the creek, where blazes become more frequent and the trail is easier to follow. Continue past the warden cabin and down to the junction with the Mystic Pass trail.

Follow the route description to reach Mystic Pass (see page 139). From Mystic Pass descend open, easy terrain. Stay in the creekbed, which steepens but not dramatically so. Once you reach the camping area, cross to the left side of the creek and locate the summer hiking trail (see page 139).

Follow the Forty Mile Creek trail to the Mount Norquay ski resort (see page 137).

Margaret Gmoser (in front), Chic Scott and Faye Atkinson set off across the Skyline Trail near Jasper on the way to Lake Louise and on to Banff. Photo Tony Hoare

Faye Atkinson and Chic Scott negotiate a difficult creek crossing. Photo Tony Hoare

Faye Atkinson crosses Pipestone Pass in glorious sunshine. Photo Tony Hoare

Faye Atkinson, under a heavy pack, follows Chic Scott along the Cline River. Photo Tony Hoare

Margaret Gmoser leads the team along the
Pipestone River. Photo Tony Hoare

Tony Hoare, Margaret Gmoser, Chic Scott and Faye Atkinson at Skoki
Lodge after a 20-day ski traverse from Jasper. Tony and Faye carried on to
Banff while Margaret and Chic skied out to Lake Louise. Photo Tony Hoare

163. SOUTHERN ROCKIES HUT-TO-HUT SKI TRAVERSE
Ski Touring, ATR 3

Grade Advanced
Distance About 125 km
Time 7–10 days
Elevation gain About 2500 m
Max elevation 2510 m

Maps Spray Lakes Reservoir
82 J/14, Mount Assiniboine
82 J/13, Banff 82 O/4, Castle
Mountain 82 O/5, Lake Louise
82 N/8

This is a fabulous tour and is some day destined for greatness. It traverses some of the most beautiful and dramatic mountain terrain in the world. There are huts most of the way, so you can travel with a lighter pack. You can ski this tour in both directions and there are several variations.

Facilities: The huts along the way are: Bryant Creek Shelter, Mount Assiniboine Lodge, Naiset Huts, Police Meadow Cabin, Sunshine Village Ski Resort, Egypt Lake Shelter, Shadow Lake Lodge, Storm Mountain Lodge, Moraine Lake Shelter, Elizabeth Parker Hut and Skoki Lodge.

Options: There are many variations of this tour that would work. You could start directly from Banff, ski up Brewster Creek and spend a night at Sundance Lodge, then cross Allenby Pass to Mount Assiniboine. From Shadow Lake Lodge you could make your way to Storm Mountain Lodge on Kootenay Highway 93, then take a high line around to Taylor Lake and on to Moraine Lake, finishing via Wenkchemna Pass and Opabin Pass to Lake O'Hara.

Access: This tour begins at the Mount Shark trailhead (see page 113). You could also start at Lake Louise or Lake O'Hara and ski south. Most of the individual sections of this traverse are described in detail elsewhere in this book. It is simply a matter of stringing them all together.

The first section of the tour follows Bryant Creek, crossing Assiniboine Pass to reach Assiniboine Meadows. This can be done in two days by overnighting at Bryant Creek Shelter. At Assiniboine you can stay at Naiset Huts or Mount Assiniboine Lodge.

The next section continues via Citadel Pass to Sunshine Village Ski Resort. There is an old log cabin at Police Meadows that can be used overnight if necessary. From Sunshine Village you can continue via Simpson Pass and Healy Pass to Egypt Lake.

From Egypt Lake Shelter you can go down Pharaoh Creek and up Redearth Creek to Shadow Lake Lodge. (**Note:** The bridges on the trail descending Pharaoh Creek were all destroyed in the floods of 2013 and have not been rebuilt.) From here you have several choices: you can descend Redearth Creek to the Trans-Canada Highway or you can cross Gibbon Pass to Twin Lakes and then down to the Trans-Canada Highway. A final alternative is to continue north beyond Twin Lakes to the Kootenay Highway via Arnica and Vista Lakes. Here it would be possible to overnight at Storm Mountain Lodge.

The last part of the traverse is open to lots of variations. If you have descended to the Trans-Canada Highway you can drive to Lake Louise, spend the night at a hotel, then ski via Deception Pass to Skoki Lodge to complete your adventure. A very adventurous possibility is to continue north along the trail to Boom Lake, then ski around the corner and along the east flank of Mount Bell and the Panorama Range via O'Brien and Taylor lakes to reach Moraine Lake. There is a camp shelter there where you could overnight in relative comfort. To complete the tour, you could cross Wenkchemna and Opabin passes to Lake O'Hara, overnight at Elizabeth Parker Hut and then descend to the Trans-Canada Highway the next day. An easier finish would be to ski along Moraine Lake Road toward Lake Louise, a hot shower and a good meal.

This traverse has great potential for the future. It needs a little more pioneering work and perhaps another cabin or two, but someday it may be one of the great ski tours in the world. It is a way to visit many of the historic lodges of the Canadian Rockies in one glorious adventure.

INDEX

Akamina Pass to Wall Lake and Forum Lake 33

Allison Chinook 45

Amiskwi Fire Road to Amiskwi Pass 280

Assiniboine to Banff via Spray River 71

Athabasca Falls Loop 313

Baker Creek 220

Baker Creek Mountain Resort 219

Baker Creek Power Line 222

Bald Hills Lookout 326

Ball Pass 161

Banff to Assiniboine via Allenby Pass 69

Berg Lake via Kinney Lake 348

Boivin Creek 43

Boom Lake 164

Bow Hut 293, 295

Bow River Loop 211

Bow Summit 296

Bryant Creek Shelter 65

Burstall Pass 108

Calgary golf courses. *See* Confederation, Maple Ridge, Shaganappi

Cameron Lake 29

Cameron Lake Cabin 32

Canada Olympic Park 50

Canmore Nordic Centre 122

Canmore to Banff via Goat Creek 129

Cascade Fire Road 125

Cedar Lake 196

Chester Lake 107

Chickadee Valley 174

Citadel Pass 148

Columbia Valley Nordic Trails (Baptiste Lake) 198

Commonwealth Creek 109

Commonwealth Lake 111

Confederation Golf Course 52

Crowfoot Pass 291

Dawn Mountain Nordic Trails 192

Dead Horse Canyon 73

Dead Man's Flat to Skogan Pass 121

Decoigne Trails 321

Dipper 28

Dog Lake 179

Dolomite Peak Circuit 288

Egypt Lake Shelter 153

Egypt Lake via Healy Pass 150

Elizabeth Parker Hut 253

Elk Lakes Cabin 102

Elk Lakes Cabin Approach 101

Elk Lake Summit 138

Ely's Dome 77

Emerald Lake Lodge 254

Emerald Lake Trails 276

Engadine Lodge 115

Eremite Valley 345

Evelyn Creek Loop 325

Fairview Loop 204

Fernie Alpine Resort Nordic Ski Trails 39

Fernie Golf Course 41

Field to Emerald Lake 274

Forty Mile Creek 137

Forum Lake 33

Fossil Mountain Loop 239

Fraser Pass 344

Fryatt Creek 308

Geraldine Fire Road 314

Gibbon Pass 163

Glacier Lake 298

Golden Golf Course Nordic Trails 197

Great Divide Trail 210

Gypsum Mine 104

Haiduk Lake 160

Hargreaves Shelter 350
Healy Creek Trail from Sunshine Village Ski Resort 149
Hidden Lake 230
Ice River Fire Road 282
Island Lake 42
Jasper to Banff Ski Traverse 354
Johnston Creek 170
Jones Bench 75
Kicking Horse Trail 277
Kiwetinok Pass 273
Lake Katherine/Lake Helen Circuit 290
Lake Louise Loop 203
Lake O'Hara Circuit 263
Lake O'Hara Lodge 251
Lake O'Hara Road 261
Leach Lake Trail 314
Little Shovel Pass 327
Little Yoho Valley 271
Loppet Trail 166
Lower Telemark Trail 209
Maligne Pass 305
Maple Ridge Golf Course 52
Marushka (Shark) Lake 116
McArthur Pass 264
Merlin Valley 240
Moat Lake 346
Monarch Ramparts 154
Moose Bath 74
Moose Lake Loop 323
Moose Lake Loop, Upper 325
Moraine Lake Road 213
Morning Glory Lakes 265
Mosquito Creek to Molar Meadows 286
Mount Assiniboine Lodge 58
Mount Edith Cavell Road 317
Mount Shark Trails 113
Mystic Pass 139
Naiset Huts 60
Natural Bridge 238
Nigel Pass 299
Nipika Mountain Resort 180, 184

Og Pass 72
Opabin Plateau 266
Opabin/Wenkchemna Circuit 267
Ottertail Valley Fire Road 281
Oyster Lake 238
Packer's Pass 241
Palisade Lookout 320
Panorama Nordic Centre 188
Paradise Valley 214
Peter Lougheed Provincial Park Trails 95
Peyto Trail 208
Pipestone Trails 218
Plain of Six Glaciers 216
Poboktan Creek 304
Pyramid Lake Resort Trail 319
Quartz Ridge 146
Radium Resort Nordic Trails 191
Redearth Creek 155
Ribbon Creek to Skogan Pass 92
Ribbon Creek Trails 89
Rock Isle Lake 145
Ross Lake Circuit 258
Rummel Lake 111
Sandy McNabb Trails 85
Shadow Lake Lodge 157
Shaganappi Golf Course 52
Shangri La 328
Shangri La Cabin 332
Shark to Assiniboine via Bryant Creek 63
Sherbrooke Lake 258
Simpson River 177
Skoki Lodge 227
Skoki Mountain Loop 234
Skoki to Lake Louise via Pipestone River 242
Skoki via Boulder and Deception Passes 232
Smith-Dorrien (Sawmill) Trails 106
Southern Rockies Hut-to-Hut Ski Traverse 365
Spray River Fire Road 127
Stanley Glacier Valley 175

Stanley Mitchell Hut 255
Summit Lake 32
Summit Lakes/Jacques Lake 322
Sundance Canyon Road/Old
    Healy Creek Road/Sundance
    Lodge 130
Sundance Lodge 134
Sundance Pass 135
Sunshine to Assiniboine via
    Citadel Pass 67
Sunwapta Falls/Athabasca River
    302
Surprise Creek Cabin 178
Sydney Vallance (Fryatt) Hut 310
Syncline Cross Country Ski Area
    47
Taylor Lake 222
Tokumm Creek (Prospector's
    Valley) 176
Tonquin Valley Backcountry
    Lodge 338
Tonquin Valley via Astoria River
    334
Tonquin Valley via Maccarib Pass
    341

Tower Lake and Rockbound Lake
    169
Trails near Castle Junction 165
Tramline Trail 207
Tunnel Mountain Trailer Court and
    Village 126
Twin Lakes 162
Upper and Lower Elk Lakes 103
Upper Moose Lake Loop. *See*
    Moose Lake, Upper
Upper Telemark Trail 209
Wabasso Campground Trails 316
Wall Lake 33
Wapta Falls 282
Wates-Gibson Hut 336
Watridge Lake 114
West Bragg Creek Trails 82
Whirlpool Campground Loop 316
Whirlpool Trail 315
Whistlers Campground Loop 318
Whiteway (Lake Windermere) 190
Wilcox Pass 301
Wolverine Valley 231
Wonder Pass 76
Yoho Valley Road 269

*"It is the people's right to have primitive access to the
remote places of safest retreat from the fever and the fret
of the market place and the beaten tracks of life."*

—Elizabeth Parker

CALLING FOR ASSISTANCE

When calling for assistance, indicate that you need a mountain rescue, and be ready to relay the following information:

- your exact location (best to give both a GPS coordinate and the name of the tour)
- what type of emergency it is and the number of victims
- your name and phone number, including area code
- the time the accident occurred

Emergency phone numbers

Banff, Yoho, Kootenay national parks: 403-762-4506 or 911
Jasper National Park: 780-852-3100 or 911
Kananaskis Country: 403-591-7767 or 911
Waterton: 403-762-4506 or 911

For all other areas, dial 911 and ask for the RCMP detachment nearest to your location.

Frequently called phone numbers

National Park Public Safety Offices

Waterton Park: 403-859-5140

Banff Park: 403-762-1470

For Kootenay Park it is recommended that you phone the Banff Park number: 403-762-1470

For Yoho Park it is recommended that you phone the Banff Park number: 403-762-1470

Jasper Park (Jasper): 780-852-6155

Visitor Information Centres

Waterton: 403-859-5133

Barrier Lake (Kananaskis): 403-673-3985

Peter Lougheed Provincial Park: 403-591-6322

Banff: 403-762-1550

Lake Louise (Thursday to Sunday during winter): 403-522-3833

Yoho (closed in winter): 250-343-6783

Jasper: 780-852-6176

Banff Lake Louise Tourism Bureau: 403-762-8421

Tourism Jasper: 780-852-6236

Travel Alberta: 1-800-252-3782

Tourism British Columbia: 1-800-663-6000

Weather Reports

Banff: 403-762-2088

Jasper: 780-852-3185

Reservations

Alpine Club of Canada huts: 403-678-3200

Banff National Park shelters: 403-762-1550

Naiset Huts (Assiniboine): 403-678-2883

Hostelling International hostels: 1-866-762-4122

"The light died in the low clouds. Falling snow drank in the dusk. Shrouded in silence, the branches wrapped me in their peace. When the boundaries were erased, once again the wonder: that I exist."

—Dag Hammarskjöld

"Ability to see the cultural value of wilderness boils down, in the last analysis, to a question of intellectual humility."

—Aldo Leopold, Sand County Almanac

"This grand show is eternal. It is always sunrise somewhere; the dew is never dried all at once; a shower is forever falling; vapor is ever rising. Eternal sunrise, eternal sunset, eternal dawn and gloaming, on sea and continents and islands, each in its turn, as the round earth rolls."

—John Muir

CHIC SCOTT

Chic Scott has over 50 years of backcountry ski experience and has completed 10 Grand Traverses, including the first successful Great Divide Traverse from Jasper to Lake Louise. He has climbed and guided extensively in the European Alps and North America. He is an honorary member of the Association of Canadian Mountain Guides, the Calgary Mountain Club, The Alpine Club of Canada and the Whyte Museum of the Canadian Rockies and is a recipient of the Banff Mountain Film Festival Summit of Excellence Award.

Chic resides in Banff, Alberta, where he makes his living giving presentations and writing books. To date, he has written ten published works, including guidebooks, histories and biographies. For more information see www.chicscott.com.

Chic Scott. Photo Kathy Madill

"We were not pioneers ourselves but we journeyed over old trails that were new to us, and with hearts open. Who shall distinguish?"

—*J. Monroe Thorington*, The Glittering Mountains of Canada

"…to tell the truth I am not sure I would trade my childhood of freedom and the outdoors and the senses for a childhood of being led by the hand past all the Turners in the National Gallery."

—*Wallace Stegner*, Wolf Willow

"In the last resort, it is the beauty of the mountain world in the inmost recesses that holds us spellbound, slaves till life ends."

—*W.H. Murray*, Mountaineering in Scotland

DARREN FARLEY

Darren Farley grew up cross-country ski racing before getting into backcountry skiing. He spends his summers helping run the Nordic ski facilities at the Haig Glacier. In the winter he guides for various ski lodges. In between ski trips he has found time for many excursions to the Himalaya and the Andes. In his travels he has spent several weeks following Tibetan pilgrims, has been an extra in a Bollywood film and was once held up at knifepoint by a gang of little kids. When not travelling Darren resides in Calgary, Alberta.

Darren Farley. Photo Matt Hadley